God

Central Problems of Philosophy
Series Editor: John Shand

This series of books presents concise, clear, and rigorous analyses of the core problems that preoccupy philosophers across all approaches to the discipline. Each book encapsulates the essential arguments and debates, providing an authoritative guide to the subject while also introducing original perspectives. This series of books by an international team of authors aims to cover those fundamental topics that, taken together, constitute the full breadth of philosophy.

Published titles

Action
Rowland Stout

Causation and Explanation
Stathis Psillos

Death
Geoffrey Scarre

Free Will
Graham McFee

God
W. Jay Wood

Knowledge
Michael Welbourne

Meaning
David E. Cooper

Mind and Body
Robert Kirk

Modality
Joseph Melia

Ontology
Dale Jacquette

Paradox
Doris Olin

Perception
Barry Maund

Realism and Anti-Realism
Stuart Brock & Edwin Mares

Relativism
Paul O'Grady

Rights
Duncan Ivison

Scepticism
Neil Gascoigne

Truth
Pascal Engel

Universals
J. P. Moreland

Forthcoming titles

The Self
Stephen Burwood

Value
Derek Matravers

God

W. Jay Wood

McGill-Queen's University Press
Montreal & Kingston • Ithaca

To Bruce Baloian, who introduced me
to the philosophy of religion

© W. Jay Wood 2011

ISBN 978-0-7735-3839-9 (cloth)
ISBN 978-0-7735-3840-5 (paper)

Legal deposit first quarter 2011
Bibliothèque nationale du Québec

Published simultaneously outside North America
by Acumen Publishing Limited

McGill-Queen's University Press acknowledges the financial support
of the Government of Canada through the Canada Book Fund for its
activities.

Library and Archives Canada Cataloguing in Publication

Wood, W. Jay (William Jay), 1954-
    God / W. Jay Wood.

Includes bibliographical references and index.
ISBN 978-0-7735-3839-9 (bound).--ISBN 978-0-7735-3840-5
(pbk.)

    1. Theism. 2. God--Proof. 3. Religion--Philosophy. I. Title.

BD555.W66 2010   211'.3   C2010-906334-1

Printed by Ashford Colour Press Ltd, UK.

Contents

Introduction

Suppose there is a personal being perfect in wisdom, power and goodness, who created the world and sustains it in existence from moment to moment, and that your highest flourishing in this life and the next depends on your being rightly related to this being. In short, suppose that God exists. This, in a nutshell, is what theists profess the world over: a belief that unites the great monotheistic religions of Judaism, Christianity and Islam. If theism is true, it is a matter of incalculable weightiness, which partially explains why theism has been of perennial interest to philosophers. Two questions dominate philosophical writings about God. First, do we have good reasons to think that theism is true? In other words, do we have good reasons to think that anything answers to the description "omnipotent, omniscient, omnibenevolent creator and sustainer of the universe"? Second, if such a being exists, what is he like and how shall we understand his relation to the world? Few questions have so engaged philosophical attention, with new books appearing each year to defend opposing answers to these questions. The first question claims some priority, for if we conclude that no good reasons can be found to think that God exists, it scarcely seems that the second question merits much attention. But the two questions are not so easily separated. For one of the chief reasons cited by some philosophers for thinking that God does not exist is that he cannot exist! Some philosophers argue that the concept of an omnipotent, omniscient, omnibenevolent God is incoherent, so nothing could answer to this description. So it is by delving into the second question about God's nature and alleged relation to the world that one gains additional insight into whether or not there is a God. Whichever their logical priority, these two questions will form the focus of this book.[1]

Why should one bother these busy days to consider these questions? Are there not more pressing matters to think about, such as war, the economy, global warming and the plight of the poor and oppressed? And have all the years of philosophical wrangling not failed to settle the matter conclusively? The famous French mathematician and philosopher Blaise Pascal thought that the question of God's existence was not merely an academic, ivory-tower concern, but one that affects how one thinks about a variety of other important matters. How one answers the question of God's existence not only influences the way one thinks about other intellectual matters, but in many cases it also influences the course of one's life, the goals one sets, the purposes and projects to which one commits oneself, the kind of person one thinks one should become. However inconclusive academic debates have proved to be, there is a perennial need for persons in each generation to address these issues themselves. At the very least, says Pascal, the questions concerning God's existence and nature are not ones about which we can be blasé. Of God's existence, Pascal writes:

> [O]ur chief interest and chief duty is to seek enlightenment on this subject, on which all our conduct depends. And that is why, amongst those who are not convinced, I make an absolute distinction between those who strive with all their might to learn and those who live without troubling themselves or thinking about it. (1995: #427, 128)

We may dispute with Pascal about the extent to which our behaviour depends on our accepting, rejecting or withholding with respect to theism. But it is hard to deny the oddity of utter indifference with respect to so significant an issue.

A ready retort suggests itself to Pascal's insistence that we attend to and settle for ourselves what will be our position towards theism. At this very moment, an alien race may be wending its way toward earth bent on planetary conquest. This too, if true, would be of tremendous moment, but surely we would not think less of someone, intellectually or otherwise, who failed to make the matter an item of serious investigation. Why should we care any more about the truth of theism? The analogy breaks down. Theism, unlike the claim about attacking aliens, has been embraced globally by a great part of the world's population, including scores of philosophy's greatest thinkers. From Augustine (and earlier) to the present day, many of the West's greatest philosophers have thoughtfully considered and embraced theism. Moreover, in many cases, they have accepted theism on the strength of arguments they found rationally persuasive. This fact, of course, is not an argument that theism is true, and many equally eminent philosophers have considered theism only to reject it. Nevertheless, the "alien invasion" hypothesis cannot boast of having received sustained and serious reflection, yet alone acceptance, by any community of intellectuals (although the likelihood that other life forms might exist has received serious attention, but that is a different matter).

The evidentialist objection to religious belief

One way to frame our investigation is to see it as a response to a challenge made famous by English philosopher Bertrand Russell. At a dinner meeting of the Voltaire Society (for which Russell was the mascot), a group of Oxford undergraduates once posed the following question to then octogenarian Russell:

> Suppose you have been wrong about the existence of God. Suppose that the whole story were true, and that you arrived at the Pearly Gates to be admitted by Saint Peter. Having denied God's existence all your life, what would you say to … Him? Russell answered without a moment's hesitation. "Well, I would go up to Him, and I would say, 'You didn't give us enough evidence.'"[2]

Russell's retort – whatever one may think about its cheekiness – raises a number of important philosophical questions. Do we have adequate evidence to show that God exists? Is the evidence available to anyone who looks for it, or must one be an expert to find and assess such evidence? Must we form all beliefs in accordance with evidence in order to be excellent intellectual agents? Russell's remark might be thought to contain an implicit belief policy, to wit: one ought to believe only those beliefs for which one thinks one has adequate evidence. So another question is: must all of our beliefs enjoy the support of adequate evidence before we can be rational in accepting them?

Evidentialism is the philosophical view about rational belief that answers our last question in the affirmative. Evidentialists think, quite reasonably, that there are responsible and irresponsible ways of accepting and rejecting beliefs, and their view insists that one should accept a belief only because one has adequate evidence for its truth. The philosopher W. K. Clifford put the thesis is a particularly strong way: "It is wrong, always, everywhere, and for anyone, to believe anything on insufficient evidence" (Clifford 2007: 109). At first blush, this may strike one as eminently good advice, perfectly in keeping with common practice in many areas of life. Suppose, for instance, that your financial broker telephones you urging you to invest your hard-earned savings in "the deal of a lifetime". You ask your broker why he thinks this is a sound investment opportunity and he mumbles something about the alignment of the stars and other astral portents. Needless to say, you will probably not believe that he is pointing you to a sound investment, and you will get a new broker. Indeed, in so many walks of life – medicine, engineering, investments, courts of law and so on – we think it prudent to form beliefs in these important areas of life only on the basis of good evidence. Just as there are responsible and irresponsible ways of acting, so too there are responsible and irresponsible ways of believing. Why should we treat religious beliefs as exempt from this everyday standard of good intellectual conduct? Should not religious beliefs also be formed in accordance with the preponderance of evidence? John Locke answers affirmatively, and does so partly for religious reasons:

> Faith is nothing but a firm assent of the mind: which if be regulated, as is our duty, cannot be afforded to anything, but upon good reason; and so cannot be opposite to it. He that believes, without having any reason for believing, may be in love with his own fancies; but neither seeks truth as he ought, nor pays the obedience due his maker, who would have him use those

discerning faculties he has given him, to keep him out if mistake and error.   (*An Essay Concerning Human Understanding* IV.xvii.24; 1959: 413–14)

Moreover, if Pascal is right, and weighty consequences attach to such beliefs, perhaps we ought to exercise an extra measure of intellectual caution before accepting religious claims. Here, perhaps more than in most areas, we should be most demanding of good evidence.

Russell's and Clifford's prescription for right belief has been formulated into what is often called "the evidentialist objection to religious belief". In brief, the objection states that the canons of good intellectual conduct require that all our beliefs enjoy the support of good evidence. Where evidence supports the truth of a belief it should be believed, where evidence points to its falsity it should be denied, and where the evidence is inconclusive we should suspend judgement. This division corresponds, roughly, to that between theists, atheists and agnostics: theists believe that God exists, atheists deny that he does and agnostics do not think the available evidence settles the matter either way.[3] So, then, evidentialists assert that theists wanting to hold their beliefs in an intellectually responsible way must do so on the basis of adequate evidence; otherwise they must be judged guilty of intellectual impropriety, of failing to meet minimum standards for rational belief. At the risk of harshness, one might reduce the evidentialist challenge to theism as this: "Put up or shut up!" Either theists must supply the evidence that shows their belief to be rational or they ought to cease believing.

Now there is much about this prescription for rational belief that cries out for clarification. How would you regard a prescription from a doctor who, as he is leaving the examination room, tosses an unmarked bottle of pills to you and, as the door closes behind him, yells "Take those!"? You would think the prescription somewhat lacking in details. What are the pills? What do they do? How many should one take? When? With meals or on an empty stomach? What are the possible side effects and interactions with other drugs, and so on? One would be hesitant to follow so vague a prescription, to say the least. The evidentialist objection, so far stated, is no less lacking in details. What is evidence? How much evidence is sufficient for a belief to be rational? Do beliefs differ in the amount of evidence needed to make them rational? How does one estimate the probative force, or weightiness, of evidence? Might one's belief fit one's evidence, and one still be in pretty bad intellectual shape? Must everyone have evidence for each and every one of his beliefs, or is it sufficient for rationality that some experts have the evidence and I rely on their testimony? Where can I get a copy of these so-called rules of good intellectual conduct? Are these rules themselves subject to debate? The efforts to clarify these and related questions have revealed deep divisions within the community of epistemologists; those philosophers who specialize in reflecting about the requirements for justified belief.[4]

We can set aside for the moment in-house philosophical disputes about how best to bring precision to the evidentialist objection to religious belief. Most persons find intuitively plausible that one can believe responsibly and irresponsibly, and that one should try, commensurate with the other demands pressing upon one, to be responsible in one's believing, and in one's denying and withholding, for that matter. Believing something on the basis of extensive scientific research is an example of the former, while resolutely believing that one's only lottery ticket will be the winner is an example of the latter. Moreover, most of us think that, all else being equal, it is a good thing to have evidence and to appreciate its force for some belief, even if one is not committed to the ironclad requirement that every belief be so supported. Also, it is commonplace that if one wishes to convince others to adopt one's own view about some controversial matter – and whether or not God exists certainly fits the bill – one is likely to advance one's efforts more successfully with good reasons, or evidence, than without. So, are there good reasons to think that God exists that will withstand critical scrutiny?

The tradition of natural theology

Philosophers who work within the tradition of natural theology think that Russell's demand for evidence can be met in the most robust terms. Natural theologians think that they can marshal evidence aplenty for God's existence; some would even go so far as to claim that they can prove that God exists. We must clarify in a moment, however, how exactly to characterize the goals of natural theology.

Natural theology is "natural" in two senses. First, the evidence on which the arguments of natural theology are based is available to us simply by using our native, inborn powers of reason: faculties such as perception, introspection, *a priori* intuition, memory and inferential reasoning. Historically, controversy surrounds the subject of classifying our native powers and deciding how epistemically valuable are the deliverances of a given power. Thomas Reid, for instance, thought that humans are equipped with a native disposition to receive and discriminate testimony, whereas David Hume and Locke disparaged testimony as a source of knowledge. Plato famously criticized the power of five senses to convey knowledge (*Resp.* VI–VII), whereas empiricists such as J. S. Mill thought that the senses lay at the foundation of all we know. Disputes about how to characterize our given intellectual nature are directly relevant to the attempt to justify theism – that is, to show that believing in God meets whatever standards must be met to avoid charges of intellectual misconduct, or to be said to believe in a truth-conducive way. As we shall see, some philosophers of religion, such as Alvin Plantinga, claim that we have a natural disposition in appropriate circumstances to believe in God. This disposition, which Plantinga, following John Calvin, calls the "*sensus divinitatis*", is like perception, memory and inferential reason, in being subject to development, so that persons can be expected to have varying levels of acuity with respect to its employment. What these disputes about intellectual faculties reveal is that epistemological standards, standards of exemplary intellectual conduct, depend in part on metaphysical beliefs about what kinds of persons we are and with what sort of intellectual equipment we are equipped.

Second, natural theology is natural in so far as the information, or data, that constitutes its premises is available simply by turning one's attention to the natural world, the "book of nature", as it were, and is therefore, in principle, accessible to all persons. Arguments for God's existence are founded upon such commonly observed features of the world as that there are things in motion, or that something cannot begin to exist from nothing, claims that at face value strike many persons as obvious. (The core insight of the ontological argument, while generally accessible, is not drawn from observations about the empirical world, and thus is something of an exception.) While the data undergirding arguments from natural theology may be accessible to all properly functioning, suitably mature persons, it may require sensitivity and skill to detect the data in all its nuances and to appreciate it for all its persuasive power. Similarly, the complex and difficult to observe behaviours of some wildlife species may require skill or training to detect, even though they are in principle open for all to see. If there is a perfectly good God who has created us and sustains us, and if our true happiness in this life and the next depends on being rightly related to God, it seems plausible to think that he would not wish us to remain ignorant of his existence, and so would make his existence known through data that is universally available and accessible without the benefit of formal education. As I shall argue later, in connection with the problem of suffering, it is also consistent with God's purposes that the awareness of his existence made possible through nature not be intellectually coercive.

Natural theology, so described, must be contrasted with "revealed theology". Common to the world's major monotheisms is the belief that not all that is important for us to know about God and his purposes for us and the world can be "read off" nature, as it were, and thus must be specially communicated by God through prophets, holy writ or through some other form of special revelation. For instance, how and when are we supposed to worship God? Should we pray facing Mecca, Jerusalem, Rome? On Saturday, Sunday, alternate Tuesdays? Should we sit, stand, kneel, assume a lotus posture? If God has specific commands on such matters, they cannot be gleaned through the "book of nature" but must be communicated through special revelation. The line dividing natural and revealed theology is porous. Thomas Aquinas, a medieval natural theologian *par excellence*, thought that most persons lacked the time, training and talent to learn of God through reason and argument, and so God included in his special revelation information that can be obtained through reason alone.

Before we look specifically at some of the traditional arguments of natural theology, we must consider its goals. Since arguments for God's existence date back over several millennia, the aims of natural theology reflect the philosophical standards of evidence and argument of various historical periods. Most natural theologians have thought that through argument one can acquire *knowledge* of God's existence. Persons have knowledge, according to the Greek gold standard, if they have self-reflective awareness that what one claims to know is certain. Augustine claims, as do many subsequent thinkers, that such self-reflective certainty comes in at least two forms. Understanding (*intellectus*) is the faculty of mind by which one grasps self-evident *a priori* truths such as mathematical and logical axioms. Knowledge (*scientia*) is the cognitive power to infer truths from self-evident starting points and, by extension, refers to the truths so inferred. Locke echoes this distinction by claiming that "intuition and demonstration are the degrees of knowledge; whatever comes short of one of these, with what assurance soever embraced, is but faith or opinion, but not knowledge" (*An Essay Concerning Human Understanding* IV.ii.14; 1959: 185). What unites these two forms of knowledge is that the knowing agent acquires them through his own cognitive powers. Upon seeing, the mind assents irresistibly and is subsequently in repose; there is no need for further enquiry into its truth. Faith and belief, according to traditional lines of demarcation, are not "seen" through our native intellectual powers, although one may have probabilistic evidence for belief.

Many contemporary epistemologists no longer distinguish sharply between belief and knowledge, making this classical division between belief and knowledge problematic. Knowledge is no longer treated as a separate genus from belief, but is often characterized as adequately grounded or warranted true belief. Nor do most contemporary philosophers think that knowledge must be invincibly certain. Indeed, they are inclined to say that scientists know facts about the world if they are supported to a very high degree of probability. And so-called externalist epistemologists, as we shall have further cause to see, deny that we must have reflective access to the grounds of our knowledge; it can arise simply out of faculties functioning properly in appropriate environments. If, for example, my remembering that I ate breakfast this morning arises out of properly functioning faculties in a suitable environment, then I have memorial knowledge, even though it is neither an instance of *intellectus* or *scientia* (see Plantinga 1993: esp. chs 1, 2). Contemporary epistemologists also devote far more attention to the requirements for rational or justified belief than did the ancients.

So how, then, shall we think about the goals of natural theology? Traditionally, natural theologians sought nothing less than undefeatable knowledge that God exists. From self-evidently true starting points and flawless logic, traditional natural theologians offered proofs for God's existence. To prove that God exists is to show that theism is the only reasonable view and anyone believing in a manner incompatible with theism is unreasonable. These days, with philosophy's increased interest in justified belief that may not attain to knowledge, we might rest content with arguments that shows God's existence to be highly probable: the most reasonable view. Even weaker forms of rational belief are possible, for instance, showing that theism is, at least, not unreasonable. At what point one abandons the demanding goals of natural theology and begins merely to argue for the reasonability of theism is difficult to say.

For anyone who has had a little experience with philosophy, or academia in general, the goals of natural theology may seem impossibly high. Philosophers seldom marshal proofs or arguments approximating proofs for most of their fondly held views. Consider, for instance, the ongoing debates about whether humans have freedom of the will, whether consciousness is simply a function of the brain, whether pleasure and absence of pain is a suitable basis for morality, what are the necessary and sufficient conditions of something's qualifying as a work of art, or even what Plato really meant to say in some later dialogue. These and most other philosophical positions remain matters under contest, and experience gives us little reason to think these contests will be decisively settled anytime soon. Debates about God's existence appear to fall into this familiar pattern, dimming the prospects of a decisive argument for theism. Philosophers are not alone, however, in facing the phenomenon of unresolved debate and protracted disagreement. Ask a roomful of economists what the effect on the market will be if the prime lending rate were to be raised 1 per cent. Then stand back and watch as the Keynesians, Marxists, supply-siders and other economists disagree. Ask a gathering of American historians for the chief cause of the Civil War, or ask a group of English professors to settle once and for all whether a play attributed to Shakespeare is actually his, or Christopher Marlowe's, or the work of some other author. It does not follow from the fact of unresolved disagreement that proofs are not possible. Maybe the Marxists have a proof, that is to say, an argument whose conclusion follows necessarily from true premises.

If so, it follows that one can have a proof for a view yet be unable to convince others to that effect.

What is important to notice is that, while philosophers and other academicians pursue their work amid unresolved disagreement, they nevertheless take sides in the matters they debate and consider themselves rational in so doing. I may consider my Marxist colleague equally as intelligent, well-trained and knowledgeable about the economical issues under discussion, but at the end of the day I respectfully disagree with his position. Perhaps I suspect that he has not felt the force of my arguments and evidence to the degree that he should, a suspicion he no doubt extends to me. Similar disagreements mark the work of scientists, although not, perhaps, to the same degree. Scientists, for instance, continue to disagree about whether the universe will expand indefinitely, the extent to which global warming is due to human activity and the anti-carcinogenic properties of various foods, among many other matters. As we shall see, what one takes to be evidence, and how one estimates its force, lie at the centre of many disagreements.

Someone may accept my sketch of academic philosophy but conclude that no one has any business adopting positions about matters that cannot be conclusively shown to be true. This sceptical position is, alas, itself a matter of long-standing and unresolved disagreement, and so, by the belief policy just enunciated, it too should not be endorsed. Moreover, this sceptical policy would affect not just my theorizing but also my everyday practical decisions. One could not, on this view, adopt convictions about how to raise one's children, where to invest one's money, what sort of foods to eat for optimal health or who to vote for in the next election, since one will find intellectual peers who take positions incompatible with one's own. The sceptical view is untenable. Instead, one should simply endeavour to look at the arguments and evidence with as keen a mind and sincere a will as one can muster, and if, after a fair and honest investigation of the matter, one finds oneself thinking that theism is true, then one can hardly be thought irrational.

So we shall look at these arguments not as a boxing match won by a single knock-out punch capable of felling all competitors, but as a match won on points. Evidentialism did not require a proof, although a proof would do. Maybe we do not have invincible knowledge, but neither do we need it in order to be rational.

1 Design arguments

The analogical design argument

We begin our study of natural theology with design arguments, not because they are logically prior to the other arguments for God's existence, but because they are grounded in so common and widespread an experience – that of beholding the complexity, grandeur and apparent design of the world around us. How many of us have cast a heavenward glance at the star-studded sky on a spectacularly clear night and been moved to the thought "surely this could not have come about by sheer accident, but must be the work of some supernatural being"? Or, for those whose wonder is moved by the microcosmic, how many of us lazily stretched out on a lawn have fixed upon a single blade of grass, contemplated the cellular machinery necessary to produce chlorophyll, and been moved to the same thought? Surely, our initial sentiments suggest that the world and all it contains could not have arisen by accident, that it must be the work of an intelligent agent; and who better than God to produce a world of such scale and intricacy?

Whittaker Chambers, who gave important evidence against convicted Communist spy Alger Hiss during the Cold War, wrote in his book *Witness*:

> But I date my break [with the Communist Party] from a very casual happening. I was sitting in our apartment in St. Paul Street in Baltimore. It was shortly before we moved to Alger Hiss's apartment in Washington. My daughter was in her highchair. I was watching her eat. She was the most miraculous

thing that had ever happened in my life. I liked to watch her even when she smeared porridge in her face or dropped it meditatively on the floor. My eye came to rest on the delicate convolutions of her ears – those intricate, perfect ears. The thought crossed my mind: "No, those ears were not created by any chance coming together of atoms in nature (the Communist view). They could have been created only by immense design". The thought was involuntary and unwanted. I crowded it out of my mind, but I never wholly forgot it or the occasion. I had to crowd it out my mind. If I completed it, I should have had to say: Design presupposes God. I did not know then, but at that moment, the finger of God was first laid upon my forehead.

> (Quoted in Gardner 1983: 196–7)

Even Immanuel Kant, thought by many to be one of natural theology's most forceful critics, nevertheless says of the argument:

This knowledge [of nature] again reacts on its cause, namely, upon the idea which has led to it, and so strengthens the belief in a supreme Author [of nature] that the belief acquires the force of an *irresistible conviction*. It would therefore be not only uncomforting but utterly vain to attempt to diminish in any way the authority of this argument. Reason, constantly upheld by this ever-increasing evidence, which, though empirical, is yet so powerful, cannot be so depressed through doubts suggested by subtle and abstruse speculations, that it is not at once aroused from the indecision of all melancholy reflection, as from a dream, by one glance at the wonder of nature and the majesty of the universe – ascending from height to height up to the all-highest, from the conditioned to its conditions, up to the supreme and unconditioned Author [of all conditioned beings].

> (*Critique of Pure Reason* A624/B652; 1961: 520, emphasis added)

Kant is careful to distinguish between the purely intellectual and the psychological force of the nature's apparent design. While he thought the "subtle and abstruse" speculations of philosophy could not fashion a logically irrefutable proof for God's existence, he nevertheless thought that the evidence of design moved the mind to "irresistible conviction" psychologically, or through what was called by Thomas Reid, "natural signs".[1]

The experience of apparent design, from the microcosmic to the macrocosmic, from the structure of single cells to the swirling stars of the Milky Way, prompts us to wonder whether the cosmos is the work of God. And, as wonder at the world's order gives rise to philosophical thought, it has fostered a family of arguments known as "teleological" or "design" arguments. William Paley, an eighteenth-century English philosopher and theologian, thought the evidence of design could be marshalled into a decisive argument for God's existence. Likening the world to a watch, Paley's version of the argument from design trades on an analogy between machines and the universe. Suppose one were to stroll along the shore and there find a beautiful gold watch keeping perfect time. Even if one lacked prior acquaintance with watches, one would not for an instant suppose that the watch had been accidentally assembled by the waves and tossed up onto the beach. We obviously think that objects of such complexity and apparent purpose – call them teleological mechanisms – cannot have come about accidentally, but only through the handiwork of some intelligent agent. Does not experience teach us uniformly that when we find teleological mechanisms whose parts appear framed and put together for a purpose – cameras, computers and cars being good examples – they are the work of intelligent agents and not the products of random or accidental forces? How much more, then, should this sentiment be strengthened as we consider that the world's subtlety, complexity and size far surpasses that of a watch.

Paley's reasoning employs a very common principle: where we see like effects, we reasonably infer like causes. This principle lies at the heart of all inductive reasoning and underlies much scientific research. A doctor, let us suppose, examines a patient and detects symptoms A, B and C, and blood tests and other diagnostic measures indicate disease D. Later in the day, the same doctor encounters additional patients with the same symptoms, and again tests point to disease D. When the sixth patient walks into her office displaying the very same symptoms, she reasonably infers disease D even in advance of results from diagnostic tests. Teleological mechanisms such as cars, cameras and computers all exhibit the harmonious interplay of parts, the means-to-end adaptation that bespeaks the work of intelligent agents. The universe, says Paley, displays these very same features or complexity and organization to a magnificent degree. In keeping with the principle that like effects presuppose like causes, is it not reasonable to suppose that the universe is the work of an intelligent agent?

David Hume, the famous eighteenth-century philosopher and religious sceptic, with his characteristic sparkling prose and evident wit, criticized arguments such as Paley's to devastating effect in his *Dialogues Concerning Natural Religion*. Hume (or Philo, thought by many to speak for Hume) objects to this analogical form of design argument on three main grounds. First, he thinks the analogy drawn between a watch and the world is weak. In order to say that with any confidence that the world resembles the watch, that teleology pervades the universe, we would need much more extensive knowledge of the vast reaches of the universe than we have. But we lack exhaustive knowledge of what is transpiring throughout the entire cosmos throughout all time. Perhaps chaos reigns in parts of the universe with which we are not yet acquainted. Perhaps the law-like regularities we presently observe are an aberration of the last couple of million years, and at other times past or yet to come, disorder will prevail.

Imagine going into an immense warehouse filled with thousands of shelves of books stretching from floor to ceiling and, upon inspecting one shelf, you observe that its books are alphabetically arranged. You could not, with intellectual propriety, conclude on the basis of that scant survey, that the rest of the books were also alphabetically arranged. (Contemporary science, however, gives us reasons Hume lacked to think that the laws of the universe are uniform throughout.) Moreover, the similarities between the world and the watch are too few. While each has multiple parts that move together in a coordinated way, we cannot easily assign a function to the universe. Washers wash, dryers dry, toasters toast; what does the universe do? Produce and sustain life? If physicists are correct to think that our sun, along with all the other stars, will be depleted of its life-giving energy and that life as we know it will one day be unsustainable, then the universe would appear to be, as much as anything else, a colossal engine of death!

Even if we grant that the universe resembles a watch by being ordered throughout, the argument still fails to establish the existence of the omniscient, omnipotent, omnibenevolent God of theism. If we suppose, as Paley does, that where we find similar effects we should postulate similar causes, then we cannot conclude that the designer of the universe is one, still exists, is infinite or, more disturbingly, is morally perfect.

To appreciate Hume's point, consider the pyramids of Egypt – immense and impressive architectural achievements. As such, they had multiple designers, all of whom are dead, none of whom were infinite in power and, given the wages and benefits given to their labour force, they fell far shy of perfect goodness. Now by strict parity of reason, something the size and age of the universe should incline us still more to doubt the current existence of a single being who created it. More disturbingly, says Hume, human wickedness and the diseases, plagues and pestilence that beset human existence, hardly betoken the efforts of a supremely good creator. Our universe, if designed, is something of a jalopy, lurching down the road in fits and starts, and far from the sleek, stylish, smooth-running Rolls Royce of a universe we would expect from an infinite being.

Finally, Hume further impugns Paley's comparison of the world to a watch or knitting loom by suggesting it might just as readily be compared to vegetative life, which appears to have the ingredients of its organization and development within itself. In thinking that foreshadows Charles Darwin, Hume repeatedly suggests in the *Dialogues* that the organization and development of the universe is due to what he calls "hidden springs and principles".

> Thought, design, intelligence, such as we discover in men and other animals, is no more than one of the springs and principles of the universe, as well as heat or cold, attraction or repulsion, and a hundred others, which fall under daily observation. It is an active cause, by which some particular parts of nature, we find, produce alterations on other parts. (Hume 1993: 49)

Hume is here gesturing in the direction of a natural rather than a supernatural explanation for the world's displaying the order and organization that is does. Hume could not, however, provide a satisfactory explanation for how natural forces such as gravity, heat, and magnetism could give rise to such complex creatures as human beings.

What Hume could only hint at, Darwin named and described in his famous 1859 work, *On the Origin of Species*. The structure, organization and development of all living things is due to repli-cating cells, random genetic mutation and natural selection, the essential elements of evolutionary explanations. Very roughly, the theory claims that natural organisms occasionally undergo random genetic mutation, resulting in some feature that other members of its kind lack: additional receptor sites on a cell wall, a longer neck or colour vision. Sometimes these adaptations prove favourable for survival in the particular environment in which the organism finds itself. The creature serendipitously finds itself in an environment where its mutation gives it greater access to food or makes it bet-ter able to elude predators. More often than not, however, these mutations are not adaptive. As Stephen Jay Gould points out, the Burgess Shale by itself contains the remains of more creatures long extinct than presently dot the face of the Earth (Gould 1989). But when random changes and environment cooperate to allow the creature to elude predators and compete for scarce resources more successfully than other members of its kind, its genetic material is more likely to be passed on to future generations.

Critics of the teleological argument deny that nature's work resembles that of a watchmaker, and think instead that appeals to intellectual agency should give way to blind chance. Richard Dawkins happily accedes to this conclusion and describes nature's processes thus: "It has no mind and no mind's eye. It does not plan for the future. It has no vision, no foresight, no sight at all. If it can be said to play the role of watchmaker in nature, it is the *blind* watchmaker" (Dawkins 1986: 5). Elsewhere, Dawkins tells us: "The universe has precisely the properties we should expect if there is, at bottom, no design, no purpose, no evil and no good, nothing but blind pitiless indifference ... DNA neither knows or cares. DNA just is. And we dance to its music" (Dawkins 1995: 133).

Logically, we are not stuck with just the two alternatives thus far surveyed, Paley's robust theism or the bleak naturalism of Dawkins. It is strictly logically possible, for instance, that pantheism is true, that the universe in its totality is itself divine, and somehow con-tains the principles of its organization and development within it, as Hume hints. Perhaps some finite creative force such as Plato's demiurge created the universe. While any number of explanations are logically possible, we will continue as though the two leading explanations for the order and organization of the universe are God or blind chance.

The argument from irreducible complexity

Versions of the teleological argument based on an analogy between the world and machines faced formidable objections from Hume, but other versions of the design argument have been formulated that claim to escape these problems. We shall look briefly at three efforts to update the general thrust of the design argument. The first is "the argument from irreducible complexity", powerfully forwarded by biochemist Michael Behe in his book *Darwin's Black Box* (1996).[2] In a nutshell, Behe claims that a tiny "molecular machine" such as the flagellum (tail) of the sperm cell and bacteria, is so elaborate, and the relationship of its parts to each other and to the cell that it propels so interdependent, that they could not have arisen in the way current evolutionary theory suggests. Darwin himself recognized the problem posed for his theory by irreducibly complex mechanisms. He writes: "If it could be demonstrated that any complex organ existed which could not possibly have been formed by numerous, successive, slight modifications, my theory would absolutely break down" (quoted in Behe 1996: 39). Behe claims to have identified precisely the sort of complex biological organisms and processes Darwin feared.

To understand the concept of an irreducibly complex machine, Behe bids us consider the humble mousetrap. It is a very simple mechanism, consisting of a spring, a hammer, a triggering device and a platform to hold the parts in place. The important point is that if you take away any one of the parts, the mousetrap will not function; it works either with every part present, or it does not work at all. Moreover, the individual parts have the function they do only when properly configured with the other parts of the trap; the bare hammer or triggering mechanism, lying off by themselves, have no function whatsoever. The irreducible complexity of the bacterium flagellum, the whip-like tail that propels the cell is even more dramatic, says Behe. This remarkable corkscrew-hair-like appendage acts like a propeller on an outboard motor, is fuelled by a delicate mixture of some thirty or so proteins, and includes a drive shaft, universal joint, bushings and bearings, rotor and a stator. According to Behe, these parts could not have developed their various functions while disconnected from one another, and then somehow have been cobbled together in the random and incremental way proposed by evolutionary theory. The better explanation, says Behe, is that these cellular structures arose as they did by benefitting from the guidance of intelligent agency.

Needless to say, since the publication of Behe's book, microbiologists have risen to the challenge, offering explanations of how the flagellum might have arisen along standard evolutionary lines. Kenneth Miller, professor of cell biology at Brown University, disputes the claim that the flagellum is irreducibly complex, noting the resemblance between the flagellum and a needle-like appendage that salmonella bacteria possess to inject toxins into host cells (see Miller 2000).[3] These needle-like structures share many elements in common with the flagellum, although they lack the proteins that propel the flagellum. The important point to grasp is that, if Miller is correct, the flagellum's parts would not be useless were they disconnected and thus could later be recruited for a new use. While Miller admits that this is not a complete explanation, still less does it explain how these individual parts came to be, it nevertheless suggests that nature is more resourceful at combining existing biological parts for new purposes than Behe believes.

I am assuming that most readers are, like me, not trained in cellular biology or biochemistry. We are therefore unable to offer scientifically authoritative evaluations of the ongoing disputes among scientists regarding allegedly irreducibly complex entities, such as the eye, the clotting system and the bacterium flagellum. Nevertheless, as philosophers, we can note several points. First, even if Behe is correct and science has not yet arrived at an authoritative evolutionary explanation of the origins and development of the bacterium flagellum (and may never do so), we cannot from that fact alone infer that God is responsible. For that matter, it is possible that both Behe and Miller are wrong, and that some as yet undiscovered natural process may one day account for this sort of scientific phenomenon. Second, even if one is inclined to favour the explanation that intelligent agency lies behind such marvellous bits of biology, this hardly constitutes an inescapable proof for God's existence, nor even a strong probabalistic argument. At best, what theists might say is that of the two leading explanations for the origin and development of the flagellum, that of evolutionary naturalism and theism, they find the theistic explanation the stronger of the two. Of course, non-believers will have precisely opposing intuitions. Can one be rational in believing something while fully aware that other persons of equal intellectual ability and sincerity deny what you believe? This is an issue to which we will return shortly.

The argument from fine-tuning

A second variation on the design argument is the fine-tuning argument, which takes its name from the fact that the physical constants that characterize the universe seem to have been fine-tuned to allow for human life.[4] Imagine a radio with a tuner whose dial – like most radios – must be adjusted precisely to the right point on the tuner in order for the radio to receive a clear signal. But unlike most radios, the dial we are imagining has ten thousand billion billion billion billion individual notches. Given our current number of broadcast frequencies, the odds that a random spin of the dial would result in a clear signal are preposterously improbable. Now imagine not just one dial, but 60 dials, each with tens of billions of notches, each of which must be precisely tuned individually and with respect to each other in order to receive a signal. Again, the likelihood of a random spin of the dials resulting in a signal is incomprehensibly small.

Such a radio is an apt metaphor, say proponents of the fine-tuning argument, for the array of physical constants in the universe whose ranges must be within spectacularly small spectrums for life to be possible. For instance, "if the initial explosion of the big bang had differed in strength as little as one part in 10^{60}, the universe would have either quickly collapsed back on itself, or expanded too rapidly for stars to form. In either case, life would be impossible" (R. Collins 1999: 49). Gravitation, the strong force, the weak force, electromagnetism, the proton–neutron mass difference and many other physical constants must fall within quite narrow ranges to be life-permitting. For example, a 3,000-fold increase in the gravitational force would decrease the life of a star to a million years, thereby preventing carbon formation, thus preventing the emergence of carbon-based life. Now a 3,000-fold increase sounds like a lot, but when compared with the whole 10^{40} range that the value might assume, it is very small: one part in a billion, billion, billion, billion. A 2 per cent increase in the strong force would decrease by 30–1,000-fold the total amount of carbon or oxygen, and would be life-inhibiting. If it were 5 per cent weaker, no helium would form and there would be nothing but hydrogen. If the weak nuclear force were a little stronger, supernovas could not occur and heavy elements would not have formed. If electromagnetic force were stronger, all stars would be red dwarves and there would be no planets. If a little weaker, all stars would be very hot and short-lived. If the cosmological constant which influences the rate of expansion of the universe were not fine-tuned to within one part in 10^{53}, the universe would expand too rapidly, and matter could never form. The same holds for many other variables. Not only must the physical constants fall within remarkably small ranges for life to occur, but so must the natural laws be life-permitting. In the nanoseconds following the Big Bang, not only did matter–energy arise but so did the physical laws that would dictate its properties. These laws too had to assume life-permitting ranges from among the broad spectrum of ranges they could have assumed. UK Astronomer Royal, Martin Rees, himself a critic of fine-tuning arguments, nevertheless admits that our existence "depended crucially on a recipe encoded in the Big Bang, and this recipe seems to have been rather special" (2003: 212).

Even if it is highly improbable that life-permitting laws and physical constants arose accidentally, it does not follow straight away that the God of monotheism established them. Cautious proponents of the fine-tuning argument tend to make the weaker claim that the "God hypothesis" is the best explanation among the leading contenders. Robin Collins here invokes what he calls, following Elliott Sober, "the likelihood principle". This general principle of reasoning says that, when confronted with competing hypotheses or explanations from some phenomenon, we should prefer whichever hypothesis makes the observations more likely (R. Collins 1999: 51). Suppose Bob, born on 11 January, gets a new car for his fortieth birthday with a number plate that reads "BOB 111". Suppose the two leading explanations are: (H1), that the number plate was randomly assigned, as most number plates are; or (H2) that it was specially ordered. Plainly, the probability of Bob's car having been assigned that plate at that time is more probable on the hypothesis of someone's having ordered it than its having been assigned randomly. Analogously, we have two leading contenders to explain the universe being fine-tuned for life: a naturalistic hypothesis, which claims the that all the life-permitting laws, constants and other boundary conditions arose purely accidentally; or (H2) that the same laws and constants arose as guided by intelligent agency. The fine-tuning argument says, simply, that the existence of fine-tuning is improbable on a naturalistic, single-universe hypothesis, but not improbable on the theistic hypothesis. So by the prime principle of confirmation, we should see the evidence of fine-tuning as providing stronger evidence for God than for atheism.

Robin Collins (2007: 354) puts the argument succinctly:

Premise 1:	The existence of a fine-tuned universe with CEL [conscious embodied life] is not highly improbable (or surprising) under theism.
Premise 2:	The existence of a fine-tuned universe with CEL is very improbable (surprising) under NSU [the naturalistic, single universe hypothesis].
Conclusion:	From premises 1 and 2 and the likelihood principle, it follows that the fine-tuning data provides significant evidence to favour the design hypothesis over the NSU.

Again, caution is called for. Just because some observation is more probable under one hypothesis than another does not, by itself, prove the hypothesis, or even show that we ought to believe it. Suppose we find the murder weapon with the defendant's fingerprints all over it. Now consider two hypotheses: (H1) that the defendant is guilty of the murder; or (H2) that the defendant is innocent of the murder. It is more probable that the murder weapon has the defendant's fingerprints on the assumption that he is guilty rather than innocent. But this does not prove that the defendant is guilty, nor does it suggest that we should believe that he is. We need to consider *all the other evidence* which bears on the case and which may exonerate the defendant. Perhaps ten outstanding witnesses all testify under oath that the defendant was nowhere near the scene of the crime when the murder occurred. Perhaps we have some reason to think that someone is trying to frame the defendant. So too in the case of fine-tuning; as we explore criticisms of the fine-tuning argument, we will see that some critics are not moved to believe in God although they admit the improbability of our universe being life-permitting. Other critics argue that if there are multiple universes, the likelihood that one should contain life is not all that improbable.

John Barrow and Frank Tipler do not dispute the narrow range of life-permitting conditions cited by writers such as Collins. If anything, they contribute additional examples of the universe's delicate fine-tuning (Barrow & Tipler 1986). Unlike Collins, however, they are not surprised by this data. Indeed, given the fact that humans exist, we should rather expect the universe to be life-permitting – if it were not, we would not be here! Say Barrow and Tipler:

> The basic features of the Universe, including such properties as its shape, size, age and laws of change, must be *observed* to be of a type that allows the evolution of observers, for if intelligent life did not evolve in an otherwise possible universe, it is obvious that no one would be asking the reason for the observed shape, size, age and so forth of the Universe.   (*Ibid.*: 1–2)

Features of the universe which, considered in the abstract, or *a priori*, strike us as startlingly improbable, cease to be surprising when viewed from the standpoint of carbon-based life forms such as ourselves who either view a universe such as the one we inhabit or we do not view one at all. This idea is summarized in what Barrow and Tipler call the "Weak Anthropic Principle": "The observed values of all physical and cosmological quantities are not equally probable but they take on values restricted by the requirement that there exist sites where carbon-based life can evolve and by the requirement that the universe be old enough for it to have already done so" (1986: 16). Our very existence, say Barrow and Tipler, acts as an "intrinsic bias" or "selection effect" for what sort of universe we are capable of observing.

What bearing does the Weak Anthropic Principle have on the fine-tuning argument? Just this: because our situation as human observers ensures that we are in a life-permitting universe, the surprise at finding ourselves so situated disappears. Our surprise thus diminished, we ought not to feel ourselves under any imperative to explain why our universe is life-permitting, still less should we look for such explanations from theology.

If we distinguish, however, as D. H. Mellor bids us, between *epistemic* and *physical* possibility, we see confusion in the claim that the Anthropic Principle eliminates our surprise at finding ourselves in a life-conducive universe. We must distinguish, says Mellor, between surprise arising from one's epistemic standpoint and surprise arising from the constitution of the physical world. Suppose, he bids us, that we toss a coin and it lands on its side. Given that we have no reason to think either our perceptual faculties or environment deceptive or misleading, then, relative to such facts, the evidence of our senses makes the *epistemic* probability that the coin landed on its side quite high. Yet this in no way explains the coin landing on its side, since these facts about our epistemic standpoint do not explain the physical probability of that event (Mellor 2003: 224). It is the *physical probability*, not just what follows from our epistemic standpoint, that induces surprise.

This last point can be strengthened by considering a well-known example by John Leslie. Suppose you were placed before a firing squad of fifty expert marksmen. Fully expecting the words "ready" and "aim" to be the last you would hear on earth, you nevertheless hear the explosion of fifty rifles and find yourself staring at your supposed executioners. It would be silly to respond "well, this is not so surprising, since, if they had not missed me I would not be here to consider the fact", given the physical improbability of fifty marksmen missing at close range. Obviously, one's being still alive is much better explained by collusion rather than that they all missed (Leslie 1988: 304). The Weak Anthropic Principle does not eliminate the physical improbability of life having arisen. So the fact that we exist still calls for an explanation.

Robin Le Poidevin objects to the fine-tuning argument on the grounds that theists who advance this argument misuse the notion of probability. What does it mean to say that a universe fine-tuned to life is improbable, especially on the assumption that the universe's coming into being is a unique, unrepeatable event? The frequency theory of probability says we should calculate the likelihood of an event by the frequency with which the event occurs in a large enough sample of cases. If we flipped a fair coin a million times, we would expect the distribution of outcomes to be even, 50 per cent heads, 50 per cent tails. According to Le Poidevin, the frequency theory, while not the only way to think about probability, "is the one most clearly relevant to this argument" (Le Poidevin 1996: 50). If probability understood as frequency is what fine-tuning arguers have in mind, then Le Poidevin is correct to think they have employed the wrong notion of probability. For frequency is relative to populations. As insurance rates attest (in fact, this account of probability originated from mortality rates used by insurance companies) the frequency of someone's getting in an automobile accident in the next year is higher for teens than it is for other segments of the driving populace. But we lack an extended population of universes with which to compare our own, since, by hypothesis there has been only one. On this way of calculating probability, it looks as though the likelihood of a life-permitting universe occurring is high, indeed 1! Says Le Poidevin: "for chance to make sense on the frequency theory, the relevant population must contain more than one member" (1996: 51).

Proponents of the fine-tuning argument, however, deny that the frequency theory is the only way to explain the sense of probability at work in the fine-tuning argument. Robin Collins, for instance, prefers either classical or epistemic probability to the frequency view. On the classical view, the probability of an event is determined by the ratio of "favourable cases" to the total number of equally possible cases: $P(s) = f/n$, read, the probability of s, some event, is equivalent to f, all the favourable outcomes, divided by n, the number of possible outcomes. So, the probability of rolling six on a normal six-sided die is 1/6. Or, the probability of an unaimed arrow shot in the direction of a target hitting the bullseye is equal to the probability of its hitting any other part of equal area.

Notice, that the classical account of probability assumes that we know all the possible outcomes that can occur and that all the possible outcomes are equally possible. So, the probability that life-permitting laws and constants obtain is the ratio of the range of life-permitting values to the total range of possible values. At this juncture, Robin Collins himself raises the crucial question: "But what," he asks, "is the total *relevant* range of possible values?" (1999: 69). Perhaps if the force of gravity were 10^{60} times greater than it is, new matter would come to exist that makes possible forms of life quite different from any of which we are currently aware.

We just do not know what is the entire range of life-permitting universes. So, the modified claim of the fine-tuning argument must be restricted to the range of values for which scientists *can* make estimates, what Collins calls "the illuminated range" of values. Even restricted to the illuminated range, however, it remains the case that the life-permitting range is extremely small. That is, "it is very improbable for the values of the parameters of physics to have fallen into a life-permitting range *instead* of some other part of the illuminated range" (*ibid.*).

A stronger objection to fine-tuning arguments concerns the possibility that there are, or have been, "multiple universes". (If the universe is all there is, it is exceedingly odd to speak of "multiple universes"; thus some proponents of this idea speak of one universe containing an "ensemble of worlds".) An easy way to see the objection is to start with the view of a cyclical universe, subject to unceasing cycles of expansion and contraction, like some sort of cosmic yo-yo. Each universe is thus temporally distinct from its predecessor. Perhaps the odds of life arising within a single cycle does beggar the imagination. But what if there have been an infinite number of big-bangs and "big-crunches"; is it so clear that the emergence of life is astronomically improbable? Like the proverbial chimp set before the keyboard, if it pecks away for a long enough period of time, it will allegedly pound out a Shakespearean sonnet. The application to the fine-tuning argument is clear; the emergence of life on an infinite number of cosmic "throws of the dice", so to speak, makes the emergence of a life-permitting universe all too likely. With a purely naturalistic explanation so ready to hand, says the critic, one need not resort to the theistic hypothesis. The strength of this objection hinges, quite clearly, on whether there are good reasons to think our universe has been through endless cycles of expansion and contraction. But as the "physics *du jour*" would have it, there is virtually no support for the idea that the universe could bounce back from such a contraction.

The notion of multiple universes finds more frequent expression and support these days in the idea of "quantum fluctuations", that produce spatially rather than temporally distinct universes. Our universe, along with all the "universes" comprising the world ensemble may have arisen out of a pre-existing but volatile superspace, an excited vacuum that is not empty, but is full of fluctuating particles of matter–antimatter appearing and disappearing. Physicist Edward Tryon, describes it this way: "If it is true that our Universe has a zero net value for all conserved quantities, then it may simply be a fluctuation of the vacuum, the vacuum of some larger space in which our Universe is embedded. In answer to the question of why it happened, I offer the modest proposal that our Universe is simply one of those things which happen from time to time" (1990: 218). Universes happen.

Some theorists extend the idea of a universe-producing vacuum state by theorizing that within an inflationary universe (a period of ultra-fast expansion in the first few nanoseconds following the Big Bang) there exists, says George Gale, the possibility for:

> an infinite number of "daughter universes" from inflationary expanding bubbles of false vacuum trapped within the domain of true vacuum. The process will most likely continue as well within nucleated regions of the daughter universes, thus bringing about "granddaughter", "great-granddaughter", "great-great-granddaughter", and so on ad infinitum. Indeed, the process of making many worlds seems inevitable, given the vacuum fluctuation + inflation model.   (1990: 198)

Imagine inflating a balloon, whose rubber wall is not of uniform thickness. As one quickly inflates the balloon, a weak section of the balloon wall allows an appendage to "sprout" from it, perhaps many appendages. And each appendage, if not of uniform thickness, and if inflated fast enough, will sprout still additional appendages, and so on. Many of these "universes" would lack life-permitting values, but, as the criticism goes, many would contain the conditions that make life possible. Thus, not only is it not surprising that the universe harbours life, but we have a non-supernatural account of how this is possible.

The physics of other universes, to which we can but gesture rather than hope to explain, is still largely at the speculative stage, with no one model enjoying a clear consensus. Setting to one side the largely speculative nature of such theories, some theists say this theoretical combination of quantum fluctuation followed by inflation still does not eliminate the surprise at finding ourselves in a life-permitting universe and the need for fine-tuning. However we are to think of the state of the pre-existing superspace, it too must have been characterized in such a way that out of its initial conditions a life-permitting universe could emerge. But why should the pre-existing superspace be so favourably configured? To some advocates of the fine-tuning argument, this simply pushes our quest for an explanation up to another level. This much is clear: however remarkable one may find a fine-tuned universe, resources are available to account for it outside a theistic framework.

So, while fine-tuning may not constitute anything remotely like a proof of God's existence, it looks as though a theist who invoked God to account for the emergence of life would not thereby be irrational. At least this is the conclusion of long-time atheist Antony Flew, whose philosophical writings for more than fifty years supported atheism, but who later became convinced that some sort of intelligent agency must be invoked to account for the origin of life and the complexity of nature. According to Flew:

> Whatever the merits or demerits of this fine tuning argument in the context of attempts to construct a natural (as opposed to a revealed) theology, it must at once be allowed that it is reasonable for those who believe – whether rightly or wrongly – that they already have good evidencing reasons for accepting the religious teachings of any one of the three great revealed theistic religions – Judaism, Christianity, and Islam – to see the fine tuning argument as providing substantial confirmation of their own antecedent religious beliefs.   (2005: 11)

Flew is not claiming that the fine-tuning argument shows theism to be true, only that theists who cite the fine-tuning argument on behalf of their theism are rational to do so. This may be cold comfort to traditional theists, however, since Flew is quick to add that the super-intelligent agency he has in mind bears little resemblance to the God of the world's monotheisms, whom he views "on the model of an Oriental despot".

The argument from reason

From the microcosmic (the cell) to the macrocosmic (a universe fine-tuned for life), design arguments point to some grand, glorious and complex feature of our world and argue that nothing short of God can account for it. Critics of such arguments deny that supernatural agency must be invoked to account for such phenomena; nature herself, in the form of matter and the laws of nature that move it, provides the resources for fully adequate explanations.[5] This divide arises again as we consider a final feature of human experience – the phenomenon of human reason. Humans are equipped, as no other animals are, with minds made for various kinds of reasoning. We enjoy a cluster of capacities that include the ability to discover and share meaning, follow chains of inferential reasoning, consider a unified field of conscious awareness, and generally to engage in what we believe to be reliable belief formation about an extraordinarily wide array of matters.[6] Yet writers such as C. S. Lewis, Richard Taylor and, most recently, Alvin Plantinga offer variations of an argument designed to show that these capacities of human reason cannot be adequately explained as the outcome of accidental evolutionary processes, but are better explained as the work of a divine agent.[7] This family of arguments claims that naturalists cannot explain various aspects of human reason solely with reference to the physical processes of the brain and to the evolutionary processes that produced the brain.

Richard Taylor and Alvin Plantinga each argue that a naturalist world view undermines our confidence in reason. Each is struck by the incongruity between the confidence we place in the reliability of human reasoning – its ability to lead us to true beliefs about a wide variety of subjects – and the naturalist's claim that reason arose from purely physical, evolutionary processes that are random, blind and fit us merely to pass on our genes. If this is so, then why suppose that the human mind has evolved as an instrument able to reason in a reliable, truth-conducive fashion? Why not adopt the view expressed in Patricia Churchland's oft-cited passage:

> Boiled down to its essentials, a nervous system enables the organism to succeed in the four F's: feeding, fleeing, fighting, and reproducing. The principle chore of nervous systems is to get the body parts where they should be in order that the organism may survive... Improvements in sensorimotor control confers an evolutionary advantage: a fancier style of representing is advantageous *so long as it is geared to the organism's way*

of life and enhances the organism's chance for survival. Truth, whatever that is, definitely takes the hindmost.

(1987: 548–9)

Churchland's claim suggests that the powers of human reason are reducible to activity of non-purposive physical processes that are indifferent to truth. But, to suppose that our mind's capacities for thought are, at bottom, unconnected with arriving at the truth about the world is to undermine our confidence in reason's outputs.[8]

Plantinga notes that Darwin himself worried about the implications for his theory on the reliability of reason:

With me, the horrid doubt always arises whether the convictions of man's mind, which has been developed from the mind of the lower animals, are of any value or at all trustworthy. Would any one trust in the convictions of a monkey's mind, if there are any convictions in such a mind?   (1993: 219)[9]

Naturalists committed to evolutionary theory are divided whether to share "Darwin's doubt", as Plantinga calls it. W. V. O. Quine voices the view of one side, saying that "creatures inveterately wrong in their inductions have a pathetic but praiseworthy tendency to die before reproducing their kind" (quoted in *ibid*.: 219). Churchland, in the quote above, voices the other. So to which side shall we incline? Is reason more or less likely to be truth conducive given evolutionary naturalism? According to Plantinga, it is reasonable to adopt an agnostic posture here, and simply withhold judgment. But if we are agnostic about a reason's reliability, we would have to be agnostic about any of reason's particular outputs, and among the outputs of reason is the claim that evolutionary naturalism is true. So to assume that our capacities for thought arose from random evolutionary processes is to be handed a defeater for a justified belief in the evolutionary process. This does not show that evolutionary naturalism is false, simply that we are irrational to believe it.

Taylor underscores the role cognitive powers play to discern meanings we regard as true. Suppose, he says, that while travelling by train, we gaze through the window and see dozens of large boulders arranged on a hillside spelling out the words "The British Railways Welcomes You to Wales" (1963: 96). Now it is conceivable, although improbable, that the rocks accidentally fell, one by one, into that configuration over hundreds of thousands of years. After all, nature sometimes produces strange and marvellous phenomena without the guiding hand of a purposive agent. Just here Taylor bids us note an important point:

> If, upon seeing from the train window a group of stones arranged as described, you were to conclude that you were entering Wales, and if your sole reason for thinking this, whether it was in fact good evidence or not, was that the stones were so arranged, then you could not, consistently with that, suppose that the arrangement of the stones was accidental. You would, in fact, be presupposing that they were arranged that way by an intelligent and purposeful being or beings, for the purpose of conveying a certain message having nothing to do with the stones themselves.   (*Ibid.*: 97)

One cannot simultaneously see the arrangement of stones as purely accidental and truth-conducive. Likewise, if the arrangement of the molecules in our brains is, to use Bertrand Russell's words, "an accidental collocation of atoms", then we cannot suppose that the mental operations it makes possible are truth-conducive. Indeed, contemporary epistemologists think that a defining feature of human knowledge is its non-accidentality (see Pritchard 2005). The mere fact that a belief of mine arose owing to luck is sufficient to disqualify it as knowledge. Yet this seems to be what philosophers such as Dawkins are willing to say about the whole of human reasoning.

Let us change the analogy: suppose we outfitted a computer with a digital voice readout, a randomizer and a program that allowed the computer to reproduce every phoneme of which the human voice is capable in strings of sounds of varying length. Upon activating the program, the computer "speaks" one random string of sounds after another. Sometimes, the computer randomly strings together thousands of sounds, sometimes only a few. Most of time the time the machine spits out strings such as "zorg glibbitch reemeeb anhuladine": sheer gibberish. Some strings may even resemble grammatically well-formed sentences, such as "Pink sleep will stroll upstream last week", but are in fact incoherent. Now suppose that having listened to the computer's outputs for a couple of hours – perhaps you find this relaxing – you hear the following string of sounds: "Lucky Jack in the third race of 3 May 2011 at the Arlington Derby is a sure winner. Bet the bank." Would anyone knowing how the computer was programmed risk a single cent? Would anyone even suppose they had received a reliable piece of information that ought to be heeded? Yet, recall Dawkins's words about nature's processes: "It has no mind and no mind's eye. It does not plan for the future. It has no vision, no foresight, no sight at all." If the brain and the mental and vocal outputs it makes possible are themselves accidental assemblages of mindless matter, why should their outputs be given any more credence than those of the computer?

Theists claim to have a superior explanation for the mind's capacity to convey meaning and reliability to lay hold of the truth, to wit, that they have been empowered for such tasks by a supremely intelligent creator who created persons with the aim of communicating with them. To invoke again Robin Collins's principle of likelihood, when confronted with competing hypotheses or explanations for some phenomenon, we should prefer whichever hypothesis makes the observations more likely. Theists claim, simply, that the human ability to reason reliably is more to be expected if our world is the product of an intelligent creator than if it is due to a successive string of improbable accidents.

Critics might respond by claiming that theists are too quick to disparage the power of mindless matter, moved by natural necessity and chance, to share information and to communicate reliably. That distinct bits of mindless matter share information is indisputable. Cells, for instance, communicate with each other. Our immune systems react to the presence of an alien virus and successfully harness T-lymphocyte cells to destroy the virus. When they do so reliably, the organism successfully fights off disease and remains alive. When, however, the information exchanged between cells is "false", as in autoimmune diseases where the body turns on itself, the organism dies. However accidental the process may have been that produced such a complex information-sharing system, that system now functions in anything but an accidental or random way, and so is disanalogous to the computer with its random outputs and the rocks assembled on the side of the hill, which *are* purely accidental and no more. So every living organism is testimony to the fact that mindless matter has, in some way, successfully shared information. Ants, bees, wolves and other examples of "hive" or "pack" mentality testify still further to nature's ability to produce through natural means, complex information-sharing networks. Why, then, should we be astounded to discover that humans outfitted with brains capable of forming mental states, and the capacity to share the content of these states, can reliably acquire information and relay that information to one another?

True, no animal considers meanings in quite the way humans do. Neither ants nor bees form theories of interpretation, ponder the multiple meanings of an ambiguous phrase, theorize about the nature of necessity or play with gestalt images. But even here, humans might be thought to enjoy an evolutionary advantage. We do not merely respond to environmental stimuli like Pavlovian dogs, but in some instances weigh competing meanings conveyed by our environment. Is that a snake in the path, a piece of coiled rope or a twisted stick? Is that tone of voice threatening, angry or merely enthusiastic? And it is quite plausible to suppose that this power allows humans to avoid needless expenditures of energy and thus confers an evolutionary advantage.

All this talk of the ability of ants, bees and chimps to share information successfully does not do justice to the complexity of human reasoning, nor to the content of what we reason about. Not all human beliefs arise simply because they have been stimulated by an appropriate environmental trigger. Humans believe and are moved to believe because of the specific propositional content of the beliefs themselves. We believe *because* of what the belief is about. Consider two propositions:

(1) Necessarily, if John is a bachelor, then John is unmarried; and
(2) If John is a bachelor, then John is necessarily unmarried.

If we are sensitive to the modal status of each claim (to what philosophers call *de dicto* and *de re* necessity, respectively) we see that (1) is true and (2) is false. But this is no purely physical response to an environmental stimulus. We affirm, for instance, that if ten is greater than eight, then it is greater than three. But this we affirm without even bothering to count. We hold this and many other beliefs because of their logical properties and relations, which are themselves non-empirical realities. Indeed, this last claim is true in all possible worlds, including worlds where physical objects do not exist. It is difficult, therefore, to tell a causal or evolutionary story about the evolutionary advantages our seeing these truths confers. In his essay "Divine Necessity", Robert Adams thus theorizes that God's own necessary existence, his knowledge of necessary truths and his having created humans with the capacity to recognize necessary truths offers some theoretical advantages to theistic belief.

> If God of his very nature knows the necessary truth, and if he has created us, he could have constructed us in such a way that we would at least commonly recognize necessary truth as necessary. In this way there would be a causal connection between what is necessarily true about real objects and our believing it be necessarily true about them. It would not be an incredible accident or an inexplicable mystery that our beliefs agreed with the objects in this. (Adams 1987: 218)[10]

I think it is safe to say that none of the design arguments here surveyed constitutes a decisive proof for God's existence, one likely to persuade all readers of good mind and sincere will. Given the remaining arguments yet to be surveyed, it is also premature to start naming winners and losers. One thing seems clear: since the advances of science bear so significantly on the status of design arguments, we can expect future advances on science to complicate and, one hopes, illuminate the issues.

2 Cosmological arguments

The *kalam* cosmological argument

We have looked at a sampling of arguments, all of which claim that the world's organization, or the functioning of its parts, can best be explained as the handiwork of God. Opponents of such arguments deny that supernatural agency must be invoked; they believe we have perfectly rational and, perhaps, superior explanations that rely solely on natural laws and processes. The cosmological argument for God's existence does not focus on the world's organization, but on its very existence. The question can be put succinctly: why is there something rather than nothing? At first glance, three options present themselves for explaining the world's existence: (i) in one form or another, the material world has always existed; (ii) the material world simply popped into being out of nothing; (iii) the material world had a beginning in time and was brought into being by something immaterial. Theists, of course, opt for the last explanation. We shall explore two versions of the cosmological argument: the *kalam* cosmological argument, which has its origins in medieval Muslim philosophy, and the argument from contingency. Each claims that theism best accounts for the existence of the cosmos.

Common sense tells us that effects have causes. If there is a fire in the garage, there must be a cause responsible, be it faulty wiring, arson, flammable chemicals or some combination of causes. The principle that all effects have causes applies to the universe as a whole. If the universe began to exist, then it too must have had a cause of its existence. William Lane Craig (2002b: 92) puts the argument very simply:[1]

1. Whatever begins to exist has a cause.
2. The universe began to exist.
3. Therefore, the universe has a cause.

Craig argues that the cause of the universe cannot be the universe itself, but something outside the natural order of things, namely God. To accept the premises, however, one must argue that the universe has not always existed and that the universe's coming to be was caused. Let us examine these premises in turn.

The claim that the universe began to exist has philosophical as well as empirical support. To deny that the universe has always existed is to claim that our universe has an infinite past. No matter how far back one goes in the world's history, there was an infinitely old universe that preceded it. This commits one to claiming that our world's history contains an actual infinite number of temporal segments, measured by whichever unit of measurement you like – days, weeks, years, decades and so on. Craig, however, argues that to say the world's history is actually infinite leads to philosophical incoherence. To see this, we must distinguish between the concept of an actual infinite series of objects and a potentially infinite one. A potentially infinite series, such as the natural numbers, is simply one to which one can add members indefinitely, increasing toward infinity but never getting there. A 100m rope can theoretically be bisected again and again without ever reaching the last division. And one need not fret the prospect of having actually littered the floor with an infinite number of rope pieces! The notion of indefinite extension is quite a different matter, however, from that of having successfully compiled an actual infinite number of things. A collection would constitute an actually infinite series if any part of it is equal to the whole of it. For example, the series of natural numbers "1, 2, 3, …" is equivalent to the series of even numbers "2, 4, 6, …" even though the natural numbers contain all the even numbers. For any natural number we pick out, there is an even number that corresponds to it that we can map onto the natural number without fear of the first series outstripping the resources of the second.

Crucial to the *kalam* argument is the claim that, while an infinite series may exist as a theoretical construct in the mind, it cannot actually exist without absurd consequences ensuing. Craig bids us imagine a library with an actually infinite number of books. As an actual infinity, it cannot be enlarged. But suppose we were to tear the first page out of every tenth book, slap a title page and binding on them, and add them to the library. According to mathematics, I would not have succeeded in enlarging the library, not even if I were to repeat the process millions of times. Nor would our actually infinite library suffer any reduction in the number of books were one to remove every other book. This strikes us as counter-intuitive. How can the library with every other book removed not be smaller than the library that includes them? Craig says the confusion arises because the ordinary operations of addition and subtraction that we use every day in, for example, giving and receiving money, do not apply to transfinite arithmetic. So, if it is conceptually absurd for the mega-library envisioned above to exist, then it is impossible for there to be an actual infinite. If this reasoning is correct, the universe cannot have existed for an infinite amount of time, nor can the present day state of the universe somehow have arisen from an infinite causal past.

Critics attack this philosophical underpinning for the *kalam* argument at several points. Philosophical intuitions differ as regards the actual infinite. Aquinas thought the world had a beginning, although he did not think it self-evidently incoherent to think that the world could have existed for an infinite past. Alexander Pruss and Richard Gale think Craig's argument trades on a confusion between numerical and parts-to-whole notions of "bigger than" (Pruss & Gale 2005: 121–2). One set is *numerically* bigger than another if the first has more members than the other has. In the animal kingdom, the set of all insects is bigger than the set of mammals. In the case of parts-to-whole, a whole pie is obviously bigger than any part of a pie. When dealing with finite amounts, a set that is bigger in the parts-to-whole sense is also bigger in the numerical sense. This is not so, however, in the case of infinite sets. For example, the library with every other book removed is smaller in the parts-to-whole sense, but not in the numerical sense, which is why, say Pruss and Gale, mathematicians take the numerical rather than the parts-to-whole sense of "bigger than" to be the defining feature of infinity.

Graham Oppy thinks that to deny the coherence of an actual infinity means "we cannot then say either that an orthodoxly conceived monotheistic god is, or that an orthodoxly conceived monotheistic god's attributes are, actually infinite" (Oppy 2006: 139). For example, if an actual infinite is impossible, so would be the notion of an actually existing infinitely powerful God. In reply, theists reject the notion that God has infinite power in virtue of having completed an infinite number of tasks. God's power, knowledge, goodness and so forth are not to be thought of quantitatively, as if omnibenevolence required God to perform an infinite number of good deeds or an actual infinite number of tasks of increasing difficulty to earn the status of omnipotence. Rather, omnipotence, for instance, should be thought of qualitatively, as the dispositional power to bring about any non-contradictory state of affairs. But what of omniscience? Does God not know an actual infinite number of truths including, say, the product of any two numbers you can multiply? Yes, but if the notion of an actual infinite series is incoherent, as Craig argues, then how can God know the defining features of an infinite number of possible worlds or the solution to an infinite number of equations? Theists might counter by claiming that God's knowledge is not discursive; he does not have to reason to the truths he holds, but simply holds all the truths there are to hold in one immediate, comprehensive vision, so that, strictly speaking, his omniscience does not require that he know an actual infinite number of truths.

What of the empirical support for Craig's *kalam* argument? That the universe had a beginning some fourteen billion or so years ago at the "Big Bang" is now the orthodox view among physicists who study cosmology. It was not always so. Early in the twentieth century, many physicists embraced a so-called "steady state" theory of the universe, according to which the universe never had a beginning. In 1929, astronomer Edwin Hubble discovered that the light reaching us from the most distant galaxies was redder than that of closer galaxies, and that this red-shift is due to the expansion of the universe. Galaxies are growing farther and farther apart, much as buttons glued to the surface of a balloon recede from each other if the balloon is quickly inflated. As scientists measured the rate of expansion, they determined that the universe was at one time compacted down to an infinitely dense mathematical point, or singularity, from which the entire cosmos exploded, creating all matter, energy, space, time and even the laws of nature (Barrow & Tipler

1986: 442). Subsequent findings, such as the discovery of cosmic background radiation – "noise" from the Big Bang itself – by Penzias and Wilson in 1965, have reinforced the Big Bang hypothesis as the standard view. Moreover, the second law of thermodynamics tells us that processes within a closed physical system tend toward a state of equilibrium or disorder (which has humorously been offered as an explanation for the messy state of our bedrooms!). If the universe is a titanic closed physical system, then, given enough time, it will tend to disorder and "wind down", as it were. But clearly, if the universe has existed for an infinite amount of time, then we would have already reached a state of maximal entropy, and the fact that we have not testifies to the finite age of the universe.

Some scientists and theologians alike were quick to note the potential religious implications of the Big Bang, causing it at first to receive a mixed reception among cosmologists. Astronomer Robert Jastrow commented:

> It seems as though science will never be able to raise the curtain on the mystery of creation. For the scientist who has lived by his faith in the power of reason, the story ends like a bad dream. He has scaled the mountains of ignorance; he is about to conquer the highest peak; as he pulls himself over the final rock, he is greeted by a band of theologians who have been sitting there for centuries. (Quoted in Silk 1994: 2)

The widespread adoption of the Big Bang model has not prevented creative cosmologists from proposing competing models, perhaps because of its alleged support for religion. In the "oscillating model", a few physicists have speculated that the universe may go through successive phases of expansion and contraction, many "big bangs" followed by "big crunches". Presently, the dominant view among cosmologists is that the universe is flat, which is to say that it will continue expanding but at an increasingly slower rate. Moreover, physics has no mechanism to explain how the universe could rebound from a "big crunch" with a "big bounce". And as we saw briefly in the last chapter, on quantum fluctuation and inflationary models, our universe may be just one of many universes to emerge from a quantum fluctuation in a cosmic vacuum filled with subatomic energy in an excited state. If, however, a primordial vacuum were birthing multiple universes, we would expect these universes to collide or intersect at some point, but there is no observational confirmation of this point. Moreover, it is not clear on this model that we escape a regress problem. Suppose our universe, with its fundamental constants of nature, arose from some "primordial soup"; how are we to explain the soup's having produced a universe with the very laws and matter that characterize our universe? Is there a deep structure behind the structure of our universe?

Quantum gravitational models, such as that offered by Stephen Hawking, attempt to avoid the difficulties for scientific explanation that arise if space and time begin in some singularity. For if the very elements of scientific explanation arise in the first few nanoseconds of the world's existence, it lacks resources to explain why there should have been a big bang in the first place. Hawking proposes that:

> The quantum theory of gravity has opened up a new possibility, in which there would be no boundary to space-time and so there would be no need to specify the behavior at the boundary. There would be no singularities at which the laws of science broke down and no edge of space-time at which one would have to appeal to God or some new law to set the boundary conditions for space-time. One could say: "The boundary condition of the universe is that it has no boundary." The universe would be completely self-contained and not affected by anything outside itself. It would neither be created nor destroyed. It would just be. (1988: 136)

Hawking is fully aware of the highly speculative nature of his proposal, inasmuch as we lack a theory that unites general relativity and quantum mechanics, and it invokes highly speculative notions such as that of imaginary time. Needless to say, the jury is still out on what is the best model of the Big Bang, or whether, as Andrei Linde proclaims, the classical Big Bang theory is dead. But what follows if we grant Craig's point that the universe had a beginning?

From the fact that whatever begins to exist has a cause, and that the universe began to exist, it follows that that the universe has a first cause. By definition, the first cause cannot itself have been caused. Nor, if Craig is right, is the first cause to be found inside the universe. But what is the nature of that cause and why should we think of the cause as God? The cause cannot be explained scientifically since, as we have seen, the raw material for scientific explanations emerge out of the Big Bang. As physicist Charles Townes observes:

> I do not see how the scientific approach alone, as separated from a religious approach, can explain an origin of all things. It is true that physicists hope to look behind the "big bang," and possibly to explain the origin of our universe as, for example, a type of fluctuation. But then, of what is it a fluctuation and how did this in turn begin to exist? In my view, the question of origin seems always left unanswered if we explore from a scientific view alone.   (Quoted in Ferris 1997: 245–6)

The cause is outside the spatial and temporal orders, since these too have a beginning, hence the cause must be eternal and non-spatial. From the fact that our universe emerged hospitable to life, we can infer that the cause of the universe was extraordinarily intelligent, powerful and concerned that human life should arise. But these qualities are precisely some of the core properties that theists ascribe to God. An appeal to the activity and intention of an intelligent agent are what philosophers call "personal explanations". We can explain the cause of a fire by adverting to the physical principles of combustion. But if the fire was set by an arsonist attempting to defraud an insurance company, the flammability of gasoline and the presence of a lit match will not be the most important explanation. Thus, according to Craig, the most reasonable and salient cause of the universe coming to be is that it was the due to the creative agency of God.

Critics say theists face a significant "gap problem". Considerable intellectual distance separates the idea of a first cause of the universe and the robust theistic conception of God. Even if we do allow personal explanations, says J. L. Mackie, "the very notion of a non-embodied spirit, let alone an infinite one, is intrinsically improbable in relation to our background knowledge, in that our experience reveals nothing of the sort" (1982: 100). Apart from the fact that creation by immaterial beings is not a routine part of our daily experience, Mackie offers no argument to support his claim that such agents are "intrinsically improbable". Indeed, his claim is subject to an obvious rejoinder. If there is only one God whose creative efforts transcend space and time, then of course it will not be a frequent datum of our experience, which is limited to space and time. But this does not entail its being intrinsically improbable in a logical or metaphysical sense. Indeed, given the highly plausible assumption that something cannot come from absolutely nothing, and given that the spatiotemporal universe did not arise from some previously existing spatiotemporal state, it may strike many as intrinsically probable that an immaterial agent of great power and intelligence brought the world into being. Craig's argument remains limited, however, to the extent that it relies on an understanding of the Big Bang that is subject to the ever-changing, highly inventive theorizing of scientific cosmologists. The worry must be ever-present that the concept of a big bang, or the particular models of it compatible with Craig's argument, will become passé. The argument thus risks the same fate as all the so-called "God of the gaps" arguments that introduce a divine cause to account for something science as yet cannot explain.[2]

The argument from contingency

The cosmos, the "whole shebang", as Timothy Ferris calls it, incites in us wonder and amazement. Among other things, we wonder why the universe exists, why there is something rather than nothing. This wonder is quickened when we pause to consider that everything with which we are daily acquainted – rocks, tables, trees, people, mountains, stars and so on – are the sorts of things that come into being and go out of being, they are born, they die. They are, to use the philosopher's term, contingent things – things whose non-existence is possible. To be sure, we may not be on hand to witness a mountain reduced to dust or a star go supernova, but we know that such things happen. The fact that everything making up the universe is contingent, that is to say, displays this rather tentative hold on being, invites the question: why are there now, and why should there have ever been contingent things? Since the universe is, from all appearances, simply the aggregate of all contingent things, and since all contingent objects might never have existed, why is there something rather than nothing at all? And even if some contingent object or collection of objects should begin to exist, they need not have persisted in being; why did the whole collection of contingent things not go the way of the dinosaurs by becoming extinct?

To answer these questions, some theists have offered another version of the cosmological argument called, appropriately enough, "the argument from contingency". The argument can be formulated as follows:

1. Whatever exists contingently requires a cause or explanation for its existence.
2. The universe (as the collection of all contingent things) exists contingently.
3. Therefore, the universe requires a cause or an explanation for its existence.
4. No contingent thing causes or explains its own existence.
5. Whatever causes or explains the existence of the universe is itself either a contingent or a necessarily existing being.
6. The existence of the universe cannot be adequately caused or explained by additional contingent entities.
7. Therefore, the universe must be caused or explained by a necessarily existing being.

Several points need clarification. First, what does it mean for something to exist necessarily rather than contingently? We will explore this concept further in relation to the ontological argument. For now, however, let us say that a necessarily existing entity is something that has always existed, exists now and will always exist, and could not do otherwise. It is impossible for a necessarily existing being to come into or pass out of existence. A necessarily existing being, if such there be, cannot fail to exist because it has existence as an essential, "irremovable" quality. Another way to express this is to say that for any possible world one can imagine, a necessarily existing being would be a part of it, as what is necessarily the case does not vary from one possible world to the next. As we will see in a moment, critics balk at applying the notion of necessity to existing things.

Second, one might ask: why should we suppose that there is an explanation for the existence of every contingent thing? Underlying premise 1 is a commitment to a strong explanatory principle, called the Principle of Sufficient Reason (PSR). Roughly, the principle says that for every fact, for everything that is the case, there is some underlying reason why it is the case. The everyday facts we encounter, things such as one's feeling ill, one's car running raggedly, a rise in inflation, the grocer being out of eggs, are facts for which there must be an underlying explanation. Something cannot be the case for simply no reason at all, according to PSR. Existence too requires an explanation. Samuel Clarke said: "Undoubtedly nothing is, without a sufficient reason why it is, rather than not; and why it is thus, rather than otherwise" (quoted in Tose 2005: 106–7). We may not know what that reason is, but that does not deter us from thinking there is one. We do not, for instance, presently know why people contract all the various forms of cancer they do, but this does not detract from our belief that there are reasons and from thinking the search for those reasons a worthy endeavour.

Care must be taken to formulate the principle of sufficient reason with the appropriate degree of strength. The above formulation – "For *every* fact, for *every* truth, there is an explanation for why it is the case" – is actually too strong, for it would require that there is an underlying explanation for the fact of God's existence. Such strong formulations of the principle lead to Schopenhauer's famous complaint of the cosmological argument, to wit, that God gets invoked as a handy explanation for everything until we ask why God exists, at which point the cosmological argument is dismissed like a taxicab one no longer needs. But this complaint is easily met by restricting the principle to contingent truths: for every *contingent* fact, there is some explanation for why it is the case. God, as a necessarily existing being, would thus not fall under the principle. Equally unacceptable are versions of the principle where a "sufficient reason" jeopardizes human and divine freedom: "For every fact *f* that is the case, there is another fact *f'* such that *f must* be the case". This would suggest that the fact of God's having created the world is itself explicable by facts that made it inevitable. (Indeed, William Rowe argues for this very conclusion, as we shall see in Chapter 8.) Yet traditional theists want to hold that God was free with respect to his decision to create.

Many critics of the cosmological argument, starting with Hume and Kant, have objected to the very notion of a necessarily existing being.[3] To apply the concept of necessity to beings, to things, rather than to restrict it to the domain of propositions is, they say, to commit an intellectual category mistake, on a par with asking "How much does the number two weigh?" The concepts number and weight make perfectly good sense, but not applied to each other. So too, say critics of the cosmological argument, of the concepts of necessity and existence. To say that something is necessarily the case is to say that it is impossible that it be otherwise, which makes perfectly good sense when applied to propositions of mathematics and logic. Squares do not just happen to have four equal sides and four equal angles; they are *necessarily* four-sided. It is impossible for them to lack these features and still be squares. Consequently, one who denies that squares have four sides says something incoherent. Again, if "All men are mortal" and "Socrates is a man", it follows necessarily that Socrates is mortal. One can deny such necessary truths only on pain of logical error. No incoherence or logical error, however, arises if one denies the existence of something. I might be factually in error to say that there are no extraterrestrial beings, but I violate no law of logic to say so. But if God is a necessarily existing being, it would follow, say critics, that to deny his existence is to say something incoherent or illogical. But one no more violates a law of first-order predicate logic to deny that God exists, than to deny that aliens exist. Hume summarizes the argument as follows:

> Nothing is demonstrable unless the contrary implies a contradiction .... Whatever we conceive as existent, we can also conceive as non-existent. There is no being, therefore, whose non-existence implies a contradiction. Consequently there is no being whose existence is demonstrable.   (1993: 91)

In sum, said Bertrand Russell in his famous debate with F. C. Copleston: "The word 'necessary,' it seems to me, is a useless word, except as applied to analytic propositions, not to things."[4]

This objection to the cosmological argument hinges on the concept of necessity having application only to propositions. This restriction on the concept of necessity reflects a highly contentious positivist orientation to metaphysics. Many contemporary philosophers, however, think that the notion of "metaphysical necessity" is perfectly applicable to things in the world, and to natural kinds and the way they possess their properties. Philosophers such as Saul

Kripke have argued that natural kind terms such as "water" have essential properties that make them the kind of thing they are (see Kripke 1977). For something to be water (H_2O), it must have two hydrogen atoms and one oxygen atom. Other things may look and feel like water, but they are not water if they lack these essential properties. We can thus say that water is necessarily H_2O. Necessity is here not restricted to a proposition, but is attributed to the way something possesses its properties. According to classical theism, God too has necessary properties. He does not just happen to be wise, he is essentially wise. He could not be God and lack perfect wisdom. The same is true of his goodness, power and, more to the present point, his very existence. If God is the ground of all contingent being, he cannot himself be the sort of thing who depends on something else for his existence. He must exist necessarily.

In his *Dialogues Concerning Natural Religion*, Hume questions why the universe as a whole needs an explanation over and above its individual parts.

> But the whole, you say, wants a cause. I answer that the uniting of these parts into a whole… is performed merely by an arbitrary act of the mind, and has no influence on the nature of things. Did I show you the particular causes of each individual in a collection of twenty particles of matter, I should think it very unreasonable, should you afterwards ask me, what was the cause of the whole twenty. This is sufficiently explained in explaining the cause of the parts. (1993: 92–3)

Suppose you approached five passengers waiting at an underground train platform, and kindly asked them to participate in a single question interview: "Why are you here at the train platform?" Being unusually cooperative, they agree to answer the question. Passenger one is commuting to work; passenger two is on holiday seeing the sights; passenger three is passenger number two's child and is being dragged along against his wishes; passenger four is doing some shopping; and passenger five is a plain clothes police officer travelling on the underground to ensure the safety of other passengers. There! You have explained why each one is waiting at the platform. Would it not be odd at this point were someone to object that, while you had explained the presence of each individual, you had not accounted for the group itself, that you had offered only a partial explanation? You might, in Humean spirit, be inclined to respond that, in so far as you explained each individual, you *had* explained the whole.

Hume's objection, however, rests on the mistaken assumption that to explain each member of a collection of dependent beings is thereby to have explained why there are dependent beings at all. Suppose we ask why a particular person, John, exists. We can explain that he is the offspring of his parents. And if we ask why his parents exist, we can advert to still earlier ancestors, and so on as far back as one cares to enquire. But this does not answer the question of why there are humans at all. The same point holds with respect to contingent beings. If we recall the question that underlies the argument from contingency – why are there now and why should there have ever been contingent things? – we see that to explain one contingent entity in terms of another is not to answer the question of why there are contingent entities in the first place. As William Rowe notes:

> When the existence of each member of a collection is explained by reference to some other member *of that very same collection* then it does not follow that the collection itself has an explanation. For it is one thing for there to be an explanation of the existence of each dependent being and quite another thing for there to be an explanation of why there are dependent beings at all. (1975: 264)[5]

The last objection we will consider questions the principle of sufficient reason, the crucial underlying assumption that undergirds the argument from contingency. Why suppose that there is an explanation for every positive fact? Customarily, those who invoke the principle of sufficient reason decline to offer an argument for it, for they take it as a presupposition of reason itself (Taylor 1963: 87). Indeed, to argue for it would seem already to assume its truth. However thoroughly the principle underlies human reasoning, it does not follow from that fact alone that the principle is true. And there are philosophers, such as J. L. Mackie, who are prepared to accept a world in which "there being a permanent stock of matter would be just a brute fact that had no sufficient reason" (1982: 91).

This conflict of intuitions proved an impasse between Copleston, who thought the contingent world required an explanation, and Russell, who saw "no reason whatsoever to suppose that the total has any cause whatsoever... I should say that the universe is just there, and that's all" (Russell & Copleston [1948] 1964: 175). "After all," Russell might say, "the only explanations I know how to give refer to matter and how it is moved about by the laws of nature. I wouldn't even know how to offer a more fundamental explanation for the matter and laws themselves." At the very least, say critics of the cosmological argument, we do not know that the principle of sufficient reason is true. And if we do not know that it is true, we do not know that the first premise of our argument is true. And if we do not know that the premises are true, we do not know that the cosmological argument is a sound argument, and thus we ought not to accept its conclusion.[6]

Here, as in so many places in philosophy, we face a fundamental conflict of intuitions. Plainly, theists are unable to establish the principle of sufficient reason as a self-evident truth that demands to be accepted by all reasonable persons, and thus they have not shown that it is unreasonable to deny God's existence. But neither have Russell's and Mackie's demurrals shown that theists are irrational to accept PSR. Theists will be inclined to think that Russell's claim not to know how to muster an explanation for the existence of matter and laws, masks a metaphysical bias against personal explanations. What if, after careful and extended reflection, one thinks the principle of sufficient reason is true, and thus that the cosmological argument is sound? While theists cannot muster an argument that compels assent on the part of all who consider it, might they nevertheless be rational in believing in God? I see no reason to think not.

3 The ontological argument

The teleological and cosmological arguments arise out of commonplace experiences of a contingent world that displays order. The ontological argument, by contrast, is purely *a priori*, which is to say, it is not grounded in everyday experience but arises from reflection alone. In a nutshell, it claims that if one truly understands the concept of God and what it is for God to be perfect, one must acknowledge that he exists, for a truly perfect being could not lack existence and still be perfect. As we will see, it is one of the more abstruse arguments in the philosophical repertoire, as it turns on complex reflections about the nature of necessity and the possibility of a necessarily existing being. Ever since it was first penned by Anselm of Canterbury nearly a thousand years ago, it has commanded considerable attention from some of philosophy's leading lights: Berkeley, Locke, Hume, Descartes, Spinoza, Leibniz, Kant, Hegel and Schopenhauer, among others, wrestled with it, some to defend and others to reject it. Even Bertrand Russell, one of the twentieth century's most famous atheists was, for a time, convinced by it.

> I remember the precise moment, one day in 1894, as I was walking along Trinity Lane, when I saw in a flash (or thought I saw) that the ontological argument is valid. I had gone out to buy a tin of tobacco; on my way back, I suddenly threw it up in the air, and exclaimed as I caught it: "Great Scott, the ontological argument is sound."   (Quoted in Oppy 1995: 6)

The argument has not lacked for supporters in the twentieth century, with admirable defences offered by Charles Hartshorne, Norman Malcolm and Alvin Plantinga. In what follows we shall explore Anselm's version of the argument from his *Proslogion*, and then we shall turn to a contemporary modal version of the argument.

Anselm of Bec, or Saint Anselm, was first a monk and then abbot of the monastery of Bec, in Normandy, before being elected (against his wishes) Archbishop of Canterbury in 1093. He wrote eleven major treatises, one of which, his *Proslogion* of 1078, concerns us here. Anselm was not entirely satisfied with the arguments he had written for God's existence in an earlier work, the *Monologion*, so he sought a simpler master argument to prove God's existence. As a clergyman writing chiefly for his fellow monks, one might wonder why he would go to such lengths to prove what everyone already believed. Anselm, following Augustine, thought that, in so far as possible, the mind should endeavour to understand what the heart already professes by faith. In so doing, he commends the whole person, body, mind, heart in devotion to God and sought to show that faith and reason are not antagonistic but compatible.

Chapter 2 of Anselm's *Proslogion* contains the following argument:

> Now we believe that you are something than which nothing greater can be thought. So can it be that no such nature exists, since "the fool has said in his heart, 'there is no God'" (Psalm 14:1)? But when this same fool hears me say 'something than which nothing greater can be thought,' he surely understands what he hears; and what he hears is in his understanding, even if he does not understand that it exists ... So even the fool must admit that something than which nothing greater can be thought exists at least in the understanding. And surely that than which a greater cannot be thought cannot exist only in the understanding. For if it exists only in the understanding, it can be thought to exist in reality as well, which is greater. So if that than which a greater cannot be thought exists only in the understanding, then that than which a greater cannot be thought is that than which a greater can be thought. But that is impossible. Therefore, there is no doubt that something than

which a greater cannot be thought exists both in the understanding and in reality. (1995: 99–100)

We can formalize Anselm's argument as follows:

1. By the term God is meant the being than which no greater can be thought.
2. The being than which no greater can be thought exists in the understanding.
3. It is possible that God exists in reality as well as in the understanding.
4. It is greater to exist in reality than to exist only in the understanding.
5. Suppose that God exists only in the understanding. [Assumption for a *reductio ad absurdum*]
6. If God exists only in the understanding, then God might have been greater than he is.
7. If God could be greater than he is, then the being than which a greater *cannot* be thought is a being than which a greater *can* be thought, which is a contradiction.
8. It is therefore false that God exists only in the understanding.
9. God must exist in reality as well.

Much about this argument requires explanation. First, it is crucial to grasp how Anselm conceives of God, as "the being than which no greater can be thought". This may be an ungainly way to refer to God, but the expression captures exactly what Anselm takes God to be: the being in whom there is no lack, but who embodies all perfections, all great-making attributes. Whatever traits it is better for a being to have than to lack – wisdom, power, goodness, personhood and creativeness being obvious candidates – God has them all to the maximal degree it is possible for any being to possess them simultaneously. For if a being were deficient with respect to even one such great-making property, it would, by that very fact, show that it is not God. Anselm is aware that not everyone conceives of God as he does. From reading his Bible, he is aware that people have, historically, worshipped all manner of idols as divine, not to mention "the fool" who denies God's existence outright. Anselm, however, wants to establish as God the superlatively great being in comparison to which all other alleged deities must fall short. Second, Anselm thinks that to be, to have life, to exist, is itself a good that it is better to have than to lack. Conjure up whatever superlative being you can think of, if it lacks existence, it cannot be as great as that same being who has all the same qualities in addition to existence. Indeed, how would any non-existent thing be a fit object of one's religious devotion? Hence, premise 4 states that something is greater if it exists in reality than were it to exist in the mind alone.

Whether or not one believes in God, Anselm thinks that when he refers to the being than which no greater can be thought, there corresponds to this expression an idea in the mind of the person who hears it. For example, if someone uses the word "unicorn", one immediately thinks of a horse (often white) with a long horn sticking out of its forehead, a lion's tail and a little goatee beard. To say that 'the being than which no greater can be thought' exists in the understanding is simply to say, as we do of a unicorns, centaurs, fauns and other fictional creatures, that one understands what is being described. Now some think God belongs in the same class as these other mythical creatures – mere figments of the imagination, with no counterpart in the real world. But from what we have already seen, if existence is a positive quality it is better to have than to lack, then no mere fictional being can qualify as God. If God does not actually exist, there is no God, nor can there ever be. For any being that came into existence would demonstrate by that very fact that it is not God. So if God exists, he exists necessarily and if he does not exist, it is impossible that he exist.

Is existence always a perfection? What would you rather have: a real piece of chalk dust or fifteen minutes of uninterrupted, vivid fantasizing about your ideal holiday? Most people, I believe, would pass on the actually existing chalk dust in favour of the fantasy holiday. This is not quite fair to Anselm, however, since we are not comparing apples to apples. Given two apples, then, alike in every respect save that one exists and one is imaginary, Anselm thinks we would have to say the existing apple is superior. But what about an actually existing cancer cell and an imaginary cancer cell? Must we say that the actual cancer cell is superior? Here again, controversially, Anselm would say that if we are comparing two identical cancer cells, A and B, that differ only in virtue of A having existence and B not, then A possesses at least one positive quality B lacks, despite all the unpleasant consequences that may arise from having it.

One final premise deserves comment. Premise 3 is actually a suppressed premise in which Anselm assumes that it is possible that there be a being than which no greater can be thought. Which is to say, that God is not to be included among the class of impossible entities: round-squares, married bachelors, objects that are simultaneously red all over and green all over, and the like. Even if one happens to believe there is no God, Anselm thinks they should at least grant that there could be a God. Presumably, readers do not believe that unicorns exist, but most would be willing to grant that there could have been unicorns. Had the twists and turns of evolutionary history gone slightly differently, we might have had unicorns rather than, say, narwhals. So, Anselm is not asking his interlocutor to grant that God *does* exist, for that would beg the question, but simply to grant that God *could* exist.

Criticism of Anselm's argument was swift in coming. Guanilo, a contemporary monk at another monastery, objected that Anselm's having conceptually linked the notions of existence and a being than which no greater can be thought in no way shows that such a being exists. In his response to Anselm, entitled "On Behalf of the Fool", Guanilo writes:

> The only reason this [being than which no greater can be thought] is said to exist in my understanding is that I understand what is said. But in the same way, could I not also be said to have in my understanding any number of false things that have no real existence at all in themselves?   (1995: 121)

Guanilo asks whether, from the fact that he can think of an island than which no greater can be thought – resplendent with whatever features you think should grace such islands – that we should give any credence whatsoever to such an island actually existing.

While Guanilo understands what is being said when one utters the words "the being than which no greater can be thought", he fails to see how accurately understanding the concept of God commits one to saying God exists. We can easily grasp Guanilo's point by considering the concept of a unicorn. Those who have the concept of unicorn recognize that one is, by definition, committed to saying that unicorns have horns, but this admission in no way commits one to saying that unicorns exist. Nor would matters be improved were we to invent the concept of a "super-unicorn", which resembles regular unicorns in all respects, save that we define them as having existence. Again, since we have built "existence" in our concept of a super-unicorn, we could not say that a super-unicorn lacks existence, but no one, I presume, thinks we have thereby shown that there is anything that answers to this description. In this way we have in our understanding "false things that have no real existence in themselves". According to Guanilo, Anselm's manoeuvre of defining the concept of God so as to include existence, likewise does not commit one to saying that God exists.

Defenders of Anselm's argument might point out by way of response that, in comparing unicorns and islands with God, we are making an unfair comparison. To call God perfect is to say, among other things, that God in no way depends on anything else for his existence. It is a part of his very essence that he exists. But islands and unicorns, even the most magnificent specimens among them, do not enjoy this sort of existence, as they are contingent; the sorts of things that might not exist and depend on something else for their existence.

Guanilo's point about "false things that have no real existence in themselves" was greatly elaborated on by Immanuel Kant, whose objections to Descartes' and Leibniz's ontological arguments have been summarized in his famous claim: "Being [or existence] is obviously not a real predicate" (*Critique*, ch. 3; 1961: 504). To predicate of something is simply to attribute properties to a subject. For instance, we might predicate of a ball that it is red, round and rubber. For several reasons, Kant claims that the term "existence" cannot legitimately serve this predicative function. Still less do we establish God's existence by adding existence to the traits of a maximally great being. Kant observed that the defenders of the ontological argument with which he was familiar rely on necessarily true "judgements" to defend the necessary existence of "things".

> Under the condition that there is a triangle ... three angles will necessarily be found in it. So great, indeed, is the deluding influence exercised by this logical necessity that, by the simple

device of forming an apriori concept of a thing in such a manner as to include existence within the scope of its meaning, we have supposed ourselves to have justified the conclusion that because existence necessarily belongs to the object of this concept ... we are of necessity, in accordance with the law of identity, required to posit the existence of its object, and that this being is therefore itself absolutely necessary.... But if we reject subject and predicate alike, there is no contradiction .... To posit a triangle, and yet to reject its three angles, is self-contradictory; but there is no contradiction in rejecting the triangle together with its three angles. The same holds true of the concept of an absolutely necessary being. If its existence is rejected, we reject the thing itself, with all its predicates; and no question of contradiction can then arise.

(*Critique* A594/B622; 1961: 502)

Kant's point might be made more forcefully if we think not of triangles, but chiliagons, closed geometric figures with 1,000 sides of equal length. Given the definition, one cannot deny that a chiliagon has 1,000 sides, but it surely does not follow that any such objects are to be discovered in the world, still less that such objects exist necessarily. Kant's point has been summarized by claiming that "one cannot build bridges from the conceptual world to the real world" (Plantinga 1974: 196).

Kant draws a sharp distinction in the passage above between the logical necessity that characterizes propositions (what philosophers call necessity *de dicto*) and the metaphysical necessity that allegedly qualifies the way something possesses its properties (necessity *de re*). As we saw in discussing the cosmological argument, many philosophers think it nothing short of conceptual confusion to extend the concept of necessity to anything other than propositions, or judgements, as Kant calls them. This is because one contradicts oneself to deny a necessarily true proposition, but one does not say something logically contradictory when one says that something does not exist. To deny that X exists may be to say what is false, but one does not say what is contradictory.

Kant is surely right to say that the word "existence" does not typically function grammatically as a predicate. It would be odd indeed to say of one's dog that he is brown, furry and floppy-eared, and what is more, he exists! Typically we assume existence of the object of which we are predicating. But not always. Imagine the following conversation:

"Hey, you will never guess what some explorers just discovered in Nepal."

"What?"

"Yetis exist".

"You're kidding me!"

"No, I'm not! You can read about it in any major news service".

Here, "existence" is being used predicatively of yetis in perfectly acceptable grammatical form, so it is not quite right to say that "existence" never functions predicatively. More importantly, though, Kant is correct to say that one does not contradict oneself or, for that matter, break any other rule of first-order predicate logic to say "God does not exist". But as we saw in relation to the cosmological argument, this does not imply that there are no other notions of necessity to which Anselm and others are appealing. Kant forwards, without the benefit of argument, the notion that necessity has no application other than to propositions. In fact, Anselm is willing to grant Kant's point about existence and necessity with respect to all but one object: God. "Everything that exists, except for you alone, can be thought not to exist. So you alone among all things have existence most truly, and therefore most greatly." Here we come to the heart of the issue. Anselm is not attributing mere existence to God, whatever one may think about using existence as a predicate; he is attributing *necessary existence* to God.

Modal ontological arguments

We have all read books or seen movies of a science-fiction sort, in which a character acquires immortality. Owing to a potion, a spell or a deal with the devil, the character cannot die, a condition most come to regret. Now imagine a character that did not have to acquire immortality but, as a matter of fact, always had it. This character would have always existed, would now exist and will always exist. But this character would still not have the quality

Anselm attributes to God. God has always existed, now exists, will always exist and cannot lose his existence in this world or any other possible world. Such a being's very essence would include his existence. But if he cannot fail to exist in this or any other possible world, then one surely errs, if not by violating a logical law, to deny this being's existence. This central point of Anselm's argument can be brought into sharper relief by considering a modal version of the ontological argument; that is, one that focuses on the concepts of necessity and possibility.

Modal versions of the ontological argument typically rely on the extremely fruitful metaphor of "possible worlds". The *actual world* is, naturally enough, the totality of all the truths that will ever obtain in our world, the world that in fact exists. But we often think that the actual world might have been different than it was, that there are alternative ways the world might have been. Novels imagine how history might have unfolded if the Nazis had won the Second World War. Someone might reasonably think that had the voting machines in Florida been working properly, Al Gore and not George W. Bush would have been elected president in 2000. If evolutionary history included a few random mutations other than the ones that actually occurred, our world might have included unicorns. If you had attended a university other than the one you did, you might have had a better education, and so on for innumerable other ways the world might have differed from what is actually the case. A possible world, then, specifies the totality of all the truths that might have obtained in that alternative scenario. These possible worlds should not be thought of as actually existing and extended in real space; rather, these possible worlds occupy what we call "logical space", much as a mathematician's perfect circles and perfect planes occupy "mathematical space".

Now, philosophers who reflect on possible worlds note that a proposition's modal status, that is, its being necessary, possible, and impossible, remains constant across possible worlds. For instance, since it is impossible for the number six to be greater than ten in the actual world, it is impossible in every other possible world. Make whatever changes you like to our world – make grass purple, make fish talk, make the human lifespan 1,000 years – it would still be impossible for six to be greater than ten in any of these other possible worlds. Similar remarks apply to what is necessarily and possibly true. If it is necessarily true in the actual world that $2 + 2 = 4$, then it is necessarily true in all possible worlds. In short, what is possible, impossible, and necessary is invariant across possible worlds.

Because a proposition's modal status does not change from one possible world to the next, most modal logicians accept as axiomatic that if some proposition P is necessarily true in some possible world, then it is necessarily the case that P is possible. But this is equivalent to saying that if it is possible that P is necessarily true, then P is necessarily true. That is, if there is a possible world where P is necessarily true, then given the constancy of a proposition's modal status across possible worlds, P is necessarily true. In fact, this is the distinctive axiom of S5, the "industry standard" among philosophers who think about the nature of necessity.[1] This insight allows us to fashion the following modal ontological argument:

1. God is, by definition, a maximally great being and thus a being whose existence is necessary rather than contingent.
2. God, so defined, could exist; in other words, he does exist in some possible world.
3. Suppose that w is a possible world in which God, so defined, exists: then it is true in w, at least, that God exists there, and, being God, exists there as a necessary being.
4. But a necessary being is one which, by definition, exists in every possible world if it exists in any possible world.
5. Hence, the God who exists as a necessary being in w is a being that exists in every possible world, including this, the actual world.
6. Therefore, God exists in the actual world; he actually exists.[2]

The crucial move is easy to see: if one admits that there is at least one possible world in which it is true that a perfect being exists necessarily, and since what is necessary does not change from possible world to possible world, then one has just admitted that it is true that a necessary being exists in all possible worlds, including the actual world. Imagine, for simplicity's sake, that there are only five possible worlds: *alpha, beta, gamma, delta* and *epsilon*. Let us designate *alpha* as the actual world. Now if someone admits that it is possible for a necessary being to exist in some world, say *delta*, then one has just admitted that there is a possible world that contains a being whose essential nature it is to exist in every other possible world, including *alpha*. Talk about giving an inch and yielding a mile!

Once one grasps the implications of admitting that it is possible for a maximally perfect being to exist, the path to blocking the ontological argument becomes clear: deny that it is possible for a maximally perfect being to exist. We must not, say critics, think of the concept of God as on a par with things such as unicorns and centaurs, possible although non-existent beings, but rather as on a par with married bachelors, round squares and other impossible entities. Recent critics thus call into question the crucial assumption that is common to all ontological arguments, in other words, that it is possible that God exist. That is, they deny that there is any possible world which might contain a maximally excellent being. But on what basis do these objectors say that it is impossible for a maximally excellent, necessary being to exist?

Objectors to the ontological argument typically use two strategies to deny that God's existence is possible: dismiss the concept of a maximally perfect God as conceptually incoherent and claim that it defies known facts. On what basis is the concept of God thought to be incoherent? The idea is to show that no being could possess the properties characteristically attributed to God, such as omnipotence, omniscience and omnibenevolence. Consider the famous "paradox of the stone", which ostensibly shows that it is impossible for God to be omnipotent. If God is all-powerful, then he ought to be able to make a stone so big that he cannot lift it. If he cannot make such a stone, then he is not omnipotent; if he can make the stone, then there is at least one thing he cannot do: lift the stone. Either way, it looks as though God cannot be omnipotent. Another strategy is to show that God cannot possess at the same time all the excellences traditionally attributed to him; these traits are said to be "non-compossible", meaning that no being can possess them simultaneously. For instance, God is said to be both perfect in goodness and perfect in power. If he is perfect in power then he can surely do anything a mere mortal can do, such as to commit injustice. But if he is perfect in goodness, God could never contravene justice. So, God is either perfectly good or perfectly powerful, but he cannot be both at the same time. The second strategy argues that a God perfect in wisdom, power and goodness defies known facts. Richard Gale, for instance, argues that the presence of morally unjustified evil in the world logically precludes the possibility of God's existence. For our world's containing unjustified suffering shows that there is at least one world that lacks a being with all God's excellences, and thus that God as maximally excellent, does not exist in all possible worlds (see Gale 1991: 204–5).[3]

Theists do not lack for responses to such objections to the concept of God and we shall explore some of them in Chapter 8. Suffice it to say, however, that despite its longevity and subtlety, the ontological argument has not proven an impressive piece of natural theology. Indeed, Plantinga, one of the argument's most capable defenders, admits as much, for he acknowledges that no one is likely to accept the crucial premise, that it is possible for maximal greatness to be instantiated, who does not already accept the claim that God exists. But Plantinga is quick to add that while the argument may not be massively persuasive, someone is not necessarily irrational for accepting the central premise as true and thus accepting the argument as sound (Plantinga 1974: 216–21). Critics will reply that because they do not know that the central premise is true – or believe that it is necessarily false – they do not know that the argument is sound, and thus cannot accept it as a persuasive proof of God's existence.

Thus far, it seems obvious that the traditional arguments of natural theology have failed to prove God's existence to a considerable number of intelligent, fair-minded folks. Even some of natural theology's most ardent supporters, such as Richard Swinburne and Aquinas, are quick to acknowledge its limitations. Even if we can establish by argument that God exists, we cannot establish the great bulk of what constitutes monotheistic orthodoxy. Nor can we establish by argument alone the central doctrines of monotheism's variants: that Jesus is God incarnate, or that there will be a general resurrection of the dead, for example. Moreover, said Aquinas, most persons are, with respect to time, ability and inclination, unsuited to the rigours of natural theology. "If the only way open to us for the knowledge of God were that of reason," wrote Aquinas, "the human race would remain in the blackest shadows of ignorance" (*Summa contra Gentiles* 1.4.4; 1975: 67). While the traditional proofs may offer evidence enough to convince someone that theism is not unreasonable, the general consensus among philosophers is that they do not show theism to be the only reasonable view, still less do they offer arguments calculated to persuade all rational persons who consider them. But as we shall see later on, most of our considered judgements and reasonable beliefs about most subjects are held on the basis of reasons we find convincing but not coercive; we know that other people of equal intelligence and good will see matters differently than we do. Thus, in subsequent chapters, we shall consider the arguments that purport to offer evidence that shows that religious belief is rational, but not rationally compelling.

The moral argument for
4 God's existence

We have surveyed a trio of famous arguments for God's existence, the teleological, cosmological and ontological arguments, which their most ardent proponents offer as "proofs" of God's existence. Many theists see these arguments in less exalted terms, perhaps as offering good reasons for thinking that God exists but not as decisive proofs that settle the issue of God's existence once and for all. Even if the arguments thus far surveyed are sound, they suffer other limitations. The teleological and cosmological arguments suffer potentially from the "gap problem", while the ontological argument suffers from a lack of cogency: no one is likely to accept its most crucial premise who is not already committed to its conclusion. In the next two chapters, we shall explore two other oft-cited bases for rational religious belief: the arguments from morality and religious experience. Each presents us with a pervasive feature of human experience and proceeds to argue that these experiences cannot be adequately explained or understood without acknowledging God's existence. Not unexpectedly, critics will contend that these phenomena can be adequately explained without appealing to supernatural causes or beings.

Moral phenomena
Let us begin our reflections about the rich and complex world of moral experience with a few simple stories. A few years ago, City of Chicago police officers witnessed a drug transaction in an alleyway. One of the men involved in the transaction pulled a gun,

whereupon the officers drew their weapons, ordering the man to drop his gun. As soon as the officers brandished weapons, the drug dealer grabbed a child to use as a human shield as he fled. The child was his own son. Such behaviour prompts in us the strongest forms of condemnation. Setting to one side our judgements about trafficking in illegal drugs and allowing children to be present at such activities, we think that anyone who would use a child as a bullet shield is cowardly and contemptible. Consider another story. A soldier (we shall call him Sam) and his twenty-man platoon are caught unawares under ferocious enemy crossfire. The barrage inflicts heavy casualties, wounding half the men. Sam's platoon receives the order to fall back, but before doing so he braves the bullets and, at great risk to his own life, works to evacuate all the wounded. He further volunteers to man a machine gun in order to cover his men's retreat. Sam is seriously wounded in the process, resulting in the loss of a leg. Sam's actions elicit a strong attitude of admiration and respect. Even if we think that Sam fought on the "wrong side" of the war, it would not change our admiration over Sam's bravery and willingness to sacrifice his own welfare on behalf of his fellow soldiers. A final example: a colleague at work receives a promotion that I desperately wanted. I begrudge the colleague's success and begin to tear down her accomplishments by gossip, by falsely accusing her of "toadying" up to the boss and inflating her sales reports. In a moment of sober self-awareness, I realize that I am in the grip of acute envy and that it has moved me unjustly to resent and to malign my colleague's well-deserved promotion. I am ashamed of myself for my pettiness and malicious gossiping.

Daily we are moved to resent, condemn, esteem, love, forgive, be grateful, admire, be disgusted by, feel shame, have hurt feelings over, be indifferent to and so on, various situations we encounter. P. F. Strawson (1982) calls these responses "reactive attitudes" and he thinks that they are inextricably woven into the fabric of our social lives and are essential to our moral frameworks. These attitudes signal our stance or posture toward the circumstances that elicit them. And Strawson underscores that these reactive attitudes are not merely mechanisms for attempting to exert social pressure or control over others; they are expressions of our moral nature. Two sprinters vying for the gold medal are running neck and neck when they accidentally become entangled and one of the sprinters stumbles and falls. "Too bad", "What a shame", we say. But notice how our reactive attitude changes should the camera reveal that one of the runners deliberately tripped his opponent. Scandalous! An outrage! The cheater should be suspended from further competition! Our charge of "scandalous" is not merely a device to control another's behaviour; it is rather an expression of our deep-seated moral estimation of what we have just witnessed.

Our reactive attitudes are more than mere "knee-jerk" emotional responses to things we may or may not find pleasant. Rather, they reveal underlying judgements that someone is behaving wrongly or rightly and that appropriate consequences are merited. We also see that our attitudes toward another can and should be applied to ourselves were the roles reversed. If someone's maliciously ridiculing me in front of others provokes resentment in me, then it is perfectly appropriate for someone else to feel resentment towards me were I doing the ridiculing. So, reactive attitudes are often directed at our own behaviour; we sometimes feel shame, contempt or, positively, various kinds of esteem or appropriate pride toward our own behaviour. And it is but a small step to the realization that if, say, cheating is contemnible when others do it, then it is contemnible when we do it, and thus we feel morally obliged not to cheat.

Finally, we also discover that the behaviours that call forth reactive attitudes – cheating, cowardice, intolerance, generosity, bravery, open-mindedness – are the sorts of behaviours that persons engage in, not rarely, but routinely. Intolerance, for example, may not occur as an isolated episode in our own or in another's life, but may have, as it were, taken up permanent residence in us. Good traits such as generosity and bad traits such as stinginess can become the "default settings" of our moral lives. From ancient times, such patterns of excellence and dysfunction in our lives were called, respectively, virtues and vices, and they are universally discussed among the reflective, theoretical cultures of the world: Indian, Chinese, Greek, Hebrew, Roman and so on. So, Confucius, in his *Analects* extols, among other virtues, those of loyalty, courage and gratitude toward one's benefactors. Buddhist writings speak out against such vices as greed, deliberate deception of others and conceit.[1] And Aristotle, in Book II of his famous *Nicomachean Ethics*, names, among many others, cowardice, envy and shamelessness as matters about which we can never be correct and that correspondingly call forth our strongest disapprobation. Not only do the great ethical traditions of the world have remarkably similar lists of virtues and vices, but remarkably similar notions of what sorts of reactive attitudes such virtues and vices merit.[2]

Simply by exploring our common reactions to the sorts of behaviour we witness on a daily basis, we are led to consider some of the deeper matters of the moral life. One datum to consider, then, is that humans the world over display reactive attitudes of positive and negative sorts in response to their own and to others' moral actions and character traits. Noteworthy too is the fact that our reactive attitudes cultivate a sense that we are sometimes under obligation, that there are things we ought and ought not to do, whether or not the doing or refraining is advantageous for us. Moreover, there is a rough consensus among the great ethical traditions of the world about what sorts of reactive attitudes various behaviours ought to elicit. Some say that this consensus betokens an objective moral standard that binds the moral lives of all persons regardless of when and where they live. Many persons also believe that it is admirable when one acts self-sacrificially on behalf of others, the way Sam did. A common pattern of moral attitudes, a felt sense of obligation, moral consensus, altruistic actions: these, then, are some of the fundamental features of the moral landscapes we inhabit. But what is the deep explanation for the common patterns of reactive attitudes we witness in our own and in other major ethical traditions of the world?

Mindful of these various features of the moral landscape, theists construct moral arguments for God's existence that often assume the following form:

1. If God does not exist, then some important feature F of the moral life is illusory or undermined.
2. Feature F of morality is not illusory or undermined.
3. Therefore, God exists.[3]

Different forms of the moral argument fix on different features of the moral landscape: for example, the existence of objective moral values, altruistic behaviour, our sense of being morally obligated, our sense that moral obligations override reasons for ignoring the demands of morality and our conviction that people should be held accountable for their failure to conform to the standards of morality. Moral arguments then endeavour to show that God's existence best explains that single phenomenon. In this chapter we shall examine moral arguments that focus on the phenomenon of altruism and the alleged objectivity of moral values. Following the pattern of earlier arguments, theists point to God as the best explanation for these two phenomena. Predictably enough, opponents of theism argue with Laplace that we have no need of religious explanations, as moral phenomena are well accounted for by various naturalistic explanations.[4]

Morality in a purely natural world

How well do purely naturalistic explanations account for the range of moral phenomena we have been considering? Consider the world Bertrand Russell thinks we inhabit as described in his famous essay "A Free Man's Worship": "Brief and powerless is man's life on earth. On him and all his race, the slow sure doom falls pitiless and dark. Blind to good and evil, reckless of destruction, omnipotent matter rolls on its relentless way" (1917: 56).[5] On Russell's naturalistic view, we are but "accidental collocations of atoms"; all human loves, beliefs, thoughts and feelings, "all the noonday brightness of human genius, are destined to extinction in the vast death of the solar system" (*ibid.*: 47–8). Russell thinks that what is most fundamental to reality is matter and the laws of nature that move it – matter that is "blind to good and evil". And as we saw earlier, Richard Dawkins shares his vision. "The universe has precisely the properties we should expect if there is, at bottom, no design, no purpose, no evil and no good, nothing but blind pitiless indifference … DNA neither knows nor cares. DNA just is. And we dance to its music" (Dawkins 1985: 133). There is a curious incongruity, to say the very least, between a world whose fundamental nature is "blind to good and evil" and the powerful sense of being morally obligated that, among other things, distinguishes humans from other creatures. No other animal feels itself constrained to honour the demands of justice, to combat intolerance, to make reparations for harms done, along with the countless other concerns that mark the moral life. Why not simply yield to anger, injustice, envy, cowardice and betrayal? What cares omnipotent matter if we abuse children, torture the innocents and buy and sell other humans on the auction block? How shall we account for the pervasiveness of moral phenomena in a world that is, according to Russell and Dawkins, fundamentally indifferent to moral concerns? Theism's critics wonder why a good God permits suffering. Theists wonder how a purely material universe gives rise to values. Dawkins's views raise "the problem of the good".

Immanuel Kant, for all his talk about doing one's duty for duty's sake, nevertheless felt the incongruity between the demands of morality and life in a purely naturalistic universe. For he recognized that in this life, submitting to the demands of morality does not always pay. Unfortunately, persons are not rewarded or made happy in proportion to their moral worthiness; in fact the opposite is sometimes the case. Clearly, many who opposed the brutal regimes of Hitler and Stalin received no rewards, no tangible benefits as they hid Jews, aided the Resistance and stood up against obvious evil. Rather, like Raoul Wallenberg, they were tossed into Gulags never to be heard from again. Others were tortured and executed for their efforts. From outward appearances, it looks as though the wicked sometimes prosper. Those who dispossess widows and orphans, wage unjust wars and shamelessly ruin the environment, often go home to a sound night's sleep, live to a ripe old age and enjoy a disproportionate share of this world's benefits.

If, as Russell believed, human life ends at the grave and a return to the "collocation of atoms" that alone are ultimately real, then one faces a serious disincentive to sacrifice this-worldly happiness to honour moral obligations that may lead to a loss of the only goods Russellians think this life has to offer. It does not make practical sense, thought Kant, to pursue a morally exemplary life if one thinks that it does not lead to one's happiness. In a naturalistic world, the demands of morality would cease to be overriding, as Kant thought they must be, and might be trumped by practical advantage. In light of the incongruity between the demands of morality and a purely naturalistic world, Kant thought he needed to postulate the existence of God to satisfy the practical concern that justice is meted out in the end. He recognized that, if nothing else, the motivation for the moral life is undermined if we live in a world that is "blind to good and evil". Kant recognized that without God, we have no guarantee that persons who ignore the demands of morality will be held accountable. Thus, he thought, the phenomenon of morality makes more sense if rooted in a universe that is itself somehow committed to morality. Dostoevsky shared Kant's intuition, by famously proclaiming: "If God does not exist, all things are permissible," by which he meant that the incentive to meet the rigorous demands of the moral life would be undermined.

In a naturalistic world "all thought *and* feeling" arise from (some say are identical with) the same physical causes and are destined for the same catastrophic end. Both our rational and emotional natures have their origin in matter and the evolutionary and physical laws that move it. Theists argue that, in such a world, altruism is undermined, since it is irrational to act in ways that are counterproductive to the only goods one is ever likely to get. The argument can be stated as follows:

1. If God does not exist, altruism is irrational.
2. Altruism is not irrational.
3. God exists.

Non-theistic evolutionary theorists, for instance, cite the principle of natural selection as a worthy replacement for religion as an explanation of altruism and other moral phenomena. In brief, evolutionary explanations of morality might claim that the survival of our genes is more likely if we do not marry our sisters, murder and steal from one another, if we do have some principled means of resolving conflicts, act altruistically and, in general, if we follow such rules as make for organized societies of any sort. In short, there is a sociobiological explanation for moral phenomena. Common sociobiological needs also serve to explain the similarities in precept and behaviour we observe among theoretically reflective cultures. We all need to eat, sleep, procreate, be nurtured by parents and conduct business in stable and relatively safe environments, so it is not at all surprising that we find similar moral thinking among different people groups. Let us explore the evolutionary explanations for altruism in greater detail.

Evolution and altruism

Consider the case of Daniel Trocme, not exactly a household name, but one worthy to be remembered and a name currently enshrined at the holocaust museum in Israel. During the Second World War, Trocme was a resident of Le Chambon-sur-Lignon, the heroic French community who defied the Vichy government's order to turn Jews over to be shipped to the Nazi concentration camps. Many Jews who fled the Nazi collaborators sought shelter in this tiny village of 3,000. The residents, many of whom were poverty-stricken and suffering from the wartime shortages of food, nevertheless offered safe haven to some 5,000 fleeing Jews, not for days or weeks, but for nearly four years. Their defiance of the Gestapo and the Vichy government, and their efforts to smuggle Jews to safety, meant that their own lives were at grave risk, yet they never refused another refugee nor did they ever betray one. Even when the Vichy government became aware of their activities and arrested several of the town's leaders, they refused to divulge the name of a single refugee. Among those arrested was Trocme, who was later murdered at the death camp Majdanek, in Poland. How do socio-biologists account for people such as Trocme?

Biologist E. O. Wilson claims that "the time has come for ethics to be removed from the hands of the philosophers and biologicised" (Wilson 1975: 562). Dawkins has eagerly embraced Wilson's vision, advancing his own account of ethics that arises from the conviction that humans are, at bottom, "survival machines – robot vehicles blindly programmed to preserve the selfish molecules known as genes" (Dawkins 1976: ix). Our physical characteristics as well as our social behaviour, like that of all other animals, is under the control of genes seeking reproductive advantages over the genes of rival animals.

Contrary to popular belief, says Dawkins, our genes are not in the business of perpetuating the species (the "group selectionist" view); rather, they seek their *own* reproductive advantage (the "individual-selectionist" view), even at the cost of other members of the species. At the level of our genes "altruism must be bad and selfishness good" (*ibid.*: 38). Individuals, then, are but hosts or, as Dawkins prefers, the machines that enable our genetic material to occupy a larger share of the gene pool over various genetic rivals. Genes do not control their host machines directly, like a puppeteer, but indirectly, like a computer programmer using coded instructions. Even human consciousness and self-awareness are developments that allow the machine to anticipate, select from alternative survival strategies and, in general, to act as an independent, executive decision-maker for our genes. Wilson and Michael Ruse claim that human minds are programmed by "epigenetic rules" that dispose us towards certain behaviours, such as fear of heights, mother–infant bonding and infant taste preferences, and against behaviours such as incest that are obviously counterproductive to the long-term survival of our genes.[6]

If our genes are selfish, we should expect the behaviour of the machines they occupy and control to act selfishly. And so they do, says Dawkins. Birds in the nest "cheat" and "lie" by screaming incessantly so that they, rather than their siblings, will get a morsel of food. Human children too cry, coo and employ various "lying, deceiving, exploiting" means to manipulate parents, especially mothers. The elaborate courtship rituals of animals, the strutting, preening, dominance displays and other behaviours are simply behaviours adapted to ensure the survival of our genes. Dawkins notes that promiscuity rather than domesticity and fidelity may in certain circumstances more effectively serve the goal of genetic survival. (Studies show, for instance, that women are more likely to cheat on a spouse during the fertile time of their monthly cycle.) Even animals living in groups and colonies may benefit from sacrificing one of their number. Penguins, for example, are known to line up along the edge of an ice floe and wait there until one member dives in to "test the waters" for the presence of predators. Dawkins tells us a good deal of pushing and shoving goes on close to the edge.

Just because our genes are selfish, it does not follow that we are incapable of cooperative behaviour. Some animals, hyenas and wolves being obvious examples, hunt and live in packs for the simple reason that they can kill much larger prey and defend themselves more effectively in groups than they can on their own. Animals will even act "altruistically" in the sense of acting "self-sacrificially" for the sake of the others. Many species have developed elaborate sounds to serve as warnings in the case of approaching predators. While the animal sounding the alarm warns its fellows, it calls attention to itself, making it a more likely target of attack. How should we explain this seemingly unselfish behaviour? "There are ways", say Ruse and Wilson:

> in which nature can bring about "altruism", in the sense of self-sacrifice for the benefit of others. If those benefited are

relatives, the altruist is still favouring genes identical to his own, even if he dies without leaving any direct offspring. Thus we say that the individual is altruistic but his genes are "selfish".   (Ruse & Wilson 1993: 309)

A worker bee, for instance, may fend off threats to honey and hive by stinging predators, which, while it may repel the invader, costs the worker bee its life. But worker bees are sterile, so their loss in no way compromises but actually serves the genetic advantage of the queen and the rest of the reproducing line. So, on the evolutionary view Dawkins defends, kinship and reciprocation are the "twin pillars of altruism in a Darwinian world" (Dawkins 2006: 218).

Animals other than humans are thus quite selective in their acts of "altruism". What to outward appearances seems to be acts of self-sacrifice turn out instead to be yet another way for our genes to prosper in the gene pool, wherein may be contained the genetic material of direct offspring and other kin. But do the accounts of Dawkins and Wilson do justice to acts of unqualified human altruism? Do they sufficiently explain the behaviour of Albert Schweitzer, Raoul Wallenberg, Daniel Trocme and others of this world upon whom we heap humanitarian awards for sacrificing, for the sake of unrelated strangers, hope of perpetuating their own genes?

Ruse and Wilson speculate that, to spur us against our usual selfish dispositions, nature, via the epigenetic rules influencing consciousness, has caused us to acquire a disinterested moral code in the form of deeply held *beliefs* about right and wrong that tell us we ought to help our fellow humans. They say that:

Morality, or more strictly our belief in morality, is merely an adaptation put in place to further our reproductive ends. Ethics as we understand it is an illusion fobbed off on us by our genes to get us to cooperate. It is without external grounding. Ethics is produced by evolution but not justified by it, because, like Macbeth's dagger, it serves a powerful purpose without existing in substance .... Ethics is a shared illusion of the human race. If it were not so, it would not work. The moral ones among us would be outbred by the immoral .... The way our biology enforces its ends is by making us think that there is an objective higher code, to which we are all subject. If we thought ethics to be no more than a question of personal desires, we would tend to ignore it. (1993: 310)

If only parts of the human race were altruistic and the other part selfish, the altruists would be the clear losers; they would be quickly out-bred. But if everyone *believes* in the benefits of cooperation, the prospects of everyone's genetic material being passed on is thereby increased. It would appear that our conscious beliefs have been hijacked by our genes and caused us to be subject to massive illusion. Nature cannot permit us – well, the masses, at any rate – to know the truth about our moral impulses, for upon learning of their illusory character, we would see past them and ignore them, the way we do the appearances of puddles on hot pavement.

Theists criticize Ruse and Wilson's account by noting the way their evolutionary story pits the concerns of survival and truth against each other. What is, strictly speaking, in the interest of our selfish genes is "qualified altruism" – altruism directed specifically toward those to whom I am genetically related (think here of a mother sacrificing herself for her children). Yet, to accomplish this end, Ruse and Wilson say that nature foists on us the illusory belief that "unqualified altruism", of the sort displayed toward strangers, is morally admirable. To act self-sacrificially toward those to whom I am genetically unrelated is not in the interests of my genes, yet nature, they say, has given me the belief that it is. Getting our genetic material thoroughly distributed throughout the gene pool comes at the cost of our being subject to massive illusion. Nature appears, then, to be working at cross-purposes; our biological gains come at the cost of epistemic loss. In short, biology trumps truth. Perhaps Ruse and Wilson happily concur with Patricia Churchland, that in matters of evolutionary survival, "truth can take the hindmost".[7]

Ruse and Wilson, at any rate, have not been hoodwinked; they see through nature's ruse. But what is to prevent other educated folk from discovering that illusory character of moral beliefs and, in so doing, coming out from under its spell? What should be the reaction of educated persons upon finding out that the biological forces behind morality, specifically altruism, do not track the truth and are, from an epistemological perspective, irrational? Anyone who accepted the truth of Ruse and Wilson's claim (assuming, for the moment, that our biology will permit this) would then be better off acting as enlightened egoists do: cooperating and sacrificing only in so far as it benefits me and mine. Let others labour under the illusion that it is good for them to be self-sacrificial towards me; I need only feign reciprocal interest. Let the other penguin jump!

Dawkins's explanation for altruistic behaviour differs slightly from that of Ruse and Wilson. Human consciousness evolved to serve the interests of our genes, but our genes may have, ironically, provided the basis for overthrowing their genomic hegemony. In a cryptic and concluding comment to his book, Dawkins writes: "We are built as gene machines, but we have the power to turn against our creators. We, alone on earth, can rebel against the tyranny of the selfish replicators" (1976: 215). Humans alone, in virtue of the independence afforded them by consciousness, can penetrate nature's schemes and its illusions. Why would we want to rebel against our genes and what would rebellion amount to?

The reason to rebel against our genes is quite simple, says Dawkins. In an interview with *The Evolutionist*, Dawkins confesses that were ethics and politics grounded solely in Darwinian principles, he "would hate it" and "it really would be a very unpleasant world in which to live". In fact, a world conformed solely to the dictates of our genes would, by Dawkins's own admission, "look like Hitler's Germany" (Dawkins 1997). While Dawkins finds it quite ironic that rational consciousness, itself wholly a product of millions of years of evolutionary processes, should be so much at variance with his genetic impulses at another level, he does not find it incoherent. There is no incoherence, he insists, in acknowledging the role of selfish genes from an academic or epistemic point of view while resisting them morally and politically.

How odd, that as with Ruse and Wilson, taking the moral point of view generates tension with the epistemic point of view. While Dawkins may be right to say there is no strict formal inconsistency in his position, it nevertheless raises anew the "queerness of morality", as George Mavrodes put it: the incongruity between the natural world at its most fundamental level and our moral sensibilities arising from the very same natural world. Theists, of course, think it preferable to search for an account of the world where morality is more at home and not at variance with epistemic consideration and the strict truth about our nature.

But can Dawkins claim that irony and not inconsistency is the only problem his position poses? In *River Out of Eden: A Darwinian View of Life*, Dawkins describes in gory detail the "macabre habits" of digger wasps, who lay their eggs in live hosts, and whose young eat their hosts alive from the inside out in order to emerge into the world. Dawkins writes:

> This sounds savagely cruel but ... nature is not cruel, only piteously indifferent. This is one of the hardest lessons for humans to learn. We cannot admit that things might be neither good nor evil, neither cruel or kind, but simply callous – indifferent to all suffering, lacking all purpose.   (1995: 96)

Critics might well wonder if it is incoherent to insist that, while natural processes at every other level are indifferent to good and evil, *moral* impulses generated by the same natural processes should be deferred to. Is there no deeper reason for honouring moral impulses than that failure to do so would lead to a world in which Dawkins would find it unpleasant to live?

We rebel, Dawkins thinks, because a world dominated by our selfish genes would have just those characteristics Thomas Hobbes famously ascribed to a purely natural state: it would be "poor, solitary, nasty, brutish, and short". Dawkins is keen to point out that just because a nature "red in tooth and claw" disposes us to have powerful appetites and desires, it does not follow that we must yield to them. We can resist on rational grounds the powerful urges to fight, flee or fornicate that our genes impose upon us. "Academically I have very clear understanding of why I feel these temptations and lustful desires", says Dawkins:

> But morally and socially, or for all sorts of other reasons, I've elected to hold them in check. There's no problem about that, we do it all the time. There's no reason why we shouldn't do the same thing with our academic understanding of why we are sometimes selfish and sometimes co-operative.   (1997)

Dawkins plainly feels the incongruity between his moral preferences and the natural world he is committed to saying is ultimately real.

Let us leave to one side the problem of whether, in a purely naturalistic world guided by physical laws, Dawkins is free to "elect" to hold anything back, as opposed to acting out whatever deterministic impulses have welled-up within him strongest at the moment. Since Dawkins wants to resist his genes on moral grounds, let us ask what would rebellion against our genes amount to? It may take the form, as noted above, of feigning commitment to general altruism while in reality letting others do the moral heavy lifting. But that is not altruism in the robust sense and not altruism of the sort even Dawkins finds most admirable. Dawkins himself favours the use of contraception, support for the aged and infirm, care for stray animals, grants of aid to the poor we shall never see and other actions that in no way serve one's genes. Nor can rebellion consist of an indiscriminate yielding to whatever impulse happens to well up within us strongest at the moment, for that would not be to escape our genetics but only to be ensnared by them at some other level.

Dawkins creates further difficulties for his view by claiming that altruism toward those outside our genetic and moral circle constitutes a "misfiring" in our genetic wiring (Dawkins 1997; see also 2006). While Dawkins thinks these misfirings "blessed" and "precious", it is crucial that one acknowledge that precisely to the extent that these are accidents or deviations from nature's prevailing evolutionary pathways, they cannot be thought of as *principled* deeds. Indeed, as aberrations or misfirings, it becomes difficult even to see how altruistic deeds can be deemed rational rather than utterly random. Moreover, whether or not Dawkins deems altruistic acts as "blessed misfirings", they are, by his own account, bound to become less and less frequent, as the majority in whom such accidents do not occur outbreed genetic aberrations such as Daniel Trocme and Albert Schweitzer.[8]

If rebellion against genetic tyranny is to count as something more than an aberrant occurrence in nature, it will itself have to be motivated by some guiding principles. Rebels have causes, creeds and manifestos that are supposed to elevate their actions above that of the unreflective, unruly mob. Dawkins is clear in the quotation above that he wants to resist the dictates of genes on *moral* grounds. So whatever principles guide human resistance to selfish genes must be subject to moral appraisal. One can, after all, escape genetic tyranny as Hitler attempted: through a programme of ruthless sterilization and eugenic engineering that sought to exterminate all persons his system of values counted as "undesirables". Surely Dawkins must have some principled basis for rejecting Hitler's form of rebellion other than that he would find it "a very uncomfortable world in which to live".

Dawkins's claim that we can liberate ourselves from the power of our selfish genes means that something other than mere biology must set itself up as biology's guide. But to what can Dawkins turn for guidance? His answer:

> [W]e decide independently what we think would be a good thing .... We don't give value judgements to the entire category, we simply look at each individual policy decision, and decide on "other grounds" – moral philosophic grounds or political philosophic grounds – what we think is a good thing.

Yet he also confesses that "the grounds on which we make that decision ... it's not entirely clear to me where they come from" (1997). Theists readily respond with an explanation that appears to elude Dawkins.

The evolutionary explanations for the phenomenon of altruism offered by Ruse, Wilson and Dawkins suffer serious drawbacks. The most glaring concerns the dichotomous relationship between truth and morality. To take the epistemic point of view is to have truth (or some other intellectual good) uppermost in mind in deciding what to believe. To adopt the moral point of view is to see and appreciate the force that the rights and welfare of other persons place upon us. Yet Ruse and Wilson confess that morality is a "shared illusion of the human race". The felt sense of the rights and welfare of others is a deception, something that, from the epistemic point of view, one should reject. Dawkins too thinks that purely epistemic or intellectual reasons underwrite a commitment to selfish genes and a world he would prefer not to live in, prompting him to become a moral rebel. Russell would no doubt accuse Dawkins of a failure of nerve. If the stone cold truth, to use Dawkins's own words, is that "the universe has precisely the properties we should expect if there is, at bottom, no design, no purpose, no evil and no good, nothing but blind pitiless indifference", and if we, the offspring of that world, are chiefly motivated by the overriding desire to pass along our genes, then Dawkins should not flinch in the face of what reason underwrites, uncomfortable though it may be. The evidentialist objection to theistic belief with which we began this book accuses theists of lacking adequate epistemic support for their belief in God. Ironically, it looks as though theism's accusers stand guilty of the very same offence.

Theists, as we shall see below, do not think that morality in general or altruism in particular is a square peg in the round hole of a universe. Rather, they think the universe was created and is sustained by a supremely good moral agent who made humans as moral beings capable of apprehending moral truths and directing their lives by them.

Theistic arguments from objective morality

Theists frequently appeal to God to explain various aspects of the moral life. Kant, as we have already noted, thought that commitment to the moral life makes *practical sense* only if there is a wise and just God who can ensure that our happiness is commensurate with our moral deserts. Others, such as Aquinas, Bishop Joseph Butler, Thomas Reid and John Henry Newman, among others, taught that all humans have a *conscience*, a moral faculty that, when suitably developed, allows us to apprehend moral first principles and, on the basis of these, to adjudicate between right and wrong. God's creative hand is offered as the best explanation for humans being so equipped. Still others think only the existence of a personal God can support our sense of *being under obligation*, under command, as it were, to obey the claims of morality upon us. Here, however, we shall explore still another form of moral argument, that points to God as the best explanation for the objectivity of moral values.

In keeping with the idea that the moral argument is an argument to the best explanation, it might be stated thus:

1. If there are objective moral values, the best explanation for them is God's existence.
2. There are objective moral values.
3. God's existence is the best explanation for objective moral values.

There are numerous places for this argument to run into trouble. One might deny premise 2, that there are objective moral values. One might accept that there are objective moral values, yet deny premise 1 by thinking they can be better accounted for in ways that do not appeal to God. Even if one grants the conclusion, one might think that God's being the best explanation does not provide enough evidence for theism to be overall rational. But before turning to the objections, let us unpack the position.

What do we mean when we say that there are objective moral values? Moral theorists agree that objective morality must be true or false, not reducible to or the result of our projecting our desires onto the world. So, to take an oft-cited candidate: torturing innocent persons is wrong. If this is objectively true, it is true at all times and in all places, whether or not persons living in a particular time and place recognize and abide by this truth. Moral judgements, if objective, thus resemble truths of mathematics. The Pythagorean theorem was true before it was discovered and true despite some people's still being ignorant of it.

J. L. Mackie, for one, finds such objective value judgements "queer", "metaphysically peculiar" and utterly unlike the ordinary empirical facts with which we have daily commerce. That our world should have such facts is, for Mackie, simply a mysterious, inexplicable, metaphysical fact. Despite their mysteriousness, Mackie nevertheless admits that "the main tradition of European moral philosophy from Plato onwards has combined the view that moral values are objective with the recognition that moral judgments are … action-guiding" (1977: 23). Of the last criterion he writes:

> The ordinary user of moral language means to say something about whatever it is that he characterizes morally, for example a possible action, as it is in itself, or would be if it were realized, and not about, or even simply expressive of, his, or anyone else's, attitude or relation to it. But the something he wants to say is not purely descriptive, certainly not inert, but something that involves a call for action or for the refraining from action, and one that is absolute, not contingent upon any desire or preference or policy or choice, his own or anyone else's.
>
> (Ibid.: 33)

To recall our discussion of reactive attitudes, the person who responds with stern reproach for the traitor does not mean to express an attitude peculiar to herself; she thinks this the attitude others should adopt and that it fosters a sense of felt obligation, "a call for action or for the refraining from action", as Mackie puts it. The traditional view, therefore, holds that moral values are not a result of our projecting our feelings and attitudes onto various bits of behaviour, but rather that something in the world "backs up and validates" our subjective concerns.

What would some examples of objective moral judgements be? Oft-cited candidates include prohibitions against incest, torturing babies, parricide, rape, genocide, punishing innocent persons and so on, as well as positive obligations to honesty, to care for and nurture one's children, to deal truthfully and justly in conferring rewards and punishments, to be grateful to benefactors, and the like. Still another stream of objectivist ethics, that of natural law, confirms Mackie's read of the history of ethics. Aristotle says in his *Nicomachean Ethics*: "One part of the politically just is natural, and the other part legal. The natural has the same validity everywhere alike, independent of its seeming so or not .... For the natural is unchangeable and equally valid everywhere" (V.7 1, 1134b19–26; 1990: 78). Or, as Cicero put it, "one everlasting and immutable law will govern all people at all times" (*De Republica* III, XXII, 33). Aristotle here distinguishes between justice that is in accordance with the laws a society has enacted (positive law) and the higher justice by which even a society's laws must be judged (supra-positive law), what is often called "the natural law". This natural law, by which human positive law is judged, is considered by some philosophers and legal theorists to be part of the objective moral order.

Aristotle's judgement coincides with that of countless legal scholars who note that societies sometimes enshrine in law practices that are immoral and unjust, such as the Fugitive Slave Act in the United States and the laws that permitted Nazis to dispossess people of their property. Such appeals to an objective natural law were indispensable in prosecuting Nazi war criminals at the Nuremberg trials. Accused Nazis could not be prosecuted under the laws of the nations participating in the trials and the actions for which they were being tried were legal under the laws of the Nazi state. One of the judgements against the Nazis thus declares:

These laws of confiscation, though clothed in the formal rules ... of a law, ... [are] an extremely grave violation of the supra-positive principle of equality before the law as well as the supra-positive guarantee of any legal order and must remain inviolable. [These provisions] were and are by reason of their unjust content and their violation of the basic demand of any legal order null and void; this law could not, even at and during the time of the Nazi regime, produce any legitimate legal effect.   (Rommen 1998: 14–15)[9]

How then do theists explain the objectivity of moral judgements and why do they think their explanation is superior to non-theistic alternatives? The God of the Judaeo-Christian religion is understood to be personal and perfect in wisdom, power and, most importantly for our discussion, goodness. God's goodness and moral knowledge are essential parts of his nature, grounded in his unchanging moral character and thus eternally and objectively true. Theists also hold that God created human persons with minds and wills that make them capable of moral agency. Given his nature, God knows for any world he creates, and for any moral agents such worlds may contain, what would constitute right and wrong, good and bad, just and unjust actions for those agents. Our moral standing is thus measured by the extent to which our moral lives, our actions, thoughts, dispositions of will and character, conform to or imitate the divine exemplar.[10] The conditions of our moral conformity to God thus depend on the particular nature with which we are created and the circumstances in which we are placed. Were God to have created the actual world to contain only spiritual beings, prohibitions against gluttony, adultery and other immoral actions requiring a body would, in that world, have had no application. Inasmuch as humans, though, have bodies that can be harmed by excessive eating and drinking, these activities become proper subjects of moral concern.

Our world, say theists, not only contains corporeal moral agents, but agents who have been equipped with faculties of mind that, when suitably mature and situated in adequately cooperative environments, are able to discern the content of the objective moral law.[11] Conscience (*synderesis*), according to Aquinas, is that faculty of reason whereby we are able to apprehend objective moral first principles, such as that we must do good and avoid evil, not cause unnecessary harm and the like. According to some theists, then, our capacity to apprehend some objective moral truths is analogous to our capacity to apprehend logical and mathematical axioms: something that is self-evident and therefore epistemically basic. To say that humans take fundamental moral truths as self-evident is to say that the mature mind in appropriate circumstances simply "sees" these claims to be true.[12] The claim that it is wrong to torture children is not a conclusion we deduce from prior premises or reach by argumentation; rather, it is immediately seen to be true upon being understood. Moreover, it is hard to imagine any premises from which we could infer such a claim that would strike us with more force and conviction than the conclusion itself. Some moral judgements, however, are such that we do not grasp them immediately; rather, we reach them through deliberation and reasoning. Delicate judgements about the just distribution of goods among rival claimants are good examples of this sort.

Theists argue that objective morality enjoys a much more natural fit in a divinely ordered world than in a naturalistic world, that latter view, as we have seen, having admitted to the "queerness" of moral properties, even going as far as to say that morality is a deceit fobbed off on us by manipulative genes. Naturalists acknowledge an oddity of morality in a purely material world analogous to the puzzle of consciousness. So Colin McGinn writes of the latter:

> Consider the universe before conscious beings came along: the odds did not look good that such beings could come to exist. The world was all just physical objects and physical forces, devoid of life .... We have a good idea of how the Big Bang led to the creation of stars and galaxies, principally by force of gravity. But we know of no comparable force that might explain how ever-expanding lumps of matter might have developed into conscious life. (1999: 15)

Still less, says the theist, do we know what natural forces might explain how ever-expanding lumps of matter came to discern objective moral truths. For theists, however, morality is neither illusory nor bewildering; it is grounded in the unchanging character of God and woven into the very fabric of the created order.

Morality is quite at home in a theistic world. To admit this is not, of course, to prove that God exists. If we knew that there is a God, some theistic story about values would no doubt be true. Theists, however, are here arguing indirectly, by an inference to the best explanation. Since we are acquainted with objective moral values and since objective moral values find little support in a naturalistic world then, according to the likelihood principle, the most reasonable explanation of the two is to say that morality finds its ultimate explanation in a divinely ordered world. Appealing to God as the ground of objective moral values also satisfies the conditions we earlier acknowledged as necessary for objective moral values. Moral claims would be either true or false in so far as they conformed to God's judgements about moral truth and falsity. Something's being moral or immoral would be necessarily true inasmuch as it is grounded in God's essential moral nature. It is also plain that, if morality were grounded in God's nature, an action's being right or wrong, just or unjust, would not depend on our desires. Finally, God's eternal moral character and our capacity to emulate him is, as William Wainwright puts it, "part of the furniture of the universe", an objectively real feature of reality.

In sum, theists claim that God's existence is the best explanation for the objectivity of morality and for the universality of moral judgements, since moral truths are not merely projections of personal or local sentiment, but in some way reflect the mind of a morally perfect being. Finally, theism, more than any naturalistic theory, best accounts for our admiration for altruists and our felt sense of obligation to conform to demands of morality, for what Mackie describes as the "call for action or for the refraining from action ... that is ... not contingent upon any desire or preference ... or choice of his own or anyone else's". If we live in a world where moral sentiments are utterly contingent and accidental, we do not necessarily feel duty-bound to comply with their demands. Indeed, like some other restrictions nature imposes, we seek ways to escape them, not bow to them. Unlike unreasoning animals that perforce conform to nature's demands, we humans seek ways to alter or avoid the hand that nature deals us. We do not accept polio and Parkinson's disease as our lot; instead, we invent vaccines and alter our genes. Why should we not do the same with our moral stirrings? Theism, better than naturalism, explains why not.

Objections to the moral argument

The argument from objective morality faces numerous objections, not the least of which is to deny that there is any such thing as objective morality. Various moral relativisms along with views that see moral phenomena merely as projections of internal emotional or other psychological states would, of course, deny that there is any genuine phenomenon to be explained. Moral relativism, however, is difficult to defend. Typically, there is at least one moral claim that virtually everyone will acknowledge to be true and binding on our behaviour, such as that one ought not to torture babies purely for the fun of it or that genocide is wrong. If there is even one moral claim that is objectively true, moral relativism fails.[13]

The more interesting objections, for present purposes, are those that acknowledge objective moral truths but think they can be explained quite adequately apart from appeals to God. Theists may put the argument for objective moral truths this way (Copan 2008):

1. If God does not exist, then objective values do not exist.
2. Objective moral values do exist.
3. Therefore, God exists.

Relativists deny the second premise. Moral Platonists and natural realists deny the first. Here we'll focus on the criticisms that objective moral truths are perfectly intelligible apart from theism.

The notion that moral laws might exist without an author is not as strange as it might at first appear. After all, we admit that there are physical laws and constants, such as those of gravitation and the speed of light, that antedate the arrival of humans. The same may be said of logical laws, such as $A = A$. Biological laws describing heredity and the genetic transference of physical traits might also reasonably be said to arise when the existence of creatures come into being who are capable of biologically bequeathing traits to offspring. These laws seem to belie the oft-cited slogan that "all laws require a law-giver".[14]

Why not say that moral laws, like the laws of logic and nature, are true? Atheistic moral realists suppose the wrongness of punishing the innocent and torturing infants was true before there was anyone to acknowledge them. Theists, after all, do not feel compelled to answer questions about where God comes from. Why can't atheistic moral realists simply say, as theists say of God, that the objective moral order is just a fundamental fact of reality: end of story?

Moral Platonists sometimes note in support of their view that we can point to instances of other laws that do not seem to depend on God as their author. Physical laws, for instance, are objectively true, coming into being when the objects whose behaviour they describe come into being, during the first few nanoseconds of the Big Bang, according to Big Bang cosmology.

The theist might concede that physical laws do not require an author, yet insist that normative principles – principles describing how we *ought* to feel and behave – do require an author. Russ Shafer-Landau points out, in reply, that logical laws are themselves normative; they govern what propositions we should and should not accept. We should not, for instance, believe contradictions and we should accept beliefs entailed by propositions we know to be true. Moreover, mathematical truths are necessary truths, truths that are forever and unalterably the case, and thus do not appear to depend on anything else for their truth. And if moral truths are necessary in the same way as mathematical truths, then, here too, it looks as though we do not require an author in order for normative principles to exist.[15]

At issue is whether objective moral truths must be anchored in something metaphysically more foundational than themselves. Craig aptly voices the theists concern:

> Moral values seem to exist as properties of persons, not as mere abstractions – or at any rate it is hard to know what it is for a moral value to exist as a mere abstraction. Atheistic moral realists seem to lack any adequate foundation in reality for moral values but just leave them floating in an unintelligible way.
> (Craig & Sinott-Armstrong 2004: 19)

If there is a God, objective moral truths would find a fitting ground. The question is whether, without God, it is unreasonable to believe in objective moral truths.

Is God a more fundamental part of reality that explains the existence of objective morality or are objective moral truths themselves fundamental, brute facts of reality?

The claim that the universe just happens to contain metaphysically brute moral facts is signally unsatisfying. Some will no doubt judge such moral facts to be as philosophically ungrounded as the metaphysically brute fact that God exists, and thus reject both. Theists, however, will object that it leaves morality without an adequate explanatory ground, a dangling metaphysical fact without any underlying explanation. Theists claim the advantage of being able to locate moral reality in an ontological reality, a necessarily existing, personal God, who is also a perfectly good moral agent. Since morality has largely to do with the way agents act toward each other, it is more fitting that the foundations of morality be found in a supreme moral agent rather than existing as bare moral data of unknown provenance. Theists also note the remarkable coincidence that the eternally true objective moral laws should be so suited to human life and well-being. Does not the fittingness of moral reality for human life cry out for an explanation other than "that is just the way it is"? This fittingness is all the more remarkable, if as Russell and Dawkins maintain, every aspect of human life is the product of an accidental collocation of atoms, evolving at every stage through blind chance. How odd (indeed, it strains the boundaries of credulity) that blind chance should, over millions of years, produce moral agents whose best judgements about good and bad, right and wrong, just happen to map onto a pre-existing, transcendental moral reality. No such coincidence arises, however, if, as theists claim, God is behind both morality and the beings to whom it pertains.

Moral naturalism and objective morality

The weaknesses of moral Platonism to explain objective morality might prompt one to look to naturalistic explanations. Richard Boyd believes objective moral truths exist without God and that humans have the cognitive wherewithal to discern them and make them a matter of scientific study. Goodness, says Boyd (1988), is analogous to the concept of health in that both are complex concepts whose elements come "homeostatically clustered". Good health requires, among many other things, that one have an internal body temperature that falls within a very limited range, that one's cholesterol levels, heart rate and blood pressure are at suitable levels, that one's vital organs be properly functioning and so on.

These aspects of health come "homeostatically clustered", that is to say, bundled together and, when suitably balanced, mutually reinforce one another, and all are supported by underlying bodily mechanisms, such as the respiratory, skeletal, muscular and endocrine systems. The elements of good health tend to rise and fall clustered together. Goodness too, says Boyd, is an ordinary natural property. We call things good that satisfy *important* human needs, physical, psychological and social, such as food, shelter, the nurture of family, love, friendship, education, as well as social and political arrangements and mechanisms that promote these.

> Moral goodness is defined by this cluster of goods and the homeostatic mechanisms which unify them. Actions, policies, character traits, etc. are morally good to the extent to which they tend to foster the realization of these goods or to develop and sustain the homeostatic mechanisms upon which their unity depends. (*Ibid.*: 203)

Boyd is not saying that these homeostatic clusters cause moral goodness or that moral goodness supervenes on these homeostatic states; rather, goodness is "defined by" or identical to such states.

Just what elements, arrangements and mechanisms promote the most favourable homeostatic cluster is not evident *a priori*, but must be uncovered through scientific research, says Boyd. That certain personal, familial, political or economic arrangements promote homeostatic goodness more than others is something amenable to scientific study. In this way, Boyd says, improving the mechanisms of moral homeostasis resembles good automotive engineering and product design. We want cars that combine reliability, performance, economy, comfort, durability and so on, and good homeostatic engineering promotes these desiderata at levels that allow for their homeostatic unity. Boyd would most likely applaud, then, the research of social scientists such as Martin Seligman, a pioneer in the recent movement in positive psychology, who claims that psychologists should be concerned not just with addressing psychological dysfunctions, such as neuroses, phobias, depression and the like, but should devote themselves also to finding ways to foster traits that positively contribute to human mental health and well-being (see e.g. Peterson & Seligman 2004).

Boyd acknowledges that the scientific study of moral goodness, like all science, depends on background theoretical beliefs and assumptions; it is paradigm-dependent, as we have come to say. Theoretical commitments to such unobservables as black holes cause us to adjust the measurement and detection procedures of our experimental procedures and, lo and behold, the results of our procedures often confirm theoretical beliefs (or approximations thereof) about unobservables. Achieving a better and better fit between theory and observation is an ongoing process that no doubt admits of adjustments back and forth, modifications of theory and experimental practice, in what Boyd, following John Rawls, calls "reflective equilibrium". "The theory dependence of the observations and their interpretation is simply one aspect of the pervasive theory dependence of methodology in science which the scientific realist cheerfully acknowledges" (Boyd 1988: 206).

But how, exactly, does the science of morality work? As with scientific observations and explanations, our moral observations and judgements are reliable only if the theories on which their interpretation depends are at least approximately true. The question, then, is whether our background beliefs about human needs and their fulfilment, the relative ranking or importance of these needs, their compatibility, the best conditions for their satisfaction and many other considerations, are at least approximately true. Given the approximate truth of our background beliefs, perhaps we are in a position to make truthful judgements about particular actions, character traits or social institutions and arrangements. But what if our "theories", our background interpretations of the moral phenomena, differ? Notice that homeostatic clusters contain a balance of "important" goods. What is considered important is not a scientific but a philosophical matter. Given the truth of Boyd's theoretical commitments about what are important goods, his "moral science" will arrive at approximately correct judgements about what behaviours are moral and immoral, just and unjust. But Boyd does not argue for his naturalistic starting point, he simply assumes it.

Notice too that Shafer-Landau, Boyd and theists agree, for example, that genocide is wrong, yet they disagree about the moral theory that accounts for that fact. How can incompatible theories arrive at identical conclusions? Curiously, Boyd, like Mackie, admits that for the most part, human reflection on morality has viewed goodness as a reflection of God's design plan, a background belief he thinks is profoundly mistaken. Yet, says Boyd, just as Newtonian physicists had mistaken theories about absolute space and time, ether, phlogiston and other matters, they were nevertheless able to make correct judgements about such matters as planetary motion and the trajectory of projectiles. Analogously, while theists and moral Platonists may be wrong about their background theory, it does not necessarily preclude religious believers from being right about the elements of the homeostatic cluster. Our basic survival as a species by evolutionary means no doubt contributed to our rough reliability at recognizing human needs and how they are homeostatically clustered.

How might critics respond to Boyd's admittedly big-picture proposal for understanding the rich array of moral phenomena we have been considering? One should note that Boyd's project does not engage the theist's claims that morality depends on God; he simply assumes theism is false and in so doing begs the question of this chapter. Still, we must consider whether his non-utilitarian consequentialism provides explanatory resources equal to or superior to theism.

While Boyd acknowledges that what counts as goodness and flourishing is theory-dependent, he fails to give sufficient attention to the fact that roughly comparable levels of homeostatic goodness are achievable under dramatically different theoretical accounts about human nature and the psychological, familial, social and political conditions – the important elements – that make such levels of goodness possible. Were we to conduct a qualitative survey in different cultures, the lives of whose inhabitants were governed by incompatible moral theories, it is plausible that we would find no one culture happier than another. Philosophical traditions offer dramatically different and, in some cases, incompatible accounts about the nature and destiny of persons and thus about what practices will satisfy their true or ultimate needs. They differ still further about what kinds of social and political arrangements are most productive of homeostatic goodness and genuine human flourishing. It is likely that many different beliefs about how the elements of homeostatic clusters are to be weighted, many different accounts of human needs and fulfilment, and many different accounts of social and political arrangements are compatible with achieving roughly similar levels of human needs satisfaction. Is it obvious that the "important" needs of humans are better met in countries that are predominantly religious than in those that are not? If roughly equivalent homeostatic goodness is achievable regardless of one's background theory, the results themselves cannot be a reason to prefer Boyd's naturalistic theory. Here is a case where the data underdetermines any particular theory, and it most certainly does not point to naturalism as superior to its theoretical alternatives. Boyd's "science" of morality relies on and is driven by theoretical commitments that, in the last analysis, go undefended.

Boyd assumes that the facts about human homeostatic clusters of goodness are the result of a long evolutionary process. Over millions of years, and a great many happy accidents, humans have emerged with many needs in common. Without so many nutrients per day, without a requisite amount of sleep, without a suitably long period of parental care and socialization, and so forth, we fail to thrive given the kinds of creatures we are. But there is still wide latitude in the way each person might configure his or her homeostatic cluster of goods. One might rank personal autonomy higher than forming family ties, one might rank wealth above wisdom and another might rank an open, experimental sexual lifestyle higher than monogamous, heterosexual sex.

Even if human needs are largely the product of evolutionary accident, why should we feel duty-bound to conform to any one given blend of homeostatic goodness? In fact, why should we not, as Dawkins suggests, rebel against the evolutionarily given package of homeostatic properties underlying a certain conception of happiness? Why not, as Michel Foucault bids us do, experiment upon the self, undertake a project in the aesthetics of self-making that finds our own preferable levels of homeostatic goodness.[16] We need not yield submissively to the "homeostatic hand" that nature has dealt us, but we can instead undertake to modify our moral preferences, sentiments, actions and character traits until we achieve our own preferred homeostatic cluster of goodness. Science may show that eating your vegetables contributes to human well-being. Science might also undertake to engineer humans to benefit equally from cake as from carrots. And there is no guarantee that one person's preferred homeostatic cluster will be compatible with that of others. Unfortunately, Boyd's proposals do not explain our sense of moral obligation, of the demands of morality on our lives being such as not to leave us free to discard them in preference to some balance of goods that suits only ourselves.

Finally, Boyd's proposals do not account – and it is hard to see how they could account – for that intricacy and subtlety of our moral lives and the judgements we make about them. Boyd's philosophy of homeostatic clusters undertakes to define but one moral term: goodness. But what of justice, temperance, courage and practical wisdom, the four cardinal virtues? How will the empirical science of homeostatic clusters render judgements about such concerns as pride, anger, envy, greed, gluttony, lust and sloth, the so-called "seven deadly sins"? What of duty, virtue, obligation, accountability and other key moral concepts? How will the notion of homeostatic clusters adjudicate such normative issues as those raised by human subject research, the environment and genetic enhancement? Boyd's response comes in a single sentence:

> On a consequentialist conception of morals such notions as obligation and justice are derivative ones, and it is doubtful if the details of the derivations are relevant to the defense of moral realism in the way that the defense of a realist conception of the good is. (1988: 205)

Even were the basic human needs of all humans to be met, moral concerns would still confront us. It is highly doubtful that all the important moral concepts that arise in the moral life are derivable from homeostatic goodness alone. Contrary to Boyd's claim, the devil is truly in the details.

The Euthyphro objection

Critics of theism are quick to charge that the objections faced by theistic ethics are as formidable as those facing moral Platonism and non-utilitarian consequentialism, so that there is no obvious explanatory advantage to theism. One of the most forceful objections against grounding objective morality in God's existence comes in the form of a powerful dilemma, first articulated by Plato in his dialogue *Euthyphro*. In the dialogue, a discussion arises about the nature of true piety. Socrates asks Euthyphro if an action is pious just because God commands it, or whether God commands only that which is pious. (For our purposes, we can substitute "morally good" for "pious".) If the former, then an action that was morally neutral *becomes* right or wrong simply by God's fiat. This view, called "divine command theory", does succeed in showing how morality depends upon God. But if something's being right or wrong has no other basis than God's say-so, God's commands appear arbitrary; he could just as well have commanded that torturing innocent children is morally obligatory. In fact, since something's being morally good depends only on God's declaring it to be so, God may declare tomorrow that what was forbidden yesterday is obligatory today. On this view, we receive no explanation as to why God has declared some things to be immoral and others moral. Divine command theory not only makes God's commands seem arbitrary, but it also evacuates the concept of good of all its meaning when applied to God. For if God's actions are good no matter what he does, simply in virtue of the fact that it is *he* who does them, then to say that God is good is devoid of content and becomes a tautology, on a par with "God is God". Finally, accepting the first horn undermines the claim that morality is objectively true, since what is morally obligatory may change as God's preferences change.

The second horn of Euthyphro's dilemma looks equally unattractive to theists. To say that God commands us to do that which is morally good, suggests that there is a moral standard independent of God to which he is beholden. God does not declare what is good and bad so much as he recognizes what is good and bad and commands accordingly. Moral goodness, on this second option, makes God's commands superfluous. Yet if God commands that which is good independently of his commands, it would seem there is some power or moral authority independent of God, and this not only threatens God's aseity (his independence of all of creation) but works against the moral argument's claim that our morality is somehow grounded in God.

As often happens with dilemmas, the wisest course lies with neither extreme, but somewhere in the middle. Theists insist that to understand God's attributes, we must analyse them not in isolation but in relation to each other and as modified by the totality of God's character. God is not powerful, *simpliciter*, but powerful as befits his also being wise and good. To say that God is perfect in goodness is to say that God's moral character embodies every moral perfection to the highest degree possible. This would mean that God is, among other things, loving, compassionate, just, merciful and forgiving, all traits readily ascribed to God by theists. And if God is essentially good, then there is indeed a standard from which he cannot deviate – the grain of truth in the second horn of the dilemma – but that standard is not independent from God but constitutive of his very nature. The first horn of the dilemma also contains a grain of truth, to wit, that the moral standards that are in force throughout creation are in some way up to God. For suppose God had never decided to create anything. There would then have been no use for commands against idolatry or moral obligations to honour God as benefactor. Or, suppose that God had created only spiritual beings such as angels. Then commands against adultery and gluttony would obviously make no sense. The moral commands that have force in the created order, then, reflect the particular creaturely natures God has chosen to instantiate and the particular conditions of their creaturely flourishing. In going between the horns of Euthyphro's dilemma, theists say that the particular moral precepts that have force in creation are partially up to God and the kinds of beings that he elects to create. But theists deny that God could create creatures and then command those things which would undermine their creaturely flourishing. But this is not to hold God accountable to a standard outside himself, but merely to require that he act consistently with his essentially loving character.

Religious experience and
5 cumulative case arguments

In 1654, eight years before his death, the brilliant French mathematician, scientist and philosopher Blaise Pascal had a powerful religious experience that lasted two hours and has come to be known as "the night of fire". From roughly 10.30pm to 12.30am, Pascal claims to have encountered God. Ever the scientist, Pascal attempted to write down what was happening to him during the experience. What he managed to write down is as follows:

> Fire
> "God of Abraham, God of Isaac, God of Jacob," not of the
>   philosophers and of the learned.
> Certitude, certitude, feeling, joy, peace.
> God of Jesus Christ.
> God of Jesus Christ.
> Thy God and my God
> "Thy God shall be my God."
> Oblivious of the world and of everything, except God.
> He is encountered only by the way taught in the Gospel.
> Greatness of the human soul.
> Just Father, the world has not known Thee, but I have known
>   Thee.
> Joy, joy, joy, tears of joy.
> I am separated from Him.
> "They have forsaken me, the fountain of living waters."
> My God will you leave me?
> Let me not be separated from Him eternally

> This is the life eternal, that they know thee, the one true God,
>   and the one Thou has sent, Jesus Christ.
> Jesus Christ.
> Jesus Christ.
> I am separated from Him, I have fled Him, renounced Him,
>   crucified Him.
> Let me never be separated from Him.
> He is only preserved by the ways taught in the Gospel.
> Renunciation, total and sweet.
>   Etc.
> Complete submission to Jesus Christ and to my Director
> Eternally in joy for one day of practice on earth
> I will not forget thy word. Amen.   (1995: 285–6)

After the experience subsided, Pascal took the piece of paper on which these words were written, folded it and sewed it into the lining of his coat next to his heart, where it remained until his death. Pascal called this experience his "second conversion". The experience proved so powerful that it altered the course of Pascal's thinking and writing until his untimely death aged thirty-nine. While not many persons have religious experiences as dramatic as Pascal's, the number of people claiming to have had some sort of religious experience is surprisingly high. According to a Gallup Poll, 54 per cent of the people polled answered affirmatively to the following question: have you ever been aware of, or influenced by, a presence or a power – whether you call it God or not – which is different from your everyday self?[1]

Varieties of religious experiences

Religious experiences are not only common but also pervasive among the world's religions. They are also diverse, as one might expect given the variety of the world's religions. Religious experiences sometimes take the form of visions, such as those Arjuna is said to have had of Krishna. They take the form of voices, such as the apostle Paul's hearing the voice of Christ on the road to Damascus, en route to persecute Christians. They take the form of mystical experiences, where subjects report being loosed from spatiotemporal consciousness and united with some ultimate, ineffable

One, that One variously identified as Nature (*à la* Wordsworth), the Void (as with some Buddhists), a Monistic One (such as the Hindu Brahman), or unity with the Trinitarian God of Christianity, as with Julian of Norwich. Indeed, as we shall see, the tremendous variety of religious experiences leads some critics to claim that they are incompatible and thus unreliable.

Since this is a book exploring theism, we will here concentrate on purported experiences of God. A quite common sort of religious experience among theists, and the one that will serve as the focus of our discussion, is what one might call an "of-God experience", a perceptual, but non-sensory experience that purports to be an encounter with God. Religious experiences of this sort are intentional; the experiences seem to refer to something existing apart from the one undergoing the experience and are thus not merely reports about the private mental state of the recipient, as would be the case when feeling depressed or having a headache. Here is an example from William James's *Varieties of Religious Experience*:

> God is more real to me than any thought or thing or person. I feel his presence positively, and the more as I live in closer harmony with his laws as written in my body and mind. I feel him in the sunshine or rain; and awe mingled with a delicious restfulness most nearly describes my feelings. I talk to him as to a companion in prayer and praise, and our communion is delightful. He answers me again and again, often in words so clearly spoken that it seems my outer ear must have carried the tone, but generally in strong mental impressions .... I have a sense of his presence, strong, and at the same time soothing, which hovers over me. Sometimes it seems to enwrap me with sustaining arms. (1929: 70–71)

Religious experiences of the sort James records differ from ordinary perceptual experiences in being perceptual yet non-sensory. God is said to be present to one, though not by stimulating one's five senses. The subject whose experience James describes claims "to feel" God's presence positively, but this feeling is not an ordinary tactile experience.[2]

In typical cases of perception, and in most instances of religious experience, one does not form an argument from the fact that one seems to see an object to the belief that the object corresponding to the experience exists. We do not, for instance, *infer* that we see an apple from the fact that we seem to experience a reddish, roundish, firm, fragrant object, and have no reason to think we are subject to demonic deception. Our belief that we see an apple follows immediately, spontaneously and *non-inferentially* from the fact that we have experiences characteristic of seeing an apple. Only in highly unusual circumstances – perhaps where a particularly clever practical jokester is known to be at work – would one construct an argument to the effect that the best explanation of one's having apple-like experiences is because one is actually seeing an apple. Typically, however, our perceptual beliefs are accepted without the benefit of argument.

That people purport to have powerful encounters with God (or some other transcendent reality) is beyond dispute. That these experiences are profoundly moving and sometimes life-changing for those who undergo them is also uncontested. The humanistic psychologist, Carl Rogers once remarked: "The touchstone of validity is my own experience. No other person's ideas, and none of my own ideas, are as authoritative as my experience" (Rogers 1961: 23). Rogers may be right that people often find experiences more persuasive than arguments. (This is often the case with those who have had a religious experience.) Whatever their psychological force may be, however, the philosophical significance of religious experiences remains an open question. What do religious experiences show? Are they veridical? Are they really experiences of God? To what extent, if any, do such experiences provide adequate grounds for thinking that God exists? Can such experiences be authoritative for anyone other than the person undergoing the experience? And can claims to veridicality be defended against the powerful objections to which they are routinely subject? These are the questions we will pursue.

One popular argument from religious experience is quite simple: experiential awareness of God – for example, his comforting presence in a time of difficulty – constitutes *prima facie* evidence for justifiably believing that God exits. In other words, such experiences should be regarded as adequate grounds for their corresponding belief unless defeating evidence gives us more reason to think the experience was illusory or unreliably formed. William Alston says that religious experiences thus function analogously to perceptual experiences of everyday objects, such as books, buildings and bicycles. Each begins with some psychological experience of something's appearing to one, some "positive-seeming", that in turn serves as the basis for an existence claim. For example, one's seeming to see a tall, three-dimensional, rectilinear structure that people are entering and exiting, gives one good reason to think one sees a building. Similarly, or so the argument goes, a person's having experienced God is supposed to give one *prima facie* reason for thinking that the object of one's experience exists. Using one's senses to form beliefs about the external world – the sensory practice, or SP, as Alston refers to it – constitutes a "doxastic practice": a normative, rule-governed, firmly established social practice for forming beliefs about the external world (Alston 1991: ch. 4). These beliefs are defeasible, that is, they are capable of being overturned should sufficient reasons arise that throw the experiences into doubt. The "mystical practice, MP", argues Alston, is analogous to the sensory practice, since it too constitutes an established social practice for forming potentially defeasible beliefs about God based on certain sorts of experiences. So the mere having of a religious experience provides *prima facie* justification for thinking that one has encountered God. If one's experience succumbs to no defeaters, we have all-things-considered or ultimate justification for the belief that we have genuinely encountered God.

Persons sceptical of religious experience might insist that religious experiences be independently confirmed as reliable *before* they may serve as an adequate ground for belief in God or any other transcendental reality. But, as Alston powerfully argues, we have no non-circular way of vindicating the reliability of sensory experiences apart from further appeals to sensory experience. If I thought my eyes were playing me false, I might reach out my hand or ask someone else to confirm that I was indeed seeing what I thought I was seeing. But these cross-checks of vision rely equally on sensory input, making any such check of perception's reliability circular. Similar remarks might be made regarding the reliability of our other cognitive powers, of memory, inferential reasoning and so forth. To insist that religious experiences meet a standard of independent confirmation not even our sensory faculties can meet is to impose a "double-standard", says Alston.

Richard Swinburne argues along lines similar to Alston by invoking what he calls "the principle of credulity". Swinburne says that we should accord to religious experiences the same presumption of veridicality that we extend to ordinary perceptual experiences. That is, ordinary perceptual experiences as well as experiences of God's being present to one should be treated as innocent unless and until proven guilty. Swinburne states his principle formally as follows: "It is a principle of rationality that (in the absence of special considerations) if it seems (epistemically) to a subject that x is present, then probably x is present: what one seems to perceive is probably so" (1979: 254).[3] Something in the neighbourhood of Swinburne's principle must be correct as regards ordinary perception, otherwise one faces the spectre of scepticism regarding all one's sensory experiences. Critics, as we shall see, resist granting to religious experiences the same presumption of veridicality we grant to sensory experiences.

What "special considerations" might prompt us to reject an experience as veridical? Alston identifies two such reasons, "rebutters" and "underminers". A "rebutter" is some independent experience or fact whose truth renders one's belief that *p* (e.g. that one has experienced God) improbable. So a person's claim to have seen Elvis at the launderette yesterday is discredited by our independent knowledge of the fact that Elvis died at his Graceland home in 1977. "Underminers" give us reasons for thinking that one's belief was formed by faculties that were functioning unreliably. So we have strong reasons to consider unreliable any religious beliefs formed while delusional or while under the influence of hallucinogens. Alston and Swinburne agree that religious experiences should be taken at face value as veridical. Absent reasons to doubt, religious experiences provide "all-things-considered" reason for thinking that God exists.

The principle of credulity faces a variety of challenges. Suppose someone of seemingly sane mind and in a non-deceptive environment were to report having seen a leprechaun. Does the principle require that we acknowledge the experience as *prima facie* veridical? If so, the principle of credulity is too permissive, extending positive epistemic status to outlandish beliefs. Defenders of the principle could argue that we have significant background information to discount such experiences. Leprechauns are known to be creatures of folklore and, unlike God, have not been the objects of thousands of experiences by persons from different cultures. Moreover, the spotting of leprechauns does not constitute a firmly established doxastic practice, as the sensory and mystical practices do. Other critics point out that Swinburne's principle, stated in the positive form, does not allow us to form justified beliefs about the *absence* of some object. Suppose I look in my garage and fail to see my car. Would this not give me good reason to think that my car is not there? Yes, of course. Granted, my failure to see my car is good reason to believe my car is not present at this location. It does not, however, give me good reason to believe that my car does not exist or that no cars exist. Similarly, one's failure to experience God, even on the part of an earnest searcher, does not show that God does not exist. It does, however, invite us to ask why a benevolent God would remain experientially absent from someone who earnestly sought God. This raises what is sometimes referred to as the problem of the hiddenness of God, an issue we shall examine in the chapter on suffering.

Do religious experiences submit to checking procedures?

Religious sceptics point out that we have excellent reasons to think that not all religious experiences are veridical, since certifiably delusional people sometimes claim to experience God. Nor are religious experiences "self-authenticating". They do not wear their authenticity on their sleeve, so to speak; they do not come with internal markers that testify to their truthfulness. So, without some basis for discriminating between fraudulent and genuine religious experiences, neither the person undergoing a religious experience nor we who receive testimony of such ought to conclude that the experience is veridical rather than delusory. Unless we know the experience is genuine, we have no basis for supposing that the experience can serve as grounds for thinking that God exists. So in the light of our background knowledge that some religious experiences are unveridical, it is too permissive to take such experiences at face value.

In reply, we should note that we have excellent reasons to believe that not all sensory experiences or memories are veridical. Delusional people hear voices and perfectly normal people sometimes see mirages. People misremember and have false memories. Yet we do not demand that persons forming beliefs on the basis of perception and memory first submit their experiences to criteria of authenticity before accepting them. Rather, we think it appropriate to take our sensory and memory reports at face value unless we acquire reasons for thinking otherwise. To demand that religious experiences labour under a burden not shared by other belief-forming faculties and practices is, once again as Alston points out, to impose a double standard.

Religious sceptics insist that forming beliefs on the basis of sensation and memory is importantly disanalogous from forming beliefs on the basis of religious experiences, such that the principle of credulity applies to the former but not the latter. In particular, sensory experiences are capable of various kinds of checking procedures whereby their genuineness can be confirmed. If I am in doubt about whether I see a deer up ahead on the path, I can ask my running buddy if he too sees a deer. Moreover, if it is a deer, we can predict that upon nearing the animal, it will bound away. Moreover, sensory objects are so situated in space and time so as to stand in the appropriate causal relationships with our experiences, whereas religious experiences are not. Richard Gale argues that:

> Whereas there are objective, agreed upon tests for determining when a person's sensory faculty is not functioning properly, there are no such tests for determining when a person's mystical faculty is not working properly. Furthermore, there is no mystical analogue to a sensory observer being properly positioned in space, since God does not stand in any spatial relations. (2005: 429)

Nor does God stand in ordinary causal relations with those who experience him. If we wanted to test whether I was in fact seeing a tree in front of me, we could run various tests to determine if my sensory faculties were being appropriately stimulated by spectra of light consistent with my seeing a tree in my particular circumstances. We could make predictions consistent with there being a tree in front of me, such as my walking headlong into it and seeing if I get a bruised noggin. No such tests allow us to check that we stand in the right causal relationship to God. Since religious experiences lack the sorts of checking procedures available to sensory experiences, we lack the means to distinguish genuine from counterfeit religious experiences and thus should not take such experiences as adequate grounds for thinking that God exists.

Gale is not demanding that ordinary empirical experiences must actually be cross-checked before we are ever justified in accepting them. For any checked experience leaves unchecked whatever experience is used to check the first. To require that our cross-checking experience also submit to cross-checking will in turn require yet another cross-check, *ad infinitum*. If we are to avoid scepticism, some experiences must simply be accepted at face value, as the principle of charity suggests. Gale's argument, rather, is that the procedures used to validate sensory experiences cannot even be applied to religious experiences and this makes religious experiences significantly different than sensory experiences, thus weakening the analogy between sensory and religious experiences.

There are very good reasons, theists point out, why the procedures used to check sensory experiences do not apply to God. For starters, God doesn't have a body. So neither X-rays, audiometers, spectrometers, nor any other device we might employ to corroborate a sensory experience will show that we stand in the right causal or spatiotemporal relations with God. Moreover, God is not an inert object subject to causal laws, but an all-powerful person who can, if he chooses, remain hidden or be experienced only by persons who have suitably prepared themselves to encounter him. Alston labels as "epistemic imperialism" the practice of making the procedures used to check sensory experience paradigmatic for epistemology as a whole (Alston 1991: 242). The beliefs we accept from *a priori* intuition, and even some highly theoretical claims of science (e.g. those that tell us about multiple universes or what happens inside a black hole) are not corroborated by empirical checking procedures, but are not necessarily unjustified on that account. The failure, then, of religious experiences to submit to checking procedures used on physical objects is not a telling disanalogy, disanalogy though it may be.

Defenders of religious experience further argue that religious experiences are subject to various checking procedures – or "overrider systems", as Alston calls them – of both a negative and positive sort. Some of the same reasons that would prompt us to disqualify ordinary sensory experiences as genuine can also override religious experiences, for example, schizophrenia, drugs or highly deceptive environments. Religious experiences might also be rejected as genuine if they contravene knowledge of God gained from natural theology, moral insight or the canonical beliefs and paradigmatic experiences of one's religious tradition. Suppose, to take an extreme and obvious case, someone in the Christian tradition who we have not heretofore had reasons for thinking insane, claims to have an encounter with God after which he is ordered to murder his next-door neighbour. This is quite obviously contrary to common moral knowledge, the dictates of a loving God and the command given by God to love one's neighbour, and so is overridden.

Gary Gutting insists that religious experiences must be subject to checking procedures in order to be justified; yet he argues they can and do pass such tests. If, indeed, one encountered an extraordinarily wise, good and powerful being who cares about us, one would expect that those undergoing such experiences would be likely to have them again, that other individuals would also be beneficiaries of such experiences and that those having such experiences would be strengthened to lead morally better lives. And this is precisely what we find, he thinks. Religious experiences are repeatable, shared by others, and lead to testable predictions (Gutting 1982: 152). "The experiences themselves give prima facie warrant to the claim that [God] exists, and the fulfillment of the expectations induced by the assumption that the experiences are veridical provides the further support needed for ultimate warrant" (*ibid.*: 152–3).

Admittedly, both negative and positive checks – the overrider system, as Alston calls it – as are applied to religious experiences are not as fine-grained and exact as those that can be applied to sensory experiences. Moreover, prophets sometimes claim to have had experiences with God that require that a religious community change its previous ways of thinking and acting, thereby nullifying the test that the experience accord with canonical practice and the paradigmatic experiences of one's tradition. Still, religious experiences do have a rough system of cross-checks.

Can religious experiences be explained away?

Even if religious experiences might be subject to a rudimentary system of cross-checks, critics claim that such experiences fail the tests, for we have compelling reasons to think that such experiences are not due to God but to purely natural causes of various sorts. Sigmund Freud famously argued that religious experiences could be explained away as so much wish-fulfilment. Daniel Dennett thinks that there are evolutionary explanations for religious experiences that defeat any claims of such experiences being reliable or serving to justify religious belief. We shall look at each of these alternative explanations as representative of efforts to explain away religious experience.

Freud, that great theoretician of the subconscious, was in no doubt that religion in general and religious experiences in particular were purveyors of falsehood. At the same time, he acknowledged that religion constituted a powerful and pervasive force in his culture and in individual lives. His task, then, was to explain why people show such a strong disposition to embrace falsehood. As a starting point, Freud largely adopted Ludwig Feuerbach's theory that belief in God originates when we select those traits deemed to be most noble and admirable in humans, magnify them to supernatural proportion, and then "project" and personify them as a divine being.[4] Freud's contribution was to locate within the human psyche the driving forces behind this propensity for projection. Two psychological forces, our relationship with our fathers (our "father-complex" as Freud calls it) and our own helplessness at fending off the various harms to which we are routinely subject, occupy the centre of Freud's account.

Children are defenceless and need protection. A child's mother is not only first to satisfy the child's needs but also first to protect the child from various dangers. Soon, however, the child turns from the mother to the stronger father, looking to the father for protection but also fearing the father as a rival for the mother's affection. With maturity, the child realizes that not even its father is able to protect it from the "crushingly superior forces of nature". "When the growing child finds that ... he can never do without protection against strange and superior powers, he lends those powers the features belonging to the figure of his father; he creates for himself the gods whom he dreads, whom he seeks to

propitiate, and whom he nevertheless entrusts with his own protection" (Freud 1964: 47). Of course, given the psychogenic origin of religious ideas and experiences, we cannot consider them
truthful. Just the opposite: "they are illusions, fulfillments of the
oldest, strongest and most urgent wishes of mankind. The secret
of their strength lies in the strength of those wishes" (*ibid.*). In
short, religion is merely a psychological coping mechanism, mere
wish-fulfilment, that helps us to confront accidents, illness and a
death we cannot prevent.

Now Freud is right that we are capable of self-deception, that
our true motives for acting are not always transparent to us. But
we did not need Freudian analysis to know this. Freud is also right
that sometimes we cope with adversity by way of wish-fulfilment.
Imagine a mother who answers a knock at her door only to discover
two army officers bearing the personal belongings of her son, killed
in action. The mother, shocked and overwhelmed by the report,
refuses to believe that her son is dead. Perhaps, she reasons, the
eyewitness reports of his having been killed were mistaken. Perhaps
it was only someone who closely resembled her son. Perhaps he
simply lost his identifying dog tags and is still alive in a prisoner of
war camp. Clearly, the mother's belief that her son is still alive is not
grounded in the facts, but in some psychological coping strategy.[5]

Is belief in God that originates in religious experience just like
the mother's belief? First, let us note that many Christian thinkers
have claimed that humans were created by God to have a natural
God-ward orientation. Alvin Plantinga, as we shall see below, thinks
that humans have a "*sensus divinitatis*", a divine sense, which forms
a part of our natural cognitive powers. Other theists claim that we
are psychologically constituted so that we can only find genuine
fulfilment as persons when rightly related to God. As Augustine
famously remarked, "our hearts are restless until they find their rest
in thee" (*Confessions* bk 1, ch. 1). So to be told by Freud that we
have a natural psychological propensity to seek security and happiness in God is not something with which theists ought automatically
to disagree. In fact, having a natural impulse to seek after God is
precisely what we should expect if we were created by a good God
who knows that our highest fulfilment depends on being rightly
related to him. The genesis of a belief, however, does not in itself
show that it is false or even unjustified.

But how are we to differentiate theistic belief in God from the mother's belief that her son is still alive? We can't by use of fMRIs or PET scans or any other empirical test detect when wish-fulfilment mechanisms are at work. No autopsy will reveal it. Clearly, the way we know that someone's belief has arisen from wish-fulfilment is when it is obviously false, massively disconfirmed by the evidence or is the kind of belief we have strong inductive reasons for believing is generally due to wish-fulfilment. The mother's belief can reasonably be so described. But, says the theist, no one has shown that theism is false or massively disconfirmed by the evidence. Nor do we have inductive reasons for supposing that religious beliefs as a whole are generally due to wish-fulfilment. The only basis, then, for claiming that theistic belief is the product of wish-fulfilment is the assumption that there is no God. But this assumption begs the question against theism, a move typically frowned upon in philosophy.

Daniel Dennett finds inspiration in Hume's efforts to explain away religion and religious experiences as purely natural phenomena. He relies heavily on the relatively new scientific research of evolutionary psychologists and anthropologists such as Justin Barrett, Scott Atran, and Pascal Boyer to argue that the impulse to belief in gods, goblins and the ghosts of dead ancestors lies in the evolutionary history of the human species. In short, religious beliefs are the by-products of cognitive mechanisms that proved advantageous for human survival by helping our ancestors detect other agents, form communities, and increase cooperation.[6]

It is reasonable to think that successfully eluding one's predators and enemies gives one's genes a better chance of surviving into the next generation. Humans capable of discriminating between the harmless movements of rushing water, rustling leaves and the activity of a predator and rivals for food and mates, stood a competitive advantage over the less discerning. Evolutionary psychologists thus reason that our remote ancestors developed a functional cognitive unit, an "agency detecting device", that identified objects in the environment as intentional agents. Since it is better to be safe than sorry, some evolutionary anthropologists argue that this cognitive faculty would be tuned by natural selection to err on the side of caution, by generating occasional false positives (think here of the startle response of a rabbit). Justin Barrett (2000), from whom

Dennett borrows the term, dubs this cognitive faculty the "hyper-sensitive agency detecting device (HADD)".

The hypersensitive agency detection device is coupled with what Barrett calls the Theory of Mind (ToM) system, or what Dennett calls "the intentional stance". Upon detecting animals, humans or any other complicated thing in the environment that "puzzles or frightens us", our evolutionary forebears began automatically to attribute to them agency, the power of being moved by beliefs, desires, purposes and the like. (He knows that I have another stone to throw.) Humans could thus form plans in response to the plans of others. Dennett further speculates that a development of the intentional stance might have been to impute agency to the spir-its of the dead, now ghosts, thus introducing the idea of invisible agency. And so, the experience of a strange noise in the dark would have triggered a response of "Who is there?" and where no obvious agent was to be seen, the idea of an invisible agent arises. In brief, HADD in conjunction with ToM is supposed to explain how the evolutionary process produced cognitive mechanisms that have as a by-product a disposition towards religious belief.

So far we have a recipe only for animism or some crude anthro-pomorphic god. A couple more ingredients must be added to Den-nett's recipe for the rise of modern religions. Our species flourished in communities, requiring that we keep track of the plans and pur-poses of many intentional agents. This gave rise to uncertainty and confusion. Who are my enemies, my allies, to whom should defer-ence be shown, to whom do I owe what? Even early humans were quite alive to the fact that no one can keep perfect track of all the alliances and social relations (what Boyer calls "strategic informa-tion") that may be vital to one's well-being. Imagine, though, that there is, in Boyer's words, a "full-access agent", someone privy to the thoughts and intentions of all humans, whose knowledge might be discovered by divination or, if properly placated, revealed to one (Boyer 2002). This would greatly lessen the weightiness of decision-making and provide something of a stamp of approval for the decisions one does make. All that remains is to explain how belief in a supremely intelligent, powerful and invisible agent coa-lesces into the religious practices we observe today.

Dennett relies heavily on the concept of a "meme" to account for the development of shamanism, creeds and cult, and organized religion. "Memes" (first introduced by Richard Dawkins in his book, *The Selfish Gene*) are bits of "cultural DNA", such as words, songs, gestures and rituals that are passed on from one human to another by non-genetic "memetic evolution". Memes are the cultural counterpart to a gene, information that is spread among humans much like viruses or parasites. A catchy jingle, slang terms, clothing fashions, among many others, have been offered as examples of memes. Like genetic replicators, cultural replicators such as the traditions, practices and teachings of religions evolve, and do so without the deliberate foresight of its practitioners. "They can arise by exactly the same sort of blind, mechanical, foresightless sifting-and-duplicating process that has produced the exquisite designs of organisms by natural selection" (Dennett 2006: 79–80). Analogously with genes, Dennett thinks some memes outcompete others by proving more useful to their hosts. Religious memes proved useful by fostering cooperation and solidarity among humans. In sum, Dennett finds that the human practice of religion and religious practices submits entirely to a natural explanation.

What shall we say about Dennett's hypothesis that human proclivity for religion and religious experiences is a by-product of an evolutionary survival mechanism? If one's standards of evidence are similar to those expressed above by Richard Gale, that is, that scientific claims must submit to agreed upon empirical tests, then one must surely take Dennett's conclusions about the connections between the rise of religion and the earliest stages of our evolutionary development with a significant grain of salt. Dennett relies on entities such as memes whose very existence remains controversial among scientists and for which persuasive experimental and predictive data is lacking. To think that human sensitivity to the presence of other agents, in conjunction with the benefits of knowing the plans of others birthed the idea of an omniscient and omnipresent God is nothing short of sheer speculation. After all, the exact conditions giving rise to the emergence of a hypersensitive agency detector are historically irretrievable and thus the theories Dennett proposes are not, indeed cannot, be subject to the rigorous empirical cross-checking critics of religious experience insist upon. Stories about the prehistoric rise of religion will, at best, be limited to inferences to the best explanation, and at worst, mere "just-so stories". Indeed, Dennett himself appears to place but limited confidence in the story he weaves. To his credit, he admits:

> I will try to tell *the best current version* of the story science can tell about how religions have become what they are. I am not at all claiming that this is what science has already established about religion. The main point of this book is to insist that we *don't* yet know – but we can discover – the answers to these important questions if we make a concerted effort. Probably some of the features of the story I tell will prove in due course to be mistaken. Maybe many of them are wrong.
>
> (Dennett 2006: 103)

To say that religious experiences rely on cognitive mechanisms that underwent a natural development no reflective religious person denies. But it does not follow from this claim that all religious experiences are *nothing but* purely natural phenomena. Quite clearly, Dennett's hypotheses are philosophical, not scientific, however much he attempts to cloak them in the work of contemporary science. Before we explain away all religious experiences as evolutionary epiphenomena of an adaptive tendency to impute agency to strange noises and bumps in the night, we must, at the very least, allow the dust to settle among the disparate accounts on offer and allow the work of evolutionary psychology, a discipline still in its infancy, to mature. Religious people can be excused for not abandoning their beliefs on the strength of what science does not know.

Let us set all questions of scientific methodology and confirmability aside and suppose that evolutionary psychology can provide a compelling case that the human impulse to religion and religious experiences has a basis in the evolutionary development of various cognitive mechanisms. Would knowing something of the religion's origins constitute good reason to think its claims false or to view religious experiences as fraudulent? Of course not. The inference is as specious as the claim that perception, memory and the other intellectual faculties are unreliable because they too depend on cognitive mechanisms that underwent evolutionary development. A consistent strain of Christian thinking, traceable through ancient, medieval and modern periods has viewed persons' spiritual lives as intertwined in important ways with our physical natures. As noted earlier, Augustine thought that our psychological constitution is such that without God we would suffer a sense of incompletion and unfulfilment, an inner longing that, if yielded to, leads one to God. Aquinas believed that "to know that God exists in a general and confused way is implanted in us by nature, inasmuch as God is man's beatitude. For man naturally desires happiness, and what is naturally desired by man must be *naturally* known to him" (*Summa Theologiae* I II, q.2 reply obj. 1, emphasis added). John Calvin believed that all humans were created with a *sensus divinitatis*, a natural instinct, that directs one's psychological and intellectual life in a God-ward direction (*Institutes of the Christian Religion* I, iii; 1981: 1). As this sense matures, it leads either automatically or when activated by the complexity and grandeur of nature to belief in God. These theologians do not resist at all the idea that religious belief arises naturally out of our human nature. They also agree that this natural knowledge is limited and confused – "a slight taste of divinity", as Calvin puts it – which may partially explain the differences in religious belief triggered by these natural impulses.

Contemporary theists affirm and clarify the sense in which religious belief is anchored in human intellectual and psychological nature. Plantinga, following Calvin, thinks that humans are naturally equipped with a *sensus divinitatis*, which he describes as a "cognitive mechanism" that is triggered in a wide variety of circumstances to form beliefs in God. "To show that there are natural processes that produce religious belief does nothing ... to discredit it; perhaps God designed us in such a way that it is by virtue of those processes that we come to have knowledge of him" (Plantinga 2000: 145). Like memory and perception, the deliverances of the *sensus divinitatis* are justified and warranted so long as they have been formed reliably, that is, by cognitive faculties functioning truth-conducively in an appropriate environment. The "*de jure*" question of the justifiability of religious belief thus turns on the "*de facto*" question of whether or not humans are equipped as Plantinga describes. Interestingly, Justin Barrett, on whose HADD research Dennett so heavily relies, defends Plantinga and the possibility of justified belief in God arising from religious experiences:

Suppose there is a Yahwist god and that one has an experience of this god. In this circumstance, according to the Reformed Epistemologist, the god-faculty is operating under optimal conditions for producing reliable religious beliefs. These experiential grounds, cognized through the god-faculty, are justifying grounds of religious belief. The development of the god-faculty through evolutionary processes prepares one for the acquisition of true religious beliefs when one has genuine religious experiences. The god-faculty produces true religious beliefs when one has genuine religious experiences. The god-faculty produces true religious beliefs in optimal environments (that is, those where one is prompted by God and not by things that go bump in the night). How those faculties were developed is irrelevant to the account of the belief's justification. Coming to learn that these faculties were developed naturally does not constitute a defeater for the justification of belief in God.

(Clark & Barrett 2010: 188)

Dennett mistakenly supposes that once we identify the natural evolutionary advantage once conferred by some cognitive power, we have thereby shown that the same power cannot have a religious purpose. But why can't our cognitive faculties serve dual purposes? This is the point of Plantinga's comment above. Surely our ancient ancestors who learned not only to identify the enemy but also to count the number of one's enemies gained an evolutionary advantage. Pity the poor Neanderthal who could not distinguish between one and a whole clan of menacing rivals. Whether to fight or flee surely depended on how many of the enemy one faced. Subtraction and addition soon followed. (One enemy down, two to go.) But the cognitive units that once counted the number of enemy evolved to produce quantified modal logic and set theory, neither of which, in my experience, helps much in procuring mates, raising offspring or conferring on one any other evolutionary advantage. Shall we say that the latter are unreliable for having been produced by faculties that originally served other purposes? Surely, the more sensible view is to suppose that some of our faculties evolved to multiple purposes.

Are religious experiences unreliable owing to the conflicting accounts of their content?

Jerome Gellman calls our final objection to religious experience "The Argument from Incompatibility" (Gellman 1997: 92ff.). A brief survey of religious experiences the world over shows them to produce incompatible outputs. Persons – especially from diverse religious cultures – claiming to have experienced God (or ultimate reality) disagree about who or what it is they have experienced: God is one, God is many; God is personal, God is impersonal; God is immanent, God is transcendent; God is quality-less, God has qualities; God is unlimited in wisdom, power or goodness, God is limited in one or all of these properties; and so on. Persons claiming to have experienced God also disagree about what they take to be God's plans and purposes for humanity: for example, God wants all people to pray facing the east, God wants all people to pray facing the west. Inasmuch as it is logically impossible for these incompatible claims to be true (or so the argument states), we have good reason to think that the religious experiences that gave rise to them are unreliable and, as they are unreliable, are incapable of justifying the beliefs arising out of the experiences.

Michael Martin puts the point succinctly: "Religious experiences … tell no uniform or coherent story, and there is no plausible theory to account for the discrepancies among them" (Martin 1990: 159). Martin, himself, does not lack an explanation of these discrepancies, to wit, that that there is no objective divine reality that is the subject of anyone's experience. Note too the disanalogy between religious and perceptual experience; while normal persons sometimes disagree about what they see or hear – consider conflicting, even contradictory, eyewitness reports at the scene of an accident – they display nowhere near the degree of disagreement found among the reports of persons claiming to have encountered God. Alston, as we have already seen, one of the chief defenders of forming justified religious beliefs on the basis of religious experience, nevertheless takes this to be the most difficult criticism of his position, reducing somewhat the overall rationality of engaging in the Christian mystical practice, although not so much as to make it irrational (Alston 1991: 275).

It should be pointed out that we are no strangers to authentic experiences receiving divergent, even incompatible, descriptions.

Think of the way two students might form different impressions on the basis of their interaction with the same professor. Owing to the circumstances of the meeting, a student may walk away thinking "he is the meanest teacher at the college". Another student, owing perhaps to very different circumstances, may leave the professor's company believing that "he is the nicest teacher in the college". Also common is the phenomenon of genuine experiences being misconstrued and therefore misdescribed. Two friends and I were once running on a path, whereupon we spied an object up ahead. One of us thought it was a dog, the other a deer, the other a cyclist. As we got closer we saw that someone had pulled a bench into the middle of the path. Each of us had a genuine experience of the same thing, but we misdescribed it.

The bearing of these illustrations for religion is easy to see. People from different cultural backgrounds and religious traditions obviously describe their experiences differently. People from Europe report having experiences of the Virgin Mary while people from India attest to visions of Krishna. But these differences of description do not necessarily show that the experiences themselves were fraudulent but only that different labels have been attached to the experiences. As the previous examples illustrate, an analogous sort of thing happens in ordinary perception. Might not differing experiences among the world's religions receive a similar explanation? Or, as the oft-cited illustration of the five blind men and the elephant suggests, maybe Hindus, Buddhists, Christians and others are simply experiencing different facets or aspects of the one ultimate reality. Critics, however, see serious disanalogies between the illustrations above and the apparent contradictory claims resulting from religious experience. To say the elephant is like a rope and is like a tree trunk is not to say what is contradictory. It would, however, be contradictory to say the elephant is both material and immaterial, and this, says the sceptic, is closer to what we face with incompatible religious experiences.

Martin complains that there is no coherent theory that accounts for the incompatible claims arising out of religious experience. This is not to say that there are not theories on offer. One of the most widely commented upon efforts to account for the inconsistencies in religious experience is John Hick's (see Hick 1989). Hick does not attempt to uncover a common theistic core of religious experiences or to show how seemingly incompatible descriptions of God can be harmonized. Rather, he attempts to explain why ultimate reality is, strictly speaking, unknowable, and thus not disclosed by any of our religious experiences. Strictly speaking, all the accounts of our religious experiences are incorrect!

Kant famously argued that our access to the empirical world is necessarily mediated by the "categories of the understanding", rendering human knowledge "phenomenal", that is conceptually mediated, rather than "noumenal", or unmediated. In an analogous way, Hick proposes that all religions are seeking to orient themselves away from self-centredness towards some good and loving divine, a transcendental reality beyond our conceptualization that Hick calls the "Real an sich". The "Real an sich", like Kant's noumenal reality, lies beyond our direct cognitive grasp. Our access to this transcendental reality is filtered through the religious concepts our cultures make available. So, none of our characterizations of the "Real an sich" are the literal truth. None should be taken at face value. On Hick's analysis, then, the problem of incompatible claims arising out of religious experience simply evaporates, since, as religious sophisticates recognize, these accounts should never have been supposed to deliver any truths at all about the ultimate reality.

Hick's views have drawn far more comment and criticism than space allows us to survey. Briefly, though, critics challenge Hick's claim that all of the world's religions are in fact moving from self-centredness toward a loving, divine reality, the cult of Kali and the bloody sacrifices of the Aztecs offering potent counter-examples.

More problematically, one wonders what underlies Hick's confidence that the "Real an sich" is good and loving, since it is supposed to lie beyond human conceptualization and predication. Hick appears prepared to make an exception in the case of "good" and "loving". Why should we not call the transcendent reality a "something we know not what"?

Finally, it is important to note that the world's religions do not share Hick's assessment that they are only dealing with a phenomenal reality filtered through concepts that ought not to be taken at face value. This certainly is not the self-understanding of most Christians who claim that religious experiences have shown Jesus to be fully human and fully divine. No doubt most Muslims, Hindus and Buddhists would likewise take umbrage at being told that they are confused regarding the central claims of their religion, that their central religious commitments are not true in the way they take them to be. So, let us take the claims about God generated by religious experiences as they are accepted, as Alston says, "on the ground", in other words, as veridical accounts of a transcendental reality. Unfortunately, this still leaves us with the problem of radical disagreement among the outputs of religious experiences.

In order for the argument from incompatibility to have force we must make a few assumptions. Suppose humans were somehow to gain in addition to our regular perceptual powers a bat's power of echolocation. The objects experienced by this faculty would appear non-coloured. The reports of vision, however, show things as coloured. Do the two faculties yield incompatible results? No, since we are not comparing apples and oranges, so to speak. We are talking about two distinct faculties and information-gathering practices.[7] For the sake of argument, then, let us assume that the Hindu religious practice, the Christian mystical practice, the Muslim religious practice and so on are not discrete practices (and this is a debatable point) but rather variations of a common mystical practice, each of which purports to tell us the truth about ultimate reality. Let us also assume that persons from various of the world's religions claiming to have experienced ultimate reality were not delusional, on drugs, in deceptive environments or in any other obvious conditions that would undermine the veridicality of their experience. Finally, let us grant that the religious experiences had by members of different religions satisfy the checking procedures internal to each religion, that is, that they are free of internal inconsistencies, line up suitably with traditional teaching and the experiences of acknowledged authorities, give rise to predicted fruits in the personal lives of those undergoing the experience and so on.

We can now put the argument a bit more precisely.[8] Let us assume that Susan is a Christian and has had a religious experience.

1. Susan is aware that practitioners of other religions have had religious experiences the propositional content of which is incompatible with her own.
2. Susan is rational in accepting the content of her own religious experience only if she has reasons independent of her own tradition for thinking her Christian religious practice and the

experiences generated by it are reliable, or more reliable than its alternatives.

3. Susan lacks independent reasons for thinking her experiences are reliable or more reliable than those of experienced by persons in other religious traditions.

4. Susan is irrational to accept her own experiences as epistemically superior to those with which it is in competition.

If one is aware that adherents of other religious traditions have had experiences with content contradictory to one's own religious experiences, the wise course is to reject all such experiential reports as unreliable and thus incapable of conferring justified religious belief. The incompatible claims "cancel each other out", so to speak.

One might address the argument from incompatibility by noting how few religious experiences issue forth in detailed claims about the nature or properties of God. We have been focusing on generic "of-God" experiences, the sort of experiences characterized by claims such as "God was present to me" and "God was comforting me", which lack detailed specifications of God's properties or nature. Gary Gutting differentiates between the "core" and the "outer periphery" of such experiences. Most religious experiences the world over might be described as a "superhuman power and love being present to one" (Gutting 1982: 175). Gutting argues that religious experience does successfully justify the claim that persons have had "contact with a reality beyond ourselves". To this "core" claim Gutting thinks one is justified in giving decisive as opposed to merely provisional or "interim" assent. "Peripheral beliefs", by contrast, the specific, detailed descriptions supplied by the creeds and theologies of the world's religions do not, according to Gutting, deserve our decisive and unswerving commitment, but rather an interim commitment.

> The greatest cognitive failure of religions throughout history has been their confusion, due to a fundamental self-misunderstanding, of the core and the outer belt of their commitment. This confusion leads to demands for decisive assent to claims that at best deserve interim assent. These demands are rightly rejected as intellectually irresponsible, with the result that religion is regarded as a thoroughly unreasonable commitment. (*Ibid.*)

Might there not be some common core to the majority of religious experiences, the differences between them being due to local cultural differences? Caroline Franks Davis, like Gutting, argues that a "common core" for what she calls "broad theism", as opposed to more highly specified accounts of God, is indeed justified by religious experiences (1989: esp. ch. 7). Her close examination of specific differences among the world's religions offers explanations for how, say, Ramanuja's Saguna-Brahman, the personal Lord of qualified, non-dualistic Hinduism and Shankara's Nirguna-Brahman, the unqualified and unknowable ultimate, can be synthesized as complementary aspects of the one Brahman. In a similar way, she shows how the Christian doctrine of the Trinity and the experience of a transcendental absolute might be viewed as complementary aspects of a whole. Imagine one were to encounter a transcendental reality of infinite love, and were to be drawn up into that love in so overwhelming a way so as to block out thought of all else. Such an experience could result in one's describing the ultimate reality as an impersonal, undifferentiated, monistic One. Were one to encounter this profound love in the experience of a supernatural person or Lord, the resulting account would likely look different, perhaps even incompatible. If there is an ultimate reality that transcends the spatiotemporal world, is eternal and more real than all else, is good, powerful, loving, a reality on which we and all else depends and in which our highest good resides, one should expect that this reality should not be graspable within the confines of a single experience but is something that can be experienced only in part. Precisely to the extent that someone thinks their finite and culturally situated experience captures the whole of ultimate reality, they have reason to think, as Feuerbach insists, that they have created their own God. While we may lack epistemic justification for highly specified accounts of deity typical of theological creeds, we nevertheless, thinks Davis, have suitable support for broad theism.

Unfortunately, says Alston, the distinction between "core" and "periphery" is not so easily preserved, for peripheral beliefs re-emerge in the form of an overrider system, that is, the system internal to each religion for checking the genuineness of claims associated with religious experiences. St Teresa of Avila had a number of religious experiences whose veracity was questioned not only by

Church authorities, but also by Teresa herself. She wondered if, perhaps, the things revealed to her in these experiences might not have been deceptions of the devil (her own version of the evil demon problem). How, then, to test their veridicality? Teresa's checking procedure required that she measure her experiences by their compatibility with scripture and the fruits one would expect to follow in her own personal moral and religious life, such as increase in humility and fervency of prayer. She writes:

> As far as I can see and learn by experience, the soul must be convinced that a thing comes from God only if it is in conformity with Holy Scripture; if it were to diverge from that in the very least, I think I should be incomparably more firmly convinced that it came from the devil than I previously was that it came from God, however sure I might have felt of this.
>
> (Quoted in Mavrodes 1978: 241)

But just here, Gutting's peripheral beliefs intrude upon the core, for the truthfulness of Teresa's experiences are weighed against claims such as that God is triune, a peripheral belief contradicted by the experiences of other mystics. To ignore the requirement that religious experiences be tested, at the very least by some internal checking procedure, invites a renewal of Gale's criticism that religious experiences lack any systems for checking their veracity.

Let us suppose that theists of various stripes and varieties lack a commonly agreed-upon test for establishing the superiority of their respective mystical practices and their corresponding claims about ultimate reality. What then? Does it follow that all persons are epistemically unjustified in accepting the accounts of ultimate reality that they do? It would seem not. Consider the long-standing, intractable disagreements that persist among philosophers. They hold incompatible views on freedom and determinism, the relationship of mind and body, the foundations of morality, not to mention the existence of God. They also disagree about matters of philosophical methodology, Plato and Descartes, among others, disparaging the power of sensory perception to convey knowledge, while Hume and logical positivists, minimized the contribution of *a priori* reason. Ironically, epistemologists divide over the very issue of the effect on my beliefs of disagreement by someone I regard as an intellectual peer (see Lackey 2010). If incompatible beliefs and the lack of a common method to resolve them make one unjustified, then philosophers, more than most, will fall on hard times. Similar remarks could be made about therapeutic psychology. What is the best way to treat clinical depression? Psychologists not only dispute what therapeutic strategies are most effective, they also lack a common methodology to resolve their disputes, since behaviourists, for instance, do not commonly accept results from psychodynamic therapy's probing of the subconscious.

If there is no compelling argument that requires one to abandon one's beliefs in the face of disagreement, then what ought a religious believer do who becomes aware that practitioners of other religions have had religious experiences resulting in beliefs seemingly incompatible with one's own? Alston recommends that one "sit tight with the practice of which I am a master", as the best prospect for gaining further understanding (Alston 1991: 274). Gutting offers similar counsel: "Given the fact that the great world religions seem to be the main loci and sustainers of our access to God, there is good reason for anyone interested in attaining such access or in more deeply understanding what it reveals to take part in the life of some established religious community" (Gutting 1982: 172–3). This seems to be sage advice. If one is to have repeated experiences, and if one seeks to test one's experiences against some overrider system, it will likely happen within the context of an existing religious community.

Cumulative case arguments, assessing evidence, and character

So far we have surveyed a handful of arguments, any one of which, according to their most ardent supporters, is supposed to underwrite the rationality of religious belief. You may not share their optimistic appraisal. Perhaps you may think that while each individual argument offers *some* evidence to think that God exists, no single argument constitutes *sufficient* evidence to justify believing in God. But what about the arguments in combination – might they have a cumulative force that they lack as separate arguments? To think that evidence can be combined to give greater strength to a conclusion is the main idea behind cumulative case arguments for

God's existence. And not just God's existence – as we shall see, cumulative case arguments are used in many intellectual contexts.

Let us take an obvious context where cumulative case arguments are used – courts of law. Suppose I were a prosecuting barrister and you were a member of the jury. "Ladies and gentlemen of the jury," I begin, "the gun used to kill the rich old widow was owned by the defendant. I rest my case." Obviously, you would find this scant evidence, however well substantiated, an inadequate basis for a guilty verdict. Suppose, further, that I add to that first piece of evidence the following: the only fingerprints found on the gun were those belonging to the defendant. Add also that the defendant had amassed substantial gambling debts and was overheard to have quarrelled about money matters with the victim in the recent past. Things are beginning to look bad for the defendant, but still you find the evidence thus far inconclusive to render a guilty verdict. Then add to the case the fact that the defendant was seen exiting the rich old widow's mansion just about the time the coroner says the lady was shot. Still unconvinced? OK. The cook and the maid swear on a stack of Bibles that they saw the defendant kill the rich old widow.

This admittedly contrived case allows one to see and appreciate the way in which various strands of evidence, no one of which is strong enough to bear the weight of a guilty verdict, can nevertheless be combined so as to support adequately one's belief that the defendant is guilty. The strategy of supporting claims on the basis of multiple strands of mutually reinforcing evidence finds application in many intellectual contexts, among them history, literary criticism and exegesis, and even science (see Mitchell 1973: ch. 3). What were the leading causes of the American Civil War? This highly debatable question finds various answers, each of which builds its case by assembling a cumulative case based on a certain ordering and weighting of the evidence. Did Christopher Marlowe or Francis Bacon write any of the works commonly attributed to Shakespeare? How did the dinosaurs die? Disputants have not been able to settle these questions by a single decisive piece of evidence – a "smoking gun", as the expression has it. Rather, the parties to these debates build their cases much the way prosecuting barristers do, strand by strand, until one has a convincing cumulative case. Notice too that a convincing cumulative case is not the same thing as a "proof". We have all watched enough detective shows to know that it is possible the maid and the cook are in cahoots to frame the defendant. It is possible, then, that one could have accumulated good evidence for the truth of some claim and yet that claim be false. Moreover, we have not yet heard from the defence barrister. What alibis does the defendant have? How do the witnesses stand up under cross-examination? What weaknesses exist in the prosecutor's case? The overall strength of a cumulative case argument is determined only after one has subtracted all the "negative evidence" from the "positive evidence".

To speak of adding and subtracting evidence makes it sound as though evidence can be weighed and measured like so many cups of flour and teaspoons of salt. If the minimal standard of rationality requires that a belief be more probable that not, or likely to a degree greater than 0.5, then how shall we judge the case for theism? How much do moral arguments count for? How much a religious experience? And is the whole collection enough to justify theistic belief? Because it is so difficult to specify with precision the exact rise in probability contributed by each strand of evidence, some theists prefer to support their belief with a close cousin of the cumulative case argument, what is sometimes called "an argument or inference to the best explanation". Here theists claim that their hypothesis, rather than that of naturalism or some other explanatory framework, receives support worthy of acceptance because it offers the best explanation for such phenomena as apparent design, intelligent life, the conditions for fine-tuning, religious experiences and so on. This difficulty of quantifying evidence aside, we shall continue to speak of the cumulative case argument.

We have surveyed design arguments of various sorts, cosmological arguments, ontological arguments, moral arguments and arguments from religious experience. Perhaps no single argument is sufficient to justify theistic belief, but can the cumulative weight of all the arguments do the job? Richard Swinburne thinks so, adding to the evidence mentioned above, arguments from consciousness, the phenomenon of miracles, and key historical evidence to support Jesus as divine (Swinburne 2004). Swinburne ends one presentation of his cumulative case argument for Christian theism as follows:

> The conclusion of this book is that the existence, orderliness, and fine-tunedness of the world; the existence of conscious

humans within it with providential opportunities for mould-
ing themselves, each other, and the world; some historical evidence of miracles in connection with human needs and prayers,
particularly in connection with the foundation of Christianity,
topped up finally by the apparent experience by millions of his
presence, all make it significantly more probable than not that
there is a God.   (1996: 139)

If it is more probable than not that God exists, more likely to be
true than false, then it is certainly rational to belief that he exists.

Critics of theism, obviously, do not estimate the force of the
assembled evidence as highly as Swinburne. Antony Flew once
remarked:

We have here to insist upon a sometime tricky distinction:
between on the one hand, the valid principle of the accumulation of evidence, where every item has at least some weight in
its own right; and, on the other hand, the Ten-leaky-buckets-
Tactic, applied to arguments none of which hold water at all.
                                                   (2005: 146)[9]

Flew, himself, as we saw in Chapter 2, changed his mind about the
force of theistic arguments. Moreover, the continued, indeed, the
increased attention given to theistic arguments, even by critics who
go on to discount their force, since Flew's comment more than
forty years ago, suggest that he was hasty to think it obvious that
the arguments hold no water at all.

We have also noticed that there is often an interpretive or subjective element to assessing the force of evidence in a cumulative
case. Religious believers sometimes cite as evidence for their belief
in God experiences and other beliefs that their critics simply do not
acknowledge as acceptable evidence. Not only do people disagree
over what counts as acceptable grounds, they also disagree over
the "weightiness" of the grounds we do commonly acknowledge.
Jurors that disagree about a defendant's guilt may not disagree that
the testimony given by the prosecution's star witness is relevant to
the case; they disagree instead as to its significance, some investing
it with tremendous import, others with less. Disagreements about
the probative force or saliency of evidence are legion, arising in

debates about history, aesthetics, exegesis, morals, law, the natural sciences, even a boxing match, and indeed anywhere that interpretive judgement is called for.

How are disagreements about the saliency of evidence settled? Typically, we invite our interlocutor to look again and see whether he or she is not as impressed as we are by what we take to be some crucial piece of evidence. Or, we may try to undermine in some way the evidence supporting a view contrary to our own. (Did you not notice how shifty-eyed and nervous the witness for the defence was under cross-examination?) Sometimes new evidence arises that throws the original evidence in a new light. Unfortunately, some of our disagreements revolve around issues buried in the past, for which we cannot reasonably expect dramatic new evidence to emerge.

We puzzle not only about how disagreements regarding saliency are settled but why they occur at all. Why should our standards of evidence be so variable? The reasons here are numerous and complex. No doubt our finitude and the limitations imposed by our cultural, historical and linguistic perspectives play a part. We are nurtured in academic cultures and influenced by mentors whose evidential standards shape our own.[10] Antecedent beliefs also bulk large in the way we estimate the force of evidence. For example, persons who think they have reasons independent of religious experience for the truth or falsity of theism will quite obviously look upon the evidence afforded by religious experience differently from one who does not share their background beliefs. Another factor is training. If I lack training in radiology, I might stare directly at an X-ray, but fail to see the black, white and grey patterns before me as evidence that the patient has a tumour. So C. D. Broad suggests that the capacity to see and appreciate the force of religious experience is analogous to having or lacking an ear for music, with sensitivity ranging from the tone-deaf to perfect pitch (Broad 1967: 180).

I want also to claim that, whether or not we are suitably positioned to see and appreciate the evidence for some claims – especially those of a valuational nature and those that touch upon our own existential well-being and the well-being of others we care about – depends on the structure of what philosophers call the "conative will", the seat of our desires, loves, cares, concerns, attachments and emotions. As much as some philosophers would have you think otherwise, humans are not entirely cerebral, utterly dispassionate, cogitating machines whose primary preoccupation consists in the judging of one proposition after another whether it be the case. Rather, what we care about, the "*ordo amoris*" as Augustine called it, influences our intellectual endeavours. At the very least if persons do not *care* about finding the truth, if truth is not something highly valued, then important truths may not be diligently sought, or if sought, judged prejudicially or gullibly.[11]

Philosophical suspicion about the role of emotions in cognitive functioning stems from the oft-observed phenomenon of emotions leading to cognitive dysfunction. Plantinga speaks for many philosophers when he says:

> [P]roper function can be impeded by pride, ambition, lust, anger, patriotism, fear, greed, impatience, buck fever, mother love, avarice, hate, undue sensitivity, excessive pessimism (or optimism) and the like; and when this happens warrant is often excluded …. loyalty and love for your friend prevents you from seeing what you otherwise might have, namely that she has been lying to you …. Now I propose to describe these phenomena in terms of "impeding proper function".
>
> (1995a: 444)

Yet a long-standing and counterbalancing tradition reaching as far back as Plato and Aristotle suggests that our cognitive powers cannot function optimally if they are *not* appropriately attuned with emotions and concerns that have been trained to virtue. In his *Symposium*, Plato advances the idea that inasmuch as the highest metaphysical reality is also a moral reality (The Form of the Good), one must simultaneously grow in wisdom *and goodness* if one is to reach reason's highest achievement. Aristotle taught clearly that we cannot think well about moral matters without ourselves *becoming* moral persons – persons whose emotions and desires are trained to virtue. Aquinas too speaks of judgements, especially as they concern morality and religion, as requiring sound reason but also a "sympathy" or "connaturality" for the matter under consideration (*Summa Theologiae* IIae, q.45, a.2). Indeed, a motif running throughout the history of Western philosophy – through Augustine, Anselm,

Aquinas, Calvin, Pascal, Edwards, James, Heidegger and up to the present in authors such as Martha Nussbaum, William Wainwright and Linda Zagzebski – argues that proper cognitive functioning is often closely linked to our having tutored emotions and a suitably cultivated moral and intellectual character.

The structure of our emotions and concerns bears not only on the having and lacking of evidence, but also on the way we *assess* such evidence as is before us.[12] Suppose Albert is a racist juror and the defendant is a person of colour. Alethea, the juror to Albert's right, by contrast, has an admirable intellectual character marked by love of truth, attentiveness, conscientiousness and practical wisdom, among other intellectual virtues. Day after day, Albert and Alethea sit shoulder to shoulder in the courtroom being treated to the same arguments, evidence, alibis, exhibits, testimonies and so on. Finally, the judge calls for the jury to render a verdict, whereupon Albert thunders, "clearly guilty!" Alethea disagrees. The other jurors join in, finding Alethea's arguments more persuasive. They also think that prejudice has caused Albert to depreciate the evidence given to exonerate the defendant and to stress too highly the evidence offered by the prosecutor. Most people would judge that Albert's lack of concern for justice and his racism, both clear moral failings, have interfered with his optimal cognitive functioning, whereas Alethea's love of truth and her sympathetic attunement to matters of justice, have arguably positioned her favourably to render a correct verdict. Sometimes, having evidence and assessing its probative force aright is not a purely dispassionate, entirely cerebral affair, but turns on matters of one's overall character.[13]

Now we must ask what bearing this discussion of rightly tuned emotions and proper cognitive function has on belief in God. According to Judaeo-Christian theism, God is a personal being perfect in wisdom, power and love, whose purpose in creating humankind was to draw us freely into a relationship of filial love and obedience wherein we find our highest happiness. God's concern with humans is not simply that they should notionally acknowledge his existence (that well-timed cameo appearances and pyrotechnical displays of divine power would guarantee) but that we should *live* in right relation to him. Theists claim that God's having created us and sustained us moment by moment, is not one more fact among many, a mere datum, but a claim that bears mightily upon our well-being, the orientation of our lives and thus upon the structure of our cares and concerns. At the very least, it implies that we owe God a debt of gratitude for our existence and obedience to his plans and purposes for humans. More specifically, the God of the great monotheistic traditions wants us to live in imitation of his moral perfection, to move from lives of self-centredness to lives in which concerns for love and justice are preeminent. Paul Moser underscores this point:

> A perfectly loving God, being morally impeccable, would seek what is morally perfect for us as long as there is hope for us, thereby giving us the opportunity to receive, without coercion, God's kind of moral goodness ... the opportunity in question, being inherently moral, would be *volitional* and not just intellectual. It would enable us to have our *wills* transformed, not just our intellects (that is our thoughts and beliefs). So, the kind of knowledge of God's reality valued by a perfectly loving God would be volitionally transformative rather than merely intellectual. It would seek a change of human will, of volitional orientation. (2008: 90)

Like Aquinas before him, Moser thinks that to see and appreciate fully the evidence for God's reality requires an "attunement" of the will and intellect, that we be maximally sensitive to available evidence for God's reality.

To speak as Moser does raises the stakes of the debate about God's existence in general, and religious experience in particular, from the merely academic to the deeply existential, touching the very core our most deeply felt concerns. In their more candid moments, philosophers sometimes provide a glimpse of the volitional core being touched by this question of God's existence.

> In speaking of the fear of religion, I don't mean to refer to the entirely reasonable hostility toward certain established religions and religious institutions, in virtue of their objectionable moral doctrines, social policies, and political influence. Nor am I referring to the association of many religious beliefs with superstition and the acceptance of evident empirical falsehoods. I am

> talking about something deeper – namely, the fear of religion
> itself. I speak from experience, being strongly subject to this fear
> myself: I want atheism to be true and am made uneasy by the
> fact that some of the most intelligent and well-informed people
> I know are religious believers. It isn't just that I don't believe
> in God and, naturally hope that I'm right in my belief. It's that
> I hope that there is no God! I don't want there to be a God; I
> don't want the universe to be like that.   (Nagel 1997: 130)

Religious believers are no less passionate about wanting to live in
a world where God provides ultimate meaning and purpose to our
lives, and will one day right all wrongs and establish a peaceable
kingdom.

The point is not to suggest that we set reason aside, that we simply
allow our passions to dictate the course of our beliefs. Rather, it is
to argue that our passional nature cannot be ignored as we reflect
on the merits of the arguments and counter-arguments we consider.
And if our emotional make-up plays the sort of role I suggest it does
in valuational matters, then a change of intellectual perspective may
hinge on a reorientation of the structure of our concerns.

The plot of many a novel revolves around the transformation of
a main character, in which we witness the events contributing to the
character's coming to see the world through new eyes. More often
than not, suffering of some sort is a principal factor in such conversions. King Lear, Thomas Gradgrind and the characters of countless other stories come into their right mind only after a period of
suffering. Real life all too often imitates art. Happily, not all such
transformational experiences involve suffering; an encounter with
great goodness can also touch our emotions in ways that result in
our coming to see and think in a new way. Raskolnikov, the nihilist
of Dostoyevsky's *Crime and Punishment*, abandons his philosophical perspective, not as the result of argument, but in response to
the powerful love of Sonya. After Raskolnikov confesses to having murdered a pawnbroker and her sister, Sonya perceives what
a wretchedly tormented soul he is, and moves to embrace and kiss
him, prompting this response:

> You're so strange, Sonya – you embrace and kiss me, when I've
> just told you about that. You're forgetting yourself .... A feel-

ing long unfamiliar to him flooded his soul and softened it all at once. He did not resist: two tears rolled from his eyes and hung on his lashes. (Dostoyevsky 1993: 412)

Could not Raskolnikov have abandoned nihilism without undergoing this experience? Perhaps. We do sometimes change our minds on the strength of purely philosophical exchanges; we read or hear a rebuttal to our favourite ways of thinking about some intellectual matter and straight away revise our thinking, with seemingly little emotional involvement. Not so, with Raskolnikov. He does not merely observe Sonya's expression of love; he *experiences himself as* loved by her. Raskolnikov, however, in virtue of his emotional experience, suddenly construes himself as an object of value in someone else's eyes. His world is suddenly suffused with values and significance his nihilism cannot allow. His experience of himself as an object of value thus constitutes a defeater to his nihilism. It cannot simultaneously be true that the world is without value (the nihilist view) and that he is himself valuable. Raskolnikov allows his experience to override his philosophical theory; Dostoyevsky's phrase "he did not resist" suggests that Raskolnikov might have resolved the tension the other way, by allowing his prior philosophical commitments to undermine his experience as unveridical.[14]

If judgements of reasonableness are influenced by the structure of our concerns, then might this not sometimes work against theism? Why not think that transformational emotional experiences could so orient the structure of one's concerns that it seemed, on balance, that God does not exist? Many testimonies of those who have abandoned religious belief attest that their experience of suffering had just this effect. Famous here is Elie Wiesel's account of the horrors of Auschwitz:

"Where is God? Where is He?" someone behind me asked … For more than half an hour [the child in the noose] stayed there, struggling between life and death, dying in slow agony under our eyes. And we had to look him full in the face. He was still alive when I passed in front of him. His tongue was still red, his eyes were not yet glazed. Behind me, I heard the same man asking: "Where is God now?" And I heard a voice within me answer him: "Where is He? Here He is – He is hanging here on this gallows…" (1985: 72)

Louise Antony's autobiographical account of her own de-conversion from Christian faith says: "But then came the day that literally changed my life – the day when I heard the argument from evil.". She reports finding the standard defences to the problem of evil, such as the free will defence, not just unpersuasive, but "morally disturbing" (2007: 49).[15]

In Chapter 7, we turn to the problem of suffering, which many philosophers consider the single most powerful objection to the rationality of religious belief. Here too the academic arguments intersect passional concerns, offering another illustration of the way heart and mind combine to lead us to adopt the positions we do.

Religious belief without
6 evidence

We began this book by considering the evidentialist objection to religious belief. The objection, as you will recall, insists that all beliefs – with religious beliefs as no exception – must enjoy the support of adequate evidence if we are to believe them rationally. Most evidentialists insist that one not only have evidence, but also that one see how and to what degree one's evidence supports the target belief. In the light of this requirement, it is quite plain how the evidentialist's demand is congruent with the natural theologian's practice of forming arguments for God's existence, whose premises and strength of conclusion are evident. In this chapter, we consider two positions that, for differing reasons, do not attempt to meet the evidentialist demand, but reject it. Pascal is famous for thinking that, even if theism cannot be underwritten by so-called proofs for God's existence, belief in God is nevertheless rational on prudential grounds, because of the good ends religious belief brings about. Second, we shall explore a position most famously forwarded by Alvin Plantinga, referred to frequently as "Reformed epistemology", stemming from the fact that he, and fellow Reformed epistemologists follow John Calvin and Martin Luther's rejection of natural theology. Belief in God, they argue, should be accepted as "properly basic", without the need for argumentative support.

Pragmatic arguments

Pascal, to whom the reader has already been introduced, was no stranger to the tradition of natural theology. From an early age, he met regularly with the leading intellectuals of the day, including Mersenne, Fermat and Gassendi, and he corresponded with René Descartes. Although he knew well the traditional arguments for God's existence, he remained unconvinced by them. He recognized that humans are more than minds encased in bodies, pure centres of cerebration. "The heart has its reasons that reason knows nothing of" is among his most frequently quoted sayings. By "heart" he does not mean mere sentiment – such as romantic infatuation – but such cares, concerns and loves that he thinks orient one toward one's true and ultimate well-being. Humans are complex beings who, if moved to embrace so potentially a life-changing belief as that God exists, will most likely do so for reasons that go beyond logic alone. "God", says Pascal, "wishes to move the will rather than the mind" (1995: #234, 72).

In his famous *Pensées*, Pascal writes: "If there is a God, he is infinitely beyond our comprehension, since, being indivisible and without limits, he bears no relation to us. We are therefore incapable of knowing either what he is or whether he is" (1995: #418, 122). The natural lights to which Pascal here refers are those of human reason, and he claims that the power and reach of our creaturely intellect is insufficient to tell us definitively what God is like or even whether he exists. Reason's failure, he says, turns on the infinite distance that separates humans reasoners, armed with 110 or so IQ points on average, and the God of theism, who is said to be omniscient and omnipotent. Trying to reason one's way to God is like trying to dig the Panama Canal with a teaspoon; the wrong tool for the job. Pascal thus begins his famous wager by stating:

> God is or is not. But toward which side shall we lean? Reason cannot decide anything. There is an infinite chaos separating us. At the far end of this infinite distance, a game is being played and a coin will come down heads or tails. How will you wager? Reason cannot make you choose one way or the other, reason cannot make you defend either of the two choices.
>
> (*Ibid.*)

Evidentialists would here council that when we are in a state of evidential equipoise, we suspend judgement. Are there an even number or an odd number of ducks in the world? There is a fifty–fifty chance that one or the other is correct but the interests of truth dictate that we commit to neither. Pascal considers and rejects this counsel in the case of religious belief. This is because nothing is at stake in the matter of ducks. A great deal is at stake, he believes, in the matter of God.

Although reason cannot tell you whether or not God exists, Pascal nevertheless says that we must wager one way or the other; it is not optional. This is because inaction, failure to choose regarding the question of God's existence, is tantamount to deciding against God. To appreciate Pascal's point, suppose you are a loan officer at a bank and I come to you on Monday seeking a home loan. Given my financial situation, you offer various rates depending on the amount and length of the loan, adding, "due to the market's volatility you must notify me by the week's end if you want to secure these rates". Tuesday and Wednesday find me still in the hunt for better rates. On Thursday I am having second thoughts about plunging into homeownership. Five o'clock Friday rolls around and I am still in the throes of indecision. My failure to contact you nets me precisely the same thing as if I had called you up to refuse your loan outright. My failure to act means I am in no position to benefit from your offer. So it is with God and the rewards he bestows on those who believe in him. If there are benefits to be had from religious belief, we shall not receive them by sitting on the fence. Fence sitting, along with outright denial, is just one more way of failing to be in the camp of believers and thus one more way to fail to position oneself to receive such rewards as God gives. In the light of reason's limitations, and so as to secure any benefits that may accrue to believers in God, Pascal recommends that we wager on God for, as he sees it, we have got everything to gain and nothing to lose.

Pascal's argument can be easily grasped in the following table:

	God exists	God does not exist
Believe	WIN	TIE
Not believe	LOSE	TIE

Either there is a God or there is no God, and we can either believe in God or fail to believe in God, as is the case with atheists and agnostics. Suppose we believe and it turns out God exists.

We are then in a position to receive such benefits as may accrue to those who believe. Importantly, Pascal thinks religious believers win both this-worldly benefits – moral virtues such as honesty, humility and gratitude and freedom from the "corrupt pleasures of high living" – and other-worldly goods, such as "an infinitely happy infinity of life". But suppose we believe and there is no God. We do not win anything. Neither do we lose anything – we are food for worms either way – so let us call it a tie. Suppose, however, we do not believe in God and it turns out that God exists. Owing to unbelief, we would then miss out on the benefits of belief. But if we do not believe and there is no God, once again we neither win nor lose. So, there is only one way to be a winner – by believing. And there is only one way to be a loser – by failing to believe. "If you win, you win everything; if you lose, you lose nothing" (Pascal 1995: #418, 123). So where is the smart money going?

We can appreciate Pascal's thinking if we consider the way rational wagers are made in casinos or at the racetrack. Rational gamblers want to maximize their gains and minimize their losses over the long run. So they wager according to a simple formula: probability of winning x payoff – cost of wagering = the rational expected value of the wager. Suppose you are a regular at the racetrack and want to know how to place your bets so as to maximize your chance of winning and minimize your chance of losing. According to Pascal, you would adopt the strategy represented by the following table (adapted from Morris 1992: 113):

Bet	Probability	Payoff	Cost expectation
Horse A	2/3 based on past races	£300	£60 = £140
Horse B	1/3 based on past races	£900	£30 = £270

Even though horse A has a higher chance of winning the race, it is still more rational to bet on horse B given the cost of betting and the possible payoff.

Suppose you wander through a casino to figure out what sort of game you would like to play. You see games of roulette, various games with dice, poker, slot machines, and more. Off in one corner of the casino, you observe a lone croupier flipping a coin. You approach and ask what game he oversees, whereupon he replies "heads or tails". "Guess correctly," he says, "and win a million pounds!" "How much does it cost to play?" you ask. "One hundred pounds," comes the reply. Even though you have no more reason to think that heads or tails will turn up, if you were practically rational, you would play that game all day long. Even if it cost £10,000 a toss, you would still be rational to play given your odds of winning and the size of the payout. Pascal thinks theism is an even better gamble. Given the fifty–fifty odds of winning, the negligible cost of wagering and an infinite reward (eternal felicity with God), it would be irrational not to bet on God. Even if the probability of atheism were high and that of theism low, theism's infinite payout compared with atheism's finite payout makes theism the more rational wager. Once infinity is factored into the formula, it trumps all other bets. Perhaps the bet Pascal holds before us could be better represented as follows:

	God exists	God does not exist
Believe	∞ GAIN	FINITE LOSS
Not believe	−∞ LOSS	FINITE GAIN

Pascal recommends that we bet on God based on considerations of prudential rather than epistemic reasoning. Prudential reasoning, or benefits-directed thinking, has as its goal securing some good for the agent. By contrast, epistemic or truth-directed reasoning has truth as its goal. A wife who detects the telltale signs that her husband is having an affair may, for her own good and the good of her children, discount the evidence as coincidental and continue believing that her husband is faithful. This may be prudentially rational but we must deny that it is rational from a purely epistemic point of view. But how do we decide which of these goods, prudential or epistemic goods, should outweigh? Interestingly, Richard Feldman and Earl Conee, defenders of evidentialism earlier referred to, think it possible that practical considerations lead one to yield to a prudential rather than an epistemic good, especially if one's reasoning leads to a conclusion one deems immoral (Feldman & Conee 2004: 91). It is also consistent with the apologetic aims of the *Pensées* to suppose that Pascal's goal in presenting the wager was but an intermediary strategy for moving indifferent persons to a place where they take religious claims seriously and, perhaps like Pascal himself, come to have a belief grounded in religious experience rather than argument.

Evaluating Pascal's wager

Numerous objections confront Pascalian wagerers. (i) Obviously, natural theologians will deny that natural reason is powerless to tip the evidential scales toward theism. (ii) Critics also take issue with Pascal's claim that by betting on God we have nothing to lose. If one believes, as Pascal does not, that reason can produce a preponderance of evidence in support of theism or atheism, then one obviously risks losing the truth. But even if one accepts Pascal's assessment of reason's limitations, one may suffer prudential losses in this life by believing in God. Was it in the prudential interests of early Christians to suffer grisly deaths in the Roman Coliseum? Clearly, belief is not without potential costs, even in this life. (iii) Even if the wager moved you, you may find that summoning up genuine belief is not subject to your voluntary control. It is not as if you can, by sheer dint of effort, produce a belief in theism any more that you can voluntarily believe that your bank account contains a million more pounds than it does. (iv) What may be the most troubling objection to Pascal's wager is not knowing which God to bet on. If, as Pascal claims, God's nature and existence are obscure to natural reason, then how are we supposed to know on which God to wager? The God of Abraham, the Trinitarian God of Christianity, some form of Hindu monotheism, Ahura Mazda, or does eternal felicity depend on our believing in some little-known, deviant deity? Maybe we should hedge our bets still further and embrace polytheism. (v) Finally, critics allege that belief grounded in prudential reasons warrants, at best, a tentative or provisional sort of endorsement, not the decisive belief adherents of the world's religions insist is necessary to receive rewards. Let us consider these objections in turn.

Anyone who has read through the earlier chapters of this book will probably have formed some opinions about the ability of human reason to show either that God does or does not exist. And if one thinks reason is capable of establishing either theism or atheism, then one will have no inclination to view Pascal's wager as anything more than an interesting thought experiment. Philosophical history gives us good reason to think this disagreement will not be settled definitively any time soon. But even if one agrees with Pascal that the evidence for God's existence is inconclusive, many philosophers deny that pragmatic arguments are an adequate basis for licensing belief. Indeed they think that accepting the wager is a blatant intellectual sin, a violation of one's duty to believe all and only what the evidence allows. Here again, one faces the competing demands of epistemic versus prudential (or moral) obligations, and it is reasonable to think there are circumstances where moral obligations outweigh. If my best intellectual efforts lead me to think that genocide is sometimes morally permissible and I am unable to see the errors in my reasoning, then I should defer to my moral or prudential judgement. "What does an epistemic peccadillo matter, compared with infinite joy or damnation?" (Lycan & Schlesinger 1996: 120).

What of Pascal's claim that "if we lose, we lose nothing". Let us grant for the sake of argument Pascal's assumption that if God does not exist, there will be no afterlife. If this is correct, then it is not as though there will be some conscious moment after death where it occurs to us that we have been suckered by betting on God. We will be worm-bait, final, period, the end. This point does nothing, however, to answer the problem of the losses we stand to suffer on this side of the grave. Again, what about the disruption to family, to a long-standing way of life, or martyrdom, losses known historically to accompany conversion to religion? Or, a little less lofty, what about my devotion to drugs, sex, rock and roll, and the life of hedonistic frenzy? Would I not be risking known pleasures for a merely possible good? Pascal's reference to "corrupt pleasures" suggests he does not think hedonism a pathway to deep and abiding personal happiness. Most contemporary psychological studies support Pascal. He thinks that even the more serious losses we might suffer in this life are "negligible" when weighed against the possibility of infinite gain. Think about having to ante up £10,000 to play the heads or tails game. Even if you had to mortgage your home to do it, it would still be a good bet. Since Pascal thinks a prudent person might risk his life in exchange for three lives, he certainly would not think it imprudent to risk this life for infinite happiness and eternal life.

Pascal himself raises the problem of the voluntariness of belief. One voice of Pascal's interior dialogue protests: "I am being forced to wager and I am not free … I am made in such a way that I cannot believe". In reply, Pascal anticipates the advice of many motivational psychologists for dealing with self-doubts and fears. A sports psychologist counselling a losing team will often advise the players to act like winners – for example, to visualize the ball going into the net, to adopt a bit of swagger – if they want to play like winners. Similarly, Pascal counsels those who would like to take advantage of the wager but find themselves psychologically blocked, to start doing the sorts of things that believers do. Go to church, pray, perform acts of charity, read Holy Scriptures and so on, and before too long, he thinks, we shall find that genuine heartfelt devotion wells up within us. Since the course of our lives will automatically be lived out as if God does or does not exist, Pascal recommends acting as if he does. We do not have direct voluntary control over what we believe, but Pascal is right to think we have a degree of indirect influence over what we believe. But is Pascal's advice here not tantamount to self-deception? It would be if we had good reason for thinking that theism is false, but as we have noted, Pascal assumes that we have no more reason for thinking theism true than false. Our passions, not our reason, are what we need to manage, and a bit of behaviourist psychology is what Pascal prescribes.

To address the "many gods" objection, Pascalians ask us to recall that our deliberations about God's existence and nature lie behind a veil that reason cannot penetrate. Can prudential considerations guide us on how to wager? Among the possible gods, some, such as the deistic God, do not dispense rewards even if believed in. From a prudential point of view, then, it is better to believe in a god who dispenses rewards. Among the gods that dispense rewards, some might do so only if believed in and others will dispense rewards even if not believed in. It makes sense to bet on the former, since we will suffer no loss by failing to believe in the latter. And among the gods who reward only when believed in, there are those that are limited in wisdom, power and goodness, and those that are not. Since nothing can frustrate the intention of an almighty God to dispense rewards, and something could potentially frustrate the will of a weaker deity, it makes sense to bet on an all-powerful God. And if one adds that there are independent *a priori* reasons for thinking that there cannot be more than one omnipotent being (as we shall consider in Chapter 8), then the God of monotheism looks like the best bet. If we further add, as Pascal does, that a life lived in devotion to God brings rewards in this life that non-belief fails to provide, then theism looks like the best bet.[1]

Finally, we consider the objection that we cannot commit ourselves wholeheartedly to beliefs grounded in prudential considerations alone. Gary Gutting distinguishes between "decisive" and "interim" assent. We give decisive assent to well-grounded beliefs for which it is appropriate to terminate the process of enquiry into the truth of the belief (Gutting 1982: 105).[2] We believe decisively that the Earth is roughly round and we do not waste time searching out more evidence to support this fact. "The book" on the Earth's shape is closed, we might say. Interim assent, by contrast, endorses a belief p while simultaneously being committed to the need for ongoing discussions of p's truth. One might have reasons for thinking that our universe contains no other intelligent life, yet "the book" on extraterrestrial life is hardly closed. Rather, we remain alert to new evidence that might move our belief one way or the other.

One might object to the pragmatic argument on the grounds that even if it licenses interim assent, this is inadequate to underwrite the decisive assent demanded by most religions. Gutting thinks that most religions demand decisive assent from their adherents (*ibid.*: 106–7). This is because religious belief marks the end of a quest for emotional and intellectual satisfaction – it functions for believers as a sort of "master passion". Yet it would be odd to say one was still in the hunt for any evidence that might move one away from the very belief that functions as a master passion. Also, interim assent is at variance with the total commitment and decisive action that the religious life sometimes calls for. Decisive actions, such as giving away all one's possessions or dying a martyr's death, call for decisive, not interim assent.

How might the Pascalian respond? First by noting that there are some prudential beliefs that demand decisive assent. Suppose a doctor tells you that you have only a fifty–fifty chance of recovering from some illness. Suppose too, that you know of research that supports the claim that people who believe wholeheartedly that they will recover have a higher likelihood of recovering from illness. Prudence dictates that we not be tentative about our recovery but that we believe fervently that we will recover. Moreover, by doing so, one may actually change the odds of recovery. Decisive assent to a prudential belief may in fact be the best way to position oneself to receive an epistemic benefit. Suppose a woman receives a marriage proposal but lacks clear evidence that her suitor will make a clearly superior husband. Worried that no other offers are imminent, she accepts. One way the woman will never find out the matrimonial merits of her spouse is by focusing on and giving voice to her doubts ("I was never too sure about you from the start", "I hope you measure up to my expectations"). Rather, her decisive but prudential assent to her husband's ability to be a superior husband is the best recipe for gaining *intellectual* grounds of his true merits. And this strategy seems to be at the heart of Pascal's wager: move a person passionally so that she is ideally situated to have the sort of religiously authenticating experience of which Pascal himself was a beneficiary.

Reformed epistemology

Alvin Plantinga's Reformed epistemology is "reformed" in at least two senses: not only does he take cues from some leaders of the Reformation in rejecting the enterprise of natural theology, but he also wants to reform some of the thinking that has structured debates about the reasonability of theistic belief. As we noted at the beginning of this chapter, evidentialists claim that the canons of good intellectual conduct require that religious beliefs be supported by evidence whose probative force we see and appreciate. On this view, the onus falls on religious believers to supply evidence that establishes God's existence as true or, failing that, highly likely to be true. Precisely this demand, that all beliefs gain their justification through evidential or argumentative support, is what must be rejected, according to Reformed epistemologists. To appreciate Plantinga's argument and the way he would reform epistemological practice, we need to look very briefly at a debate within the larger discipline of epistemology: that between epistemological internalists and externalists.

The evidentialist's demand that all justified beliefs receive their support through propositional evidence of whose force we are aware is expressive of a larger view in the discipline of epistemology called "internalism". Although there are species of internalism, the core idea is that epistemic justification requires that agents, in principle at any rate, have access to the grounds of their belief.[3] Typically, one has access to these grounds through introspection, by turning inward, as it were, and surveying the mind's ideas. So if I were to ask you why you believe the stock market is going to rebound from recent losses, you might reflect momentarily and then cite a slight drop in the unemployment rate, a surge in orders for durable goods and a more favourable balance of trade over the last quarter with our economic competitors, and so on. In this way, you would show to anyone who enquired after or challenged your belief, that you have reasons that clearly support that belief. Since this requirement bears on religious beliefs, theists too must be able to advert to the grounds of their belief in God. And this requirement leads to arguments for God's existence and the general enterprise of natural theology.

Yet the requirement that all rational beliefs enjoy the support of reasons and arguments whose force we see and appreciate is highly contentious.[4] For one thing, it looks as though there is a welter of beliefs we take ourselves to be perfectly rational in accepting for which we lack argumentative support. Most of us believe that there is an external world and that this belief is not an illusion foisted upon us by some malign demonic force. What evidence could we muster in support of this belief that might not also have its origin in demonic deception? Most of us believe that our sensory faculties are reliable guides to truths about the external world, although we lack non-circular reasons for thinking this. We believe in the reliability of inductive inference and the uniformity of the laws of nature, although most persons cannot marshal arguments to support these beliefs (and it is doubtful that philosophical efforts to do so have succeeded). We believe that if $A = B$ and $B = C$, then $A = C$, but we do not believe this because we have an argument to support it. We think it is wrong to inflict unnecessary pain on others but not because we first had to adduce evidence or gather experimental data to support this belief. These are beliefs we take as "properly basic", that is justifiably believed in the absence of reasons and arguments to back them up. In short, there look to be plenty of exceptions to internalism's demand.

Internalism faces additional difficulties. Most persons – certainly not children – are not up to the task of supplying reasons and arguments for what they believe. This means that most people are unjustified in most of what they believe. Perhaps only a few philosophers – and this is a matter on which reasonable minds differ – can meet internalism's demands for all they believe. This grates against our common sense conviction that most people are justified in most of what they believe. If most believers are not capable of summoning evidence and arguments for the elementary beliefs about the natural world, how much more difficult will summoning such evidence be when treating things supernatural? Even the pre-eminent natural theologian Aquinas thought that most persons lacked the time, training and aptitude to provide arguments for God's existence. Indeed, as quoted earlier, he remarked: "If the only way open to us for the knowledge of God were solely that of the reason, the human race would remain in the blackest shadows of ignorance" (*Summa contra Gentiles* I.4.4; 1975: 67).

The problems besetting epistemological internalism have prompted many thinkers to embrace epistemological externalism, a view of epistemic justification that waives the access requirement characteristic of internalist views. Externalists think a belief's justification depends on its causal ancestry, on the "reliability" or "proper functioning" or "virtuous functioning" of the cognitive faculties causally responsible for producing a belief.[5] If our cognitive faculties are functioning properly in a non-deceptive environment for which they are suited, then they have a high statistical likelihood of conveying to us truths relevant to the scope of their reach. Consider, for example, the simple perceptual experiences one might have of an apple. Upon seeing, smelling or tasting the apple, you immediately, spontaneously and non-inferentially form the belief that you perceive an apple. You do not *reason* to the belief in anything like the following manner: I am being appeared to in red, round, firm, sweet and aromatic way characteristic of apples I have eaten in the past; I have no reason to think this is a clever imitation apple; I have no reason to think I have ingested drugs that would induce apple hallucinations, nor do I have any reason to think I am the unhappy victim of a post-hypnotic suggestion or any form of trickery or deception; therefore, I believe there is an apple before me. One does not adduce reasons for most perceptual beliefs; one simply forms a belief in response to the appropriate sort of experiential stimulus. Suppose you ask me where I left the keys to my car, and without hesitation I reply, "they are at home on my dresser". This memorial belief is not formed on the basis of my first having collected evidence and arguments. Instead it is simply triggered by an experiential stimulus, in this case, your question about the whereabouts of my keys and my vivid memorial impression. If my memory is functioning properly, then I am justified in my belief about my keys. Nor do externalists require that we be aware of or have justified beliefs about our faculties functioning reliably. Just as my internal organs can function properly to make me healthy without my awareness, so too can my cognitive faculties function properly to produce justified belief without my awareness. It need only be the case that they function reliably, not that I have beliefs about this.[6]

We are now in a position to consider Plantinga's objections to the evidentialist's demand that theists support their belief in God with arguments or propositional evidence. If externalists are correct, then all of us accept many of our beliefs without the benefit of first having gathered supporting propositional evidence for them. It is sufficient for their justification that they have been produced by our cognitive powers in suitable environments in a truth-conducive way. We take the outputs of these faculties as properly basic, as justified without argumentative support. But if perceptual and memorial beliefs, among others, can be accepted as properly basic, then why can't belief in God's existence be accepted in the same way? At the heart of Plantinga's rejection of evidentialism is his defence of the idea that one's theistic beliefs – beliefs such as God is comforting me or God has created all this – are properly basic in the right circumstances (Plantinga 1983: 73ff.).

If properly basic visual beliefs are produced by the underlying faculty of vision, and if properly basic memory beliefs produced by the underlying faculty of memory, then what faculty produces theistic beliefs? When Reformers such as John Calvin claimed that belief in God is not justified through argument, they did not mean that it popped into being out of thin air, that there were no justifying circumstances for it. Calvin, and Plantinga following him, believes that a part of our overall repertoire of cognitive powers is what Calvin called a "*sensus divinitatis*", a natural part of our noetic endowment with which all humans are endowed. This divine sense, when triggered by various circumstances in appropriate environments, leads us to accept theistic beliefs in the properly basic way.

> God has so created us that that we have a tendency or disposition to see his hand in the world around us. More precisely, there is in us a disposition to believe propositions of the sort *this flower was created by God* or *this vast and intricate universe was created by God* when we contemplate the flower and behold the starry heaven or think about the vast reaches of the universe. (*Ibid.*: 80)

So to say that belief in God is properly basic is not to say that it is groundless, that its production is independent of experiential triggers and the cognitive powers they act upon. In the same way that sensory and memorial beliefs arise out of experiential triggers acting upon noetic faculties, so too is properly basic belief in God produced. Triggers leading to awareness of God also include, says Plantinga, experiences such as "feeling the presence of God" or "being frightened, feeling grateful, delighted, foolish, angry, pleased, and the like" (2000: 183).

Notice that the experience of seeing the starry heavens above is not being used as a premise for the construction of a design argument (although it can and has been used this way); that would be to duplicate the inferential reasoning of the natural theologian. Instead the experience is being invoked for its emotive and psychological power to trigger a basic belief through the intellectual faculty of the *sensus divinitatis*, the purpose of which is to enable us to have true beliefs about God. Even Immanuel Kant, who denied reason's power to prove God's existence, nevertheless acknowledged the psychological force of experiences such as beholding the starry firmament. To recall the passage cited in Chapter 1, Kant writes:

> This knowledge [of nature] again reacts on its cause, namely, upon the idea which has led to it, and so strengthens the belief in a supreme Author [of nature] that the belief acquires the force of an irresistible conviction. It would therefore not only be uncomforting but utterly vain to attempt to diminish in any way the authority of this argument. Reason, constantly upheld

by this ever-increasing evidence, which, though empirical, is yet so powerful, cannot be so depressed through doubts suggested by subtle and abstruse speculations, that it is not at once aroused from the indecision of all melancholy reflection, as from a dream, by one glance at the wonder of nature and the majesty of the universe – ascending from height to height up to the all-highest, from the conditioned to its conditions, up to the supreme and unconditioned Author [of all conditioned being]. (*Critique* A624/B652; 1961: 520)

Although Kant still speaks of the heavens as offering evidence, he also seems aware of the power of such experiences to produce belief that is spontaneous, immediate and non-inferential – what Plantinga dubs a properly basic belief. The American pragmatist philosopher Charles Sanders Peirce appears to share a view similar to Kant's. Compare the following quotation with Kant's:

A man looks upon nature, sees its sublimity and beauty, and his spirit gradually rises to the idea of God. He does not see the Divinity, nor does nature prove to him the existence of that Being, but it does excite his mind and imagination until the idea becomes rooted in his heart.
(Quoted in Plantinga 2000: 174 n.10)

Both Kant and Peirce, then, appear to affirm Calvin's (and Plantinga's) claim that we have a native disposition for our thinking to take a "God-ward" turn in response to appropriate triggering circumstances, rather than in response to an argument.

It is also important to mention that the justification conferring conditions for perceptual, memorial and theistic beliefs is a *prima facie* justification. My justifiably accepting in the properly basic way that my car keys are at home on my dresser, can be overridden, for example by my wife calling me on the phone to say she is staring at the top of my dresser and the keys are not there. (It could also happen that my wife's defeater for my memorial belief could itself be defeated. Perhaps my keys are on my dresser but, unbeknown to my wife, are hidden by a pair of socks.) Religious beliefs that are taken as properly basic are also capable of being overridden, perhaps by a powerful argument from the problem of suffering. Plantinga also admits that just as one's vision or memory can be damaged or malfunction, so too might the *sensus divinitatis* malfunction, perhaps as a result of being in a cultural setting that suppresses or extinguishes it (2000: 173 n.9).

In his magisterial trilogy on warrant, Plantinga refines his account of belief in God as properly basic. He clarifies the chief term of positive epistemic appraisal possessed by properly basic beliefs as "warrant", not justification. Warrant is that quality, enough of which, when added to a true belief, makes that true belief an instance of knowledge. Plantinga refines the conditions a basic belief must satisfy to be warranted. It must (i) be produced by properly functioning cognitive faculties whose function is to produce true beliefs, which they reliably do; (ii) in a non-deceptive, congenial epistemic environment for which one's cognitive faculties are suited; (iii) where the degree of warrant is a function of one's felt inclination to believe the proposition in question when produced by properly functioning faculties (Plantinga 1993: 46–7). Plantinga even devises a model for warranted religious belief called "The Extended Aquinas/Calvin Model", that attempts to show how warrant could attach to specifically Christian, as opposed to merely theistic beliefs, such as that God is reconciling the world to himself through Christ. This model is more controversial still to non-believers as it incorporates the role of the Bible and the Holy Spirit in coming to warranted Christian belief.

Evaluating Plantinga's Reformed epistemology

Among the first objections likely to be posed to Plantinga's claim that belief in God can be warranted as properly basic, is that there is no consensus in the philosophical community about the *sensus divinitatis* being part of our standard issue cognitive faculties. In fact, atheists and agnostics would undoubtedly take the stronger position that no such faculty exists. As we have seen, just what intellectual faculties humans have is a perennial topic of philosophical disagreement. There is virtually no dispute about our perceptual faculties as they are associated with prominent organs on the face. But what about introspection and *a priori* intuition? These commonly acknowledged intellectual faculties not only fail to be correlated with obvious organs on the face, it is not clear that they are identical to or even causally linked to the activity in some specific region of the brain. As noted in the Introduction, what cognitive powers we possess, and the degree to which they are truth-conducive, is contested. Plato and Descartes eschewed perception as a source of knowledge; British empiricists took the opposite view. John Locke was leery of testimony as a reliable source of knowledge, yet Thomas Reid thought all normal humans were endowed with a credulity disposition that inclined us to accept testimony. Reid also thought we possess a native aesthetic sense whereby we detect and appreciate beauty. Others stoutly reject any such faculty. Aquinas thought humans possess a moral conscience, Bertrand Russell thought otherwise. And so on. For Plantinga to be told that other philosophers disagree with the claim that we have a *sensus divinitatis* puts in him some pretty good company, and by itself does not constitute a compelling objection to his views.

More worrisome than whether we have a *sensus divinitatis* is the question over the conditions of its properly functioning. Central to Plantinga's epistemology is the claim that a basic belief is warranted if, among the other conditions, it arises from the activity of a properly functioning faculty. But what are the conditions for the *sensus divinitatis* functioning properly? Neither Plantinga, nor Calvin before him, provides a lot of specifics. We are told, as we have already noted, that the *sensus divinitatis* is subject to malfunction. But what exactly causes it to go awry? The short answer, says Plantinga, is a wayward will, a corrupt heart – in a word, "sin". But this answer will likely find favour only with people antecedently convinced of Judaeo-Christian religion and thus is not of much polemical use. We are also told that the proper function of the *sensus divinitatis* is subject to having been properly nurtured and is moreover susceptible to dysfunction due to one's living amid a culture that stifles the development of the *sensus divinitatis*. Even with these qualifications, the parameters of a properly functioning *sensus divinitatis* remain unclear. Suppose, for instance, that one gazes up into the starry heavens above and immediately, spontaneously and non-inferentially finds oneself believing that Gaia or Brahman created all this. Would these beliefs be the output of a properly functioning *sensus divinitatis*? It is hard to say.

Plantinga admits that, although the activity of the *sensus divinitatis* may prompt us to take belief in God in the basic way, its doing so depends on a lot of other factors: the culture we are a part of, the training and nurture we have received from parents, the communities in which we were reared, the contribution of churches. The proper functioning of the *sensus divinitatis* also depends on the absence of factors that suppress its proper functioning, such as an orientation of the will opposed to God and the things of God. Given all these other factors, one might wonder how "basic" this properly basic belief in God really is. If all these factors were contributing to the production of one's belief in God, would it not be accurate to attribute it more to teaching and acculturation rather than to the mysterious operation of some divine sense? Is one's belief in God still *properly basic* if subject to these and other influences, or is it instead a belief reached, not through overtly rehearsed inferential reasoning, but through some sort of implicit synthetic reasoning occurring over a period of time? Here, I think Plantinga could respond by pointing out that in this regard the *sensus divinitatis* is not different in kind (although perhaps in degree) to the rest of our cognitive powers. Our perceptual and memorial cognitive powers are, like the *sensus divinitatis*, also subject to training, acculturation, and nurture. Numerous studies confirm, for instance, the power of training and expectation to shape vision. Memory too is susceptible to "interrogative suggestibility", as happens when, say, police question witnesses with questions such as "and was the black man you saw in the store tall?" (see Schacter 2001, esp. chs 5, 6). False memories can also be induced as attested by the infamous "guided imagery exercises" of a few years ago that resulted in people falsely accusing their parents of having sexually molested them as young children. The deliverances of memory are susceptible to being shaped by some of the same forces that shape the *sensus divinitatis*, yet many of its outputs are no less properly basic for that.

A related objection addresses Plantinga's admission that the warrant conferred by the *sensus divinitatis* is defeasible. This can happen in two ways. One's belief in God can be undermined if one has reasons to think that one's *sensus divinitatis* was not working properly in a congenial epistemic environment. One's belief in God can potentially also be refuted by a philosophical argument, such as the problem of suffering. To each of these types of objections, the theist will try to offer defeaters of the potential defeaters, that is, arguments that nullify the force of both sorts of criticisms. These arguments are often very technical and elaborate, as we will see in the next chapter.

One might object that by making use of an elaborate defence against an argument such as the problem of suffering, my belief in God is no longer held as basic; it now rests on all the reasons I put forward to defend my belief against this and other charges. According to Philip Quinn, this is precisely the predicament of most sophisticated adult believers in our culture; they are all too painfully aware of a raft of potential defeaters of theism, among them the problem of evil, Marxist critiques of religion, objections stemming from some evolutionary theorists and so on. Quinn doubts that any theists are so favourably situated as to defeat all the objections arrayed against theism. Even if they were, however, their defensive efforts would show that the status of their belief in God would have shifted; instead of being taken as basic, it would now be based on the host of arguments and defenses used to defend theism.

> I would insist ... that many, perhaps most, intellectually sophisticated adult theists in our culture must, if their belief in God is to be rational, have a total case for the rationality of theistic belief which includes defenses against defeaters which have very substantial support. (Quinn 1985: 484)[7]

Does it follow, however, that if I offer reasons to counter the objections posed against my belief in God that it is no longer basic for me? As Plantinga points out, parrying criticisms against one's faith is not the same thing as offering evidence for the faith. One could engage in the task of negative apologetics, as it is sometimes called, the task of defeating objections posed against the justifiability of religious belief, and still not base one's own belief on argument.

It might have already occurred to readers to wonder if Plantinga's strategy of taking theistic belief as properly basic might not be adaptable to other religious contexts. If theists are warranted in taking belief in God as the properly basic output of the *sensus divinitatis*, then why is this not the basic model for securing epistemic warrant available to practitioners of other religions? And might not these other religions be incompatible with theism? For instance, why couldn't a Hindu polytheist develop an account of warranted religious belief that appealed to "Brahman *divinitatis*"? What is to prevent a pantheist from taking belief in Gaia as properly basic based on sublime experiences of the powers of nature? Michael Martin poses just this objection to Plantinga's position. He argues that Plantinga's model for justifying Christian beliefs would seem to allow any belief at all to become basic from the point of view of some intellectual community. Although Reformed epistemologists would not have to accept voodoo beliefs as rational, voodoo followers would be able to claim that in so far as they are basic in the voodoo community they are rational and, moreover, that Reformed thought was irrational in this community. Indeed, Plantinga's proposal would generate many different communities that could legitimately claim that their basic belief are rational and that these belief conflict with basic beliefs of other communities (Martin 1990: 272).

Plantinga's reply requires that he first disambiguate Martin's terms. Plantinga is concerned with that form of positive epistemic appraisal he calls "warrant", not rationality. If rationality is simply a matter of living within one's intellectual lights as best one can, or being within one's intellectual rights in believing as one does, or some similar weak term of epistemic appraisal, then there is no argument, since Plantinga agrees that voodooists could be rational in these weak senses. Warrant, however, is accorded to those beliefs that arise from properly functioning faculties, in other words, from truth-conducive faculties functioning in an appropriate environment, and Plantinga denies that voodooists satisfy this condition. For Martin's objection to have force, says Plantinga, it would have to be put more like this:

> If the claim made by a Reformed epistemologist – namely that belief in God is properly basic with respect to warrant – has warrant, then for any proposition *p* (no matter how bizarre) accepted by some community, if the epistemologists of that community were to claim that p is properly basic with respect to warrant, their claim would itself have warrant. (2000: 347)

Warrant, as we have seen, is a much stronger term of epistemic appraisal, requiring that the beliefs which have it be formed by properly functioning, truth-conducive faculties, in an appropriate environment. But clearly voodoo beliefs, worshippers of the gods of Mount Olympus, the Heaven's Gate worshippers (the community who committed mass suicide in order to board a spaceship trailing the Hale-Bopp comet), are not warrant-basic. But what about other theistic religions: what is to prevent them from claiming that their core beliefs are properly basic and warranted? Here Plantinga concedes that his model for securing warrant for theism (and other Christian beliefs) might be applied to Judaism, Islam and some theistic forms of Hinduism, even some forms of American Indian religion.

But how does Plantinga know that *his* religion is warranted? What arguments does he offer to support the claim that his theistic beliefs have been formed by properly functioning, truth-conducive faculties in a suitable environment for those faculties? The short answer is: no arguments at all. Recall, that externalist accounts of justification deny that in order for beliefs to be justified, one must be able to access the grounds of one's beliefs and see how they bear on the truth of the target belief. It is sufficient for justification that they are in fact reliably produced, not that one be aware of this, and still less that one be able to offer an argument that they are so produced. Plantinga openly admits that he has not *shown* his model for properly basic religious beliefs to be true and thus has not *shown* that his theistic beliefs are warranted. His claim is conditional and thus more modest: *If* theistic belief is true, then the model involving the *sensus divinitatis* (or something closely approximating it) is true and theistic beliefs have warrant (Plantinga 2000: 168–9). If this is correct, then it follows, says Plantinga, that there are no *de jure* objections to theism (objections that accuse theism of lacking all epistemic support) that are independent of *de facto* objections (objections that purport to show that theism is false.) If you want to show that theism is without warrant, says Plantinga, you must show that it is false and that, he thinks, no one has done.

Many readers (particularly theists) may find it unsatisfying to be told that their belief in God is warranted *if* it is true. Surely the chief question participants to this debate want answered is just this: "Is it or is it not the case that God exists?" And the model for securing warrant for theistic belief that relies on the *sensus divinitatis* does not attempt to establish by argument that God exists. Curiously, in a footnote, Plantinga writes: "it doesn't follow that theistic belief can't get warrant by way of argument from other beliefs; nor does it follow that natural theology and more informal theistic argument is of no worth in the believer's intellectual and spiritual life" (2000: 179 n.16). Yet if natural theologians such as Aquinas are correct in claiming that most people cannot produce such arguments, then if they are to be justified or warranted in their beliefs, they must secure it some other way. Plantinga's account of properly theistic belief is one such alternative.

7 The problem of suffering

John Rawls, author of *A Theory of Justice*, arguably the most influential treatment of the subject in the twentieth century, grew up a faithful Christian. His Christian convictions were fully on display in his undergraduate thesis at Princeton University, titled "A Brief Inquiry Into the Meaning of Sin and Faith". His ardent faith foundered, however, by what he experienced as a soldier during the Second World War. Rawls (as so many others) was particularly troubled by the Holocaust. "How could I pray," wrote Rawls, "and ask God to help me, or my family, or my country, or any other cherished thing I cared about, when God would not save millions of Jews from Hitler?" (Rawls 2009: 263). Rawls is but one of untold numbers of people whose commitment to classical theism has been severely challenged and even abandoned by the obvious incongruity between an all-loving, all-powerful, providential God and the world's pervasive pain and suffering. If an infinitely loving God has all power and knowledge at his disposal, could he not have thwarted the genocidal campaign of the Nazis? Surely it would pose no problem for the almighty to turn back a tidal wave or two, to prevent the AIDS virus from jumping to the human gene pool or, at the very least, to ensure that suffering does not befall innocent children and animals. The chief question we must wrestle with is whether or not the extent and severity of the world's suffering undermines the rational credibility of theism.

Suffering and the case against theism

To note an incongruity between extensive suffering and the classical conception of God is not yet to offer an argument that belief in God is irrational or unjustified. Not to worry – arguments abound that purport to show theism is either improbable or impossible, and thus that belief in God is irrational. In this section we rehearse a handful of the more well-known objections to theism grounded in the problem of suffering. These arguments focus on "moral evil", the physical and emotional suffering caused by human actions and negligence – torture, rape, genocide and cruelty being clear examples – as well as so-called "natural evils", those arising independently of human agency, such as natural disasters and disease.[1] As we shall see, the multifaceted nature of the problem of suffering is part of what makes this objection to theism so formidable for theists.

The logical argument from evil

It is a truism to say that one ought not to believe what is impossible, the claims of Lewis Carroll's queen notwithstanding.[2] For instance, no one should believe contradictory claims such as that one is simultaneously less than 1.8m tall and more than 1.8m tall. Even if one were somehow able to believe the impossible, it would nevertheless constitute a paradigmatic case of intellectual irrationality. Yet, this is precisely the charge J. L. Mackie levels at theists. Here is a slightly modified version of Mackie's (2001: 78) argument:

1. God is omnipotent and perfectly good.
2. A perfectly good God would eliminate evil so far as it can, and there are no limits to what an omnipotent being can do.
3. Evil exists.

Mackie argues that these three claims constitute an inconsistent set and that theists are committed to affirming all three claims. One can accept any two of the three propositions, but one cannot, on pain of contradiction, he says, accept a third. Plainly, Mackie accepts propositions 2 and 3, and rejects 1. For it seems obvious to Mackie that a perfectly loving and all-powerful God would not want his creatures to suffer and has the power to effect the same. So why, then, does suffering abound?

Traditional theists do not attempt the desperate strategy of avoiding Mackie's charge by denying premises 2 and 3. To deny that suffering exists seems palpably absurd. Even if one thinks our everyday pains are illusory in some ultimate sense, they hurt nevertheless. The pain of a phantom limb still hurts, even if I am mistaken about its origin (one might even think this adds insult to injury), and this pain is enough to generate the problem of suffering. To deny that God is perfect in knowledge, power and goodness, is to abandon traditional theism. As we shall see, defenders of theism think the charge of contradiction fails, thereby avoiding the need for any such desperate measures.

The evidential argument from evil

William Rowe bids us considers scenarios such as the following:

(i) A fawn is horribly burned in a forest fire caused by lightning. It lies on the forest floor suffering terribly for five days before death relieves it of its suffering.

(ii) A five-year-old girl is brutally beaten, raped and strangled in Flint, Michigan, on New Year's Day a few years ago.

These ghastly vignettes underscore the fact that the innocent are sometimes the victims of terrible suffering. No credible story could possibly support the claim that either the fawn or the little girl deserved their unfortunate fates. Nor is it plausible, says Rowe, to suppose that their suffering was indispensible either for bringing about some great good that otherwise would not have occurred, or staving off some worse evil. Were we to discover, for instance, that that one fawn's dying as it did was necessary to keep the entire ecosystem intact, God would certainly have had a justifying reason for allowing it (although one may wonder why God did not create an ecosystem other than the one he did). But from everything we can tell, this is not the case. These are instances, says Rowe, of "gratuitous suffering" – pointless suffering without any redeeming value. In the light of examples such as these, Rowe offers the following argument, frequently called "the evidential argument from evil":

1. There exist instances of intense suffering that an omnipotent, omniscient being could have prevented without thereby losing some greater good or permitting some evil equally bad or worse.
2. An omniscient, wholly good being would prevent the occurrence of any intense suffering it could, unless it could not do so without thereby losing some greater good or permitting some evil equally bad or worse.
3. There does not exist an omnipotent, omniscient, wholly good being.   (1996: 2)

Rowe admits that he cannot know with invincible certainty that premise 1 is true. Who knows, in the infinite depths of the divine mind there may exist some justifying reason beyond our ken that explains why innocent creatures must suffer. But if there are such reasons, they are utterly unfathomable to us and thus Rowe concludes that the evidence available to us supports the claim, not that it is impossible that God exists, but that it is improbable that he does. And if it is improbable that God exists, atheism is the most reasonable position to take toward the existence of God.

God's failure to make the best of all possible worlds

In the 1970s the Ford Motor Company produced a car called the Pinto, which had the unfortunate tendency to burst into a ball of flames upon a rear impact. This resulted in a number of highly publicized lawsuits brought against Ford by the families of those who lost loved ones in accidents involving the Pinto. During the trials it came to light that Ford knew about the problem and had access to a modified design that would have remedied the car's defect, costing the company approximately $11 a car. The executives at Ford chose not to retool the car and wound up paying out millions in lawsuits. Now if God is perfect in wisdom, power and goodness, and sets out to create a world, we can be sure that he would not let some third-rate, half-baked, Pinto of a universe roll off the divine assembly line. He would, in the words of Leibniz, so wonderfully parodied by Voltaire's Pangloss, create the "best of all possible worlds".

We can metaphorically imagine God contemplating whether or not to create a universe and, if so, what sort of universe to create. He could have created a universe with only one star, or millions of stars but no life, or a universe containing vegetative, but no animal life. Omnipotent and omniscient, for him not even the sky's the limit. One would suppose that also being perfectly good, God would select from the incalculable number of possible worlds just those states of affairs that, when combined, would make for the best of all possible worlds. To do anything less, to create a Pinto of a universe when he would could so easily create a Rolls-Royce of a universe would appear to reflect ill on God's goodness and perhaps also on his power and wisdom. Theism's God must create the best of all possible worlds, yet all of us can imagine possible worlds superior to the one we inhabit. How about a world devoid of AIDS? Would that one adjustment not make for a better world? Yet, what do we discover as we survey our world? One of Hume's characters in *Dialogues Concerning Natural Religion* gives clear voice to the results of one such survey:

> The whole earth is cursed and polluted. A perpetual war is kindled amongst all living creatures. Necessity, hunger, want, stimulate the strong and courageous: Fear, anxiety, terror, agitate the weak and infirm. The first entrance into life gives anguish to the new-born infant and to its wretched parent: Weakness, impotence, distress, attend each stage of that life: And it is at last finished in agony and horror.   (1993: 96)

Surely an omniscient God foreknew what sort of world he was bringing into being. And since God, being perfectly good, must always act for the best, it would seem as though this world with its incalculable list of woes must indeed be the best of all possible worlds. But this conclusion, says the atheist, simply strains the boundaries of credulity; the world's suffering should rather lead us to conclude that God does not exist.

The problem of divine hiddenness

After Mother Teresa's death, and against her express wishes, portions of her private diaries were publicized. People familiar with this saintly Christian and international face for the plight of the poor were shocked as they read of her prolonged "dark night of the soul". In her diary Mother Teresa wrote:

> Now Father – since 49 or 50 this terrible sense of loss – this untold darkness – this loneliness this continual longing for God – which gives me that pain deep down in my heart – Darkness is such that I really do not see – neither with my mind nor with my reason – the place of God in my soul is blank – There is no God in me – when the pain of longing is so great – I just long & long for God – and then it is that I feel – He does not want me – He is not there – ... God does not want me – Sometimes – I just hear my own heart cry out – "My God" and nothing else comes – The torture and pain I can't explain.
>
> (2007: 1–2)

Experiences such as those of Mother Teresa's have formed the basis of a new problem of suffering which has come to be called "the problem of divine hiddenness". The problem, in short, is that persons earnestly desiring that God provide reassurance of his existence find that their entreaties go unanswered. In examining religious experience, we noted that instead of experiencing God, some people testify to a palpable sense of God's absence, analogous to what one might feel walking into the house of a loved one recently departed. Yet if God were perfect in wisdom, power and goodness, it seems plausible to think that evidence of his existence would be provided to all who sincerely seek it, that none should seek and fail to find, that none should knock and find the door slammed shut.

John Schellenberg asks us to imagine the plight of a child suffering severe amnesia from a blow to the head. The child cannot recall who his mother is, or indeed whether or not he has a mother, so day after day he searches diligently for his mother, walking up and down the streets calling out "Muuuummmm", but all to no avail. Schellenberg asks: "Is this what we should expect if you really have a mother and she is around, and aware of your search?" (Schellenberg 2004: 31). Yet the boy's plight is analogous to that of many persons who seek but fail to find God, which leads Schellenberg to conclude that there is no God. His formal argument states:

(P1) If God exists and is perfectly loving, then for any human subject *S* and time *t*, if *S* is capable of relating personally to God, *S* at *t* is in a position to do so (i.e. can at *t* do so just by choosing to), except insofar as *S* is culpably in a contrary position at *t*. (1993: 28)

Schellenberg realizes that some people culpably shut themselves off from any divine overtures and God's respect for our human freedom may require him to allow us to turn a deaf ear to his voice. Nevertheless, we are not in a position by sheer dint of will to summon up genuine belief in God; it is not subject to our direct voluntary control. But then, says Schellenberg, we can infer the following:

(P2) God exists and is perfectly loving, then for any human subject *S* and time *t*, if *S* at *t* is capable of relating personally to God, *S* at *t* believes that God exists, except insofar as *S* is culpably in a contrary position at *t*. (1993: 31)

It simply follows from the fact that God is perfectly loving, that there will be no sincere seekers after God who fail to find him. But by Schellenberg's lights, this is not the case. Therefore, those who seek and fail to find God have a reason for rejecting theism.

Unpromising strategies for dealing with suffering

Several approaches to dealing with the problem are signally unhelpful. As noted above, denying the reality of evil as somehow illusory does not deal with the problem of apparent or phantom pain, which still hurts. Some philosophers teach that evil does not exist in its own right but is rather a privation or lack of goodness. So we might think that greedy people simply display a lack of generosity, or that those who imprison the innocent lack justice. Herbert McCabe explains:

[I]f I have a hole in my sock, the hole is not anything at all, it is just an absence of wool or cotton or whatever, but it is a perfectly real hole in my sock. It would be absurd to say that holes in socks are unreal and illusory just because it isn't made of anything and is purely an absence. *Nothing* in the wrong place can be just as real and just as important as *something* in the wrong place.

(1991: 29)

While viewing evil as a privation may allow the theist to say that God only creates good things and that evils are simply absences of good things, it does not by itself solve the problem of suffering. A drought may be viewed as an absence of rain, but if a benevolent and all-powerful God controls the weather, we must ask why he allows significant absences that bring disaster upon his creatures.

Another simple solution would be to deny the first premise of Mackie's argument by limiting God. Why not back off ascribing to God the traditional attributes of omnipotence, omniscience and omnibenevolence? Perhaps God is only finitely good, wise and powerful, and this world with all its suffering is the best such a deity can do.[3] Suppose, for instance, that God is not perfect in goodness. Suppose that once in a blue moon God goes into an irrational rage, smiting Earth's inhabitants hip and thigh. To deny God's moral impeccability does not solve the problem of suffering, it merely compounds it, for now God himself is another direct source of evil and suffering. If God is not all-knowing and all-powerful, then it is not clear that God can provide compensatory goods for the ills we do suffer. Promises of paradise and other redemptive efforts might be thwarted by circumstances God either did not see or could not counteract. This strategy makes one wonder whether such a God would be altogether worthy of worship or trustworthy.

Theologians have been known to say that God is so far removed from our cognitive grasp so as to be beyond our categories of good and evil. What we view as evil from our human perspective may, for all we can tell, turn out in God's eyes to be a good thing. Maybe from God's perspective, and despite all human appearances to the contrary, the world could not be any better. To justify God's ways to men by putting him utterly beyond our cognitive reach would, perhaps, bar us from blaming God, but it would also bar us from praising God or attributing to him any other attributes such as mercy, love and forgivingness, concepts that lie at the heart of theistic religion. This strategy would also undermine natural law traditions and other arguments that attempt to ground human morality in divine goodness, since whatever God may think about right and wrong, justice and injustice, would remain hopelessly opaque to us.

While some theistic defenders do not go so far as to say that God's views about morality are utterly opaque, neither do they admit that God's standards concerning matters of justice and injustice are completely transparent. If God has justifiable reasons for allowing us to suffer, they more than likely turn on his plans and purposes being carried out across all time and throughout the whole of creation. Humans cannot even predict next week's weather accurately, let alone chart the exact balance of goods and evils being realized throughout all history. Even if God were to appear in the midst of our philosophy of religion class and state his justifying reasons for allowing evil, it is not clear that, equipped with such cognitive powers as we have, we could fathom God's reasons in all their detail. Considerations such as these move most philosophers of religion to decline to offer a "theodicy", that is, a comprehensive and exact account that explains why God permits all the various ills we suffer. Instead, we must be content to offer a "defence", which simply attempts to offer a *possible* (and perhaps plausible) explanation that reconciles theism and human suffering. We turn, then, to several of the major theistic defences for God's allowing us to suffer.

The free will defence

The free will defence is one of the most famous efforts at reconciling the goodness and justice of God with our suffering, variations of which having been offered by Alvin Plantinga, Richard Swinburne and John Hick, among others. If God is unsurpassably great, as theists suppose, what could possibly be his reason for creating us? Aquinas claims:

> We pay God honor and reverence, not for His sake (because He is of Himself full of glory to which no creature can add anything), but for our own sake, because by the very fact that we revere and honor God, our mind is subjected to Him; wherein its perfection consists.   (*Summa Theologiae* II–II, q.81, a.7)

On Aquinas's view, if God created us, it is not because he is lonely, needy or in any sense incomplete. He creates us not to receive a benefit but to confer one. One important benefit, say theists, is to draw us into friendship with himself, wherein, according to the Judaeo-Christian tradition, consists our highest happiness. But if God wishes to draw us into deep friendship with himself, one with genuine reciprocity or exchange of love, then he must make us free with respect to himself. The logic of friendship precludes coercion. We enter this kind of friendship freely or not at all. But in order for us to respond to God voluntarily, we must be created with freedom of the will, which freedom leaves open the possibility that we will refuse God's offer of friendship. For God cannot create us free and simultaneously *guarantee* that we will choose friendship with him. We might instead exercise our freedom to reject his offer and rebel against his plans and purposes for us. So there is tremendous value in our having been created with free will. God has not accorded his creatures a shallow freedom that ranges over trivial issues – "Dare I eat a peach? Shall I wear the bottoms of my trousers rolled?" – but freedom that is deep, significant, and which carries weighty consequences for us and others. And according to the free will defender, a great deal of the physical and emotional suffering we experience is attributable to human malevolence, negligence and rejecting God's purposes for us.

It is important to note that if God creates genuinely free creatures with respect to himself and other morally significant actions, then God has, as it were, imposed a limit on the exercise of his own power. It is logically possible, for instance, that all humans whatsoever should always have exercised their freedom in concert with God's perfect will. But if this scenario were to come to pass, God could not engineer it directly. God can only bring about this state of affairs indirectly, by creating beings who *freely* cooperate with his purposes. One might wonder, then, why God did not populate the Earth with a different batch of humans – humans that in his omniscience he knew "in advance" would never abuse their freedom by causing suffering to one another. Here too is a scenario that is not under God's *direct* creative power. If such a world comes to pass, it is through the free choices of whatever creatures God brings into being. And it is also logically possible that, for any batch of free people God brings into being, they go wrong morally.

Alvin Plantinga's influential "Free Will Defence" is widely regarded by philosophers of religion as having decisively addressed

Mackie's logical problem of evil (Plantinga 1977). All that is required to undermine Mackie's claim that evil and God's existence are incompatible is to show (i) that morally significant freedom is a great good we are better off to have than to lack and (ii) that it is possible for any free creatures God creates to go on to make morally bad choices. Plantinga even suggests that it's logically possible that there are other supernatural agents (Satan and his demonic host) whose exercise of creaturely freedom accounts for some of the natural evils that befall us. Do note that Plantinga is not saying that (i) and (ii) are *actually* the case, only that they are *possibly* the case. With the correction to Mackie's claim that there is no limit to what an omnipotent being can do, we see that Plantinga's two claims just noted, when added to the premises of Mackie's argument, entail that evil exists. But that is all he needs to undermine the claim that evil is logically incompatible with an all-powerful and all-loving God. Most critics of theism have now abandoned the logical argument in favor of the evidential argument from evil.

Free will defences will fail, however, for both logical and evidential versions of the problem of evil if, for reasons scientific, philosophical or theological, one believes that humans lack the requisite sense of freedom of the will. If, for example, one accepts certain versions of naturalism, which hold that humans are, at bottom, merely material creatures, subject to the same laws of physical determination that govern the rest of the physical world, then one will most likely deny that we have freedom of choice over morally significant actions. Or, if one has so robust a view of God's sovereign control over the world that he directly causes everything that comes to pass, there will be no room for the libertarian freedom of the will that is central to free will defences.

Critics of the free will defence raise additional worries. Why does God permit humans to abuse their creaturely freedom to the degree that they do? Consider an analogy: it is reasonable to suppose a perfectly competent parent will not intervene to settle every sibling squabble. It is good for children to learn to work such matters out on their own. But when one sibling grabs the kitchen meat cleaver with malevolent designs upon her older brother, we think that freedom to settle such matters on their own comes to an end. In fact, we would judge any parent who did not intervene in such a situation as unfit for parenting. Why then, the critic of religion asks, has God not done more to circumscribe the range within which our free choices take place? At the very least, should God not have disallowed the free choices that resulted in the Holocaust or Stalin's pogrom of Ukraine?

Theists could respond by claiming that there are no clear lines to demarcate acceptable and unacceptable uses of freedom. Were God to override every murderous impulse that wells up within humans, we would then wonder why he does not override manslaughter. And if God were to override acts of manslaughter, we would ask why he allows acts of assault and battery. For any place one would have God draw the line, there would be a "worst evil" that we would want God to bar. Moreover, it may be that, were God to circumscribe the scope of our freedom that permits such evils, we would lose the freedom to initiate other valuable goods. Despots who starve the populace to fatten their wallets abuse their creaturely freedom in especially egregious ways. Such wickedness, however, makes possible the free, magnificent acts of generosity in the form of food aid, medical care and other means of assistance to those unfortunately afflicted. Free will defenders also insist that God's allowing us expansive and morally significant freedom does not mean he has granted unbounded freedom. Popular movies and television to one side, humans do not possess superpowers enabling them to incinerate their enemies with X-ray vision or scramble the minds of others with telepathic powers. And, as Richard Swinburne adds, despots die, bringing the worst reigns of terror to an end. Swinburne's response, while true, may strike some persons as cold comfort, especially as we witness the expanding powers of humans to bring about nuclear and environmental annihilation.

More troubling still is the fact that the greater part of the suffering we experience does not arise from wrongly exercised moral freedom, but is due to what insurance companies call – with no irony intended – "acts of God". The Tangshan earthquake in 1976 in China wiped out a quarter of a million people in a day. A tsunami in the Indian Ocean on 26 December 2004, which hit Thailand, Sumatra and other islands, killed an estimated 275,000 people. These disasters pale, however, before the destructive power of epidemic diseases. The Spanish flu pandemic of 1914–18 wiped out millions, more than 16 million in India alone. We have yet to see how many the scourge of AIDS will claim before vaccinations for the disease are discovered. Obviously, these catastrophes were not owing to human moral malfeasance. Free will has precious little, if anything, to do with such calamities. So how do theists address suffering produced at the hands of nature?

The greater good defence

The greater good defence proposes that a God perfect in wisdom, power and goodness might justifiably allow instances of human suffering if, by allowing suffering, he is able to bring about great goods he would not otherwise be able to bring about, or is able to forestall even greater suffering. Consider two worlds, A and B. World A has no suffering but on balance, is able to generate 750 units of goodness. (Of course, these are arbitrary numbers for the sake of the example.) Now consider World B, which, while containing suffering, generates on balance 1,500 units of goodness. Theists think God has good reason to create World B and is certainly not obliged to create World A. To speak of units of evil is to speak of evil abstractly. Some atheists concede that some evil – of a none-too-serious sort – may be compatible with the perfections attributed to God. What they find objectionable are the concrete evils of this world, with their particular distribution, duration and severity (see Tooley 1991).

Several conditions traditionally qualify any acceptable greater good defence. First, the world God creates must, on balance, contain more good than evil. Most people's intuitions tell them that if the best world God could create contains more evil than goodness, then a morally perfect God should refrain from bringing such a world into being. It is not consonant with perfect goodness to create a world that is chiefly an engine for inflicting pain. Second, a perfectly good and powerful God will not permit pointless suffering – suffering that has no purpose or redemptive value. Eleanor Stump states a strong version of the condition:

> A perfectly good entity who was also omniscient must govern the evil resulting from the misuse of … significant freedom in such a way that the sufferings of any particular person are outweighed by the good which the suffering produces *for that person*: otherwise, we might justifiably expect a good God

> somehow to prevent *that particular suffering*, either by inter-
> vening (in one way or another) to protect the victim, while still
> allowing the perpetrator his freedom, or by curtailing freedom
> in some select cases. (1985: 411)

Theists will have to answer critics of theism who claim that it is
palpably obvious that some human lives are, on balance, marked
by considerably more suffering than goodness – Rowe's example of
the five-year-old girl's rape and murder leaps immediately to mind.
Notice that the second premise of Rowe's argument above offers
a weaker condition for gratuitous suffering. It is consistent with
his condition that, while goodness does not necessarily outweigh
in each individual life, the sufferings of each person nevertheless
contribute in some way to a positive overall balance of the world's
aggregate goodness. Rowe, however, sees no reason to think that
even this weaker condition is satisfied. The last requirement for
greater good defences says that the goodness that God brings about
through suffering is such that it could not have been achieved in any
other way. Were God able to get 1,500 units of goodness in World
B while avoiding the suffering, then he should have done that.

So what are these goods deemed so valuable so as to be worth
the suffering required to obtain them? John Hick famously argues
that it was never God's intention to plant us immediately amid
his celestial glory (as is claimed of angels), nor into a hedonistic
paradise on Earth, the human equivalent of an ideal hamster habi-
tat. Rather, it is God's purpose that this world function as a place
of "soul-making", a proving ground, so to speak, in which free
creatures struggling with the temptations and vicissitudes of daily
existence become the kind of creatures that can love God and be
rightly related to him and to one another, now and in the life to
come. Pivotal to the soul-making process is that humans have the
genuine freedom to preside over their own moral and spiritual
formation, and that this is more valuable than God's having created us with our characters ready-made. In order that we have a
genuinely free hand in our own moral and spiritual formation, God
must keep a certain "epistemic distance", says Hick. Were God to
appear to people with the power and intensity of Pascal's "Night of
Fire", God would overwhelm us with his presence, thereby coerc-
ing belief.[4]

For free creatures to be rightly related to God, they must become the sorts of persons whose inner character is so formed as to find the prospect of such a relationship with God desirable. In short, our character must come to resemble God's. And Hick believes that the school of hard knocks provides the best backdrop for our cultivating virtues such as generosity, compassion, forbearance and forgivingness. After all, how could one cultivate compassion in a world where no one suffered or patience in a world where one never bore pain? How could one cultivate generosity in a world where no one needed anything or courage in a world where you could not possibly suffer a scratch? We do not possess these virtuous traits inherently, so we must acquire them. Greater good defenders thus argue, better a world where we know pain and can cultivate virtue than a world where we know neither.

To cultivate character, one needs to live in a stable world in which we guide our conduct by uniform laws of moral cause and effect. If bread nourishes and cyanide poisons today, then if I am to learn kindness and avoid negligence, I will have to live in a world that operates in accordance with fixed, uniform laws. A law-like world makes possible moral knowledge as well as scientific and other sorts of knowledge. And here too arises the opportunity for persons freely to cultivate intellectual virtues such as open-mindedness, love of truth, intellectual autonomy, practical wisdom and more, as opposed to close-mindedness, self-deception, dogmatism and unteachability. But laws of gravity, force, laws governing weather and the movement of tectonic plates, in addition to all the salutary benefits they confer, also visit disaster on humans who are not knowledgeable enough or lack the initiative to counteract their potentially destructive effects. Still, the greater good defender argues that it is better to live in a law-like world, with the knowledge and potential for great good that it makes possible, rather than to live in a world that has neither.

The greater good argument, like the free will defence, faces formidable objections. Critics note that the very same circumstances that make it possible for us to cultivate virtues also make vice possible. In circumstances that might call forth compassion, one can respond with indifference, adding sin to already existing suffering. Needy persons whose plight might have stimulated generosity can also provoke stinginess. These vicious responses compound the evil, for now in addition to the original suffering we must add the morally counterproductive responses. Whether one responds to adverse circumstances positively or negatively is, of course, a further display of human freedom, which is a great good in itself, making the better versions of the greater good defence ones that incorporate the free will defence.

If we cannot attain to the great goods of character and deep responsibility for one another's welfare without suffering, then why not let suffering abound that character and other goods might increase? If some suffering results in morally important goods, then why not think more suffering would be better? Would not the belief that suffering is a necessary condition for the realization of these important goods foster, at best, an indifference to suffering and, at worst, the desire that suffering might increase? The trouble with this objection is the supposition that humans have the proper perspective from which to assess just how much suffering is sufficient to produce desirable results. Whereas the typical hardships one encounters in life may be sufficient for fostering virtue, overwhelming adversity would most probably swamp our capacity to face it head-on. Facing up to the class bully or taking on the challenge of an arduous and somewhat dangerous mountain climb may foster courage, whereas the prospect of martyrdom in the arena might overwhelm us and fail to foster courage. So God is presumably like a wise doctor, who knows that some degree of poison – in the form of chemotherapy – will kill the cancer but too much will kill the patient. In the absence of any accurate knowledge of just how much suffering is sufficient, our best tack would be to eliminate all the evil we can.

The religious sceptic protests. Even if contending with suffering fosters moral character and other goods, it is a bad bargain. Whatever goods we may gain from the school of hard knocks is not sufficient to justify the amount of suffering we must endure to attain them. Were we to weigh suffering in one hand and the various goods of which it may be productive in the other, suffering outweighs. Another way to put this point is to say that we suffer far in excess of what is necessary to bring about moral character and related goods. Consider a little cocaine baby, addicted in the womb, born in agony with nerve endings afire. It persists in this state for a few days, a few weeks perhaps, then dies. The baby certainly did not learn any important moral lessons, and whatever lessons the rest of us may derive from its death do not warrant the infant's suffering.[5] Or consider, as Rowe bids us, the case of the fawn burned horribly in a forest fire, whose agony endures for days before it succumbs to death. The fawn certainly does not gain any moral lessons and, on the supposition that the event is unobserved, neither do any humans. In a word, says Rowe, the world contains "gratuitous" evil, pointless evil that subserves no greater good, and for this reason he judges theism unlikely to be true.

Refinements to theistic defences

We have spoken thus far as if all parties to this discussion about the problem of suffering affirm a common account of moral values, of right and wrong, good and bad, justice and injustice. We have also spoken as if God's goodness lies strictly with his moral goodness and that his status as moral agent *par excellence* consists in his complying perfectly with the same sorts of moral obligations that befall humans. (So God is perfectly good because he never tells lies, envies his neighbour's mansion, breaks promises and so on.) To respond to the charge of gratuitous suffering requires that we question both assumptions. That philosophers fail to embrace a common account of moral value is a commonplace. The protracted debates between deontologists and utilitarians, moral relativists and objectivists, suffice to make this clear. But these disagreements are relevant to the charge that there is an imbalance between suffering and the goods of which it is productive, requiring that we ask by what metric the goods and evils are being calibrated. To say that suffering outweighs good in our world presupposes some standard of measurement. Suppose one is a utilitarian, then goodness consists solely in the maximization of pleasure and the minimization of pain. While it is hard to know just how anyone would compute the net amount of pain and pleasure in the world, it is no stretch of the imagination to speculate that pain outweighs. But why think that judgements about the balance of good and evil in the world are to be weighed on the "pleasure-scale"? Hick and others expressly deny that pleasure and the absence of pain is an overriding good. Rather, Hick thinks that virtues are of such supreme and overriding value and that we should willingly countenance a lot of pain in order to achieve them. Other theists argue that the supreme and overriding value of being eternally united with God outweighs any suffering we undergo that moves us to recognize our need for God and leads to our turning to him in friendship. Whether or not one accepts Hick's virtue-metric or the "friendship with God metric", it is important to grasp that judgements about the balance of good and evil in the world will vary as one or another standard of value and measurement is applied, and that these standards are contested. If one rejects a utilitarian calculus, the claim that our world is imbalanced in favour of suffering becomes much more difficult to justify.

Stephen Wykstra claims that humans lack the cognitive where-withal to assert with any confidence that our world contains gra-tuitous evil, thereby calling into question Rowe's balancing or probabilities against theism (Wykstra 1996). Wykstra argues that religious sceptics often employ a "noseeum argument" (named for the tiny, difficult to see, biting flies of the American upper Mid-west) that reasons as follows: since I cannot see any greater good to which much of the world's evils contribute, there is not any greater good, and thus the world contains pointless suffering. Sometimes the inference from "I do not see X" to "X is not there" is perfectly acceptable – if I open my dresser drawer and fail to see any socks, it is reasonable to conclude there are no socks in there. Suppose, however, that you and your police partner are in hot pursuit of a thief who ducks into a huge warehouse. You arrive first, crack open the door and stare into a warehouse the size of several foot-ball fields, filled from wall to wall and floor to ceiling with crates, machines, loading equipment and so forth. Your partner arrives seconds later and asks if you see the thief. "No," you say, "I cannot see him, so he must not be in there." Clearly the noseeum inference concerning the socks is acceptable and that concerning the thief is not. So what is the difference between acceptable and unacceptable noseeum inferences? Just this: unacceptable inferences fail because we lack the cognitive powers that would allow us to reason from something's failure to appear to us, to the conclusion that it does not exist. Suppose a rank neophyte at chess watches a chess match between grandmasters and remarks, "I do not see a way out for white; black has him beaten". From the fact that an inexperienced beginner fails to see a good move for white, it certainly does not follow that none exist. The neophyte's lack of ability bars him from concluding that white has no reasonable response. It is on a par with my concluding there are no ants in my neighbour's lawn across the street because I cannot see any from my living room. Even if there were ants, I lack the cognitive power to perceive them even if they were there.

Wykstra argues that religious sceptics lack the cognitive resources to say that some of the world's suffering is pointless. As was noted earlier, if God has a morally justifiable reason for allowing his creatures to suffer, it no doubt turns on his plans and purposes being realized across the cosmos and throughout the whole of time. We cannot act as God's accountants here, toting up the balance sheet of goods and evils, because our perspective is too limited. We are to God's providential guidance of the world as the chess neophyte is to the play of grandmasters. How can beings that cannot even predict what the stock markets will do next week assert with any confidence that some of the sufferings of this world serve no purpose now or at any time in the future? So, since the noseeum argument that underwrites Rowe's evidential argument is illicit, theism has not thereby been shown to be unreasonable. We do not know that there is gratuitous suffering, hence we do not know that the first premise of Rowe's argument is true. The evidential argument thus neutralized, theists argue that the positive evidence for God's existence consisting of religious experiences, fine-tuning and the rest, shows theism to be reasonable overall.

Rowe admits that we do not *know* – we cannot be certain – that there is no conceivable good to which the fawn's suffering may contribute. Atheists point out, however, that theists suffer the same cognitive limitations, and cannot say with any assurance that good will outweigh. As regards the rippling effects of suffering throughout eternity and throughout the cosmos, both sides must plead ignorance. Sceptics then reason that, inasmuch as both sides are arguing from ignorance about the remote balance of goods and evils, the only basis that remains to us on which we can make judgements about the balance of goods and evils, and thus on the reasonableness of theism, is what we see in the world around us. And based on what we have to go on, it looks as though some suffering is gratuitous. Consider Rowe's fawn. Who could it benefit? Not the fawn. It would have been better off had God made it comatose before death. Again, if we stipulate that the fawn's death goes unobserved by humans, then we derive no benefit. Nor can God benefit from the fawn's suffering if he is as theists conceive him to be. Moreover, only idle speculation would prompt us to suppose that alien beings hover about benefitting from the fawn's suffering.

William Hasker, unlike most theists, argues that theists should reject premise 2 of Rowe's argument: in other words, they should reject the claim that a good and all-powerful deity will never allow gratuitous suffering. Hasker thinks that God operates by a "principle of divine moral intention" that conflicts with Rowe's requirement. The principle states that: "It is an extremely important part of God's intention for human persons that they should place a high priority on fulfilling moral obligations and should assume major responsibility for the welfare of other human beings" (Hasker 2008: 193).[6]

How is this principle at variance with the premise of Rowe's argument that claims that a good God would never allow suffering that did not contribute to a greater good, the realization of which required the suffering? Hasker thinks Rowe's requirement would undermine our incentive for acting morally and working to bring about the welfare of other humans. To grasp Hasker's reasoning, suppose that I am contemplating some morally suspect action, the pursuit of which might harm someone else. If God is as Rowe claims he must be, I need not worry overly much about the harm my action may cause, since, if God lets me do it, it must have been necessary for some greater good. If the harm I am contemplating would not bring about any needed benefit then, on Rowe's view, God would not let me perform the action. Since God is oversee-ing the welfare of all persons, any harms I may cause others must have been essential to bringing about their good, and any harms I prevent will, if essential to their ultimate good, arise in some other quarter in some other way.[7] Thus, my thinking "it will all work out for the best" undercuts one's incentive to assume major responsibility for the welfare of others. If my acting out some morally wrong course of action is up to God, then I need not worry overly much about it, since it is up to God whether my actions ever get realized. This attitude, however, undermines moral motivation and moral seriousness. Proper moral motivation, therefore, must allow that God permit gratuitous suffering. If this is correct, Rowe's evidential argument is undermined.

Hasker anticipates an obvious perplexity about his argument. On the one hand, he claims that the possibility of gratuitous suffering is necessary for proper moral motivation. If, however, the gratuitous suffering God allows is necessary for our becoming morally mature and being deeply responsible for one another's welfare, then in what sense is the suffering God allows gratuitous? Any evils God allows are forwarding the great good of our moral maturity and thus are not gratuitous.

In response, Hasker bids us consider an illustration: suppose a crowded symphony hall applauds a performance enthusiastically. Even if one or two members of the audience had been prevented from clapping, the performance would still have been enthusiastically received. In like manner, were God to prevent one instance of gratuitous suffering, our moral motivation would not thereby be undermined. But if God were to prevent all instances of gratuitous suffering, moral incentive would be undermined. Rowe himself summarizes Hasker's position saying that "the class of gratuitous evils is not gratuitous" (1988; quoted in Hasker 2008: 195), since God could not have prevented the entire class of gratuitous sufferings without undermining moral motivation.

Rowe replies to Hasker's argument by insisting that God could delete not just one or two instances of gratuitous sufferings from the class of all evils – he could eliminate quite a few without thereby undermining moral motivation. True, he could not eliminate them all without undermining moral motivation. But however many are needed to spur moral motivation would then cease to be gratuitous as they play the indispensible role of spurring moral concern and action! Think again, insists Hasker, of an agent contemplating some serious moral misdeed who thinks Rowe is right, that a good God would allow only those evils that serve some greater good. It matters not whether the good served is moral motivation or some other good. What is salient for our wayward moral agent is the knowledge that whatever suffering may arise from her evil action will be compensated for by some good for which the evil action was an indispensable cause. But this, says Hasker, is just the sort of view that undermines morality.

God and the greatest possible world

Before turning to explicitly theological defences to the problem of suffering, we must examine how theists respond to the objection that God is obliged to create the best of all possible worlds. The argument says that if God exists and if God creates a world, then that world must be the best of all possible worlds. This world is not the best of all possible worlds. Therefore, God does not exist. But why accept the consequent of the first premise? First, the idea of the best of all possible worlds is arguably incoherent. Recall Gaunilo's objection to Anselm's ontological argument that relied on the notion of a "best of all possible islands". We noted that the concept is incoherent, since whatever great-making qualities serve to make an island great – palm trees, artesian springs, mountains and so on – admit of no intrinsic maximum. If palm trees contribute to the greatness of an island, then the more the merrier. There seems to be no non-arbitrary stopping point after which one has exceeded the perfect number of palm trees for the best of all possible islands. A parallel argument can be made regarding the notion of the best of all possible worlds. If stars, planets, vegetation, people and the like make for a good universe, then there is no upper limit to how good God could make the universe. He could always add more and never "run out of room", as it were. If this is correct, then the objection that God has failed to create the best of all possible worlds is always in place no matter what world he creates, which is strong reason for rejecting that any such obligation exists.

Robert Adams rejects the claim that a perfectly good God must create the best of all possible worlds. God's failure to do so would not necessarily wrong any person or show that God's character is defective (R. Adams 1987: 51–64). On the assumption that a best of all possible worlds is coherent, then suppose, says Adams, that God were to create a world W that satisfied the following conditions: (i) None of the creatures it contains would exist in the best of all possible worlds. (ii) None of the creatures has a life so miserable that it is better that it never existed. (iii) Every creature in the world is at least as happy on the whole as it would have been in any other possible world in which it existed (*ibid.*: 53). It follows from these criteria that whatever creatures make it into W would not have been happier in any other world they inhabit, so it is difficult to see how God wrongs them by putting them in W. Nor does Adams think it plausible to think that God wrongs the merely possible beings that would have existed had he created the best of all possible worlds, since Adams denies that we – or God – have moral obligations to merely possible beings. Indeed, were God to create W, it looks as though God would not harm anyone.

This conclusion is subject to a powerful objection. Suppose a couple desires to bear a mentally disabled child and to that end the mother takes drugs that alter the foetus's developing genetic structure. The parents lavish love and the best of care for this child so that the child is happy, on the whole.[8] Many people's moral intuitions tell them that the parents have done something grievously wrong. Critics of theism argue that God would do an analogous wrong were he to bring about any world less than the best, even if its inhabitants are on balance happy and would not have existed in any other possible world. Adams points out, however, that had the child been born without its mental disability, then it would not have been the child in question, since *its* genetic material would have been different. And if the child is not worse off had it never existed, and wouldn't have existed except as disabled, then it is not obvious that *its* rights have been violated.

The parents in the example above have done something wrong, agrees Adams. Their fault, however, does not lie in the fact that they willingly brought into existence a being less excellent than they could have brought into existence. We would not, for example, fault a pet owner for raising chinchillas rather than stronger and more intelligent chimpanzees. Nor would we judge parents moral malefactors who forsook genetic enhancements to give their offspring superhuman strength and intelligence. The fault lies rather in the parents violating a more specific principle, in other words, that one ought not knowingly and willingly bear offspring notably deficient physically or mentally by comparison with *normal* human beings. Robert Adams defends this principle along Judaeo-Christian lines. If God is our creator and sustainer then we not only owe him a debt of gratitude, but we ought not act in ways that would contravene his overall purposes for us. Genetic manipulation to bring about physically and mentally defective offspring could hardly be said to make such children better able to enter into God's purposes for human life. But from the fact that it would be wrong for *humans* to bring about defective offspring given their created and dependent status, it does not follow that God would be wrong to create creatures that are less excellent than the best possible.

Marilyn Adams raises a more troubling objection to the previous argument. From all appearances, it looks as though our world fails condition two, which requires that any world a good God creates be such that the lives of its inhabitants are not so overwhelmingly swamped by suffering that it would have been better had they never existed. We turn next to consider the problem of what Marilyn Adams calls "horrific suffering".

Theological defences

So far we have examined philosophical responses to the problem of suffering from the standpoint of what Rowe calls "standard restricted theism", a minimalist conception of the deity as a being perfect in wisdom, power and goodness (Rowe 1984). Yet the great monotheistic traditions of the world affirm much more about God and his plans and purposes for the world. Some theodicists argue that a satisfactory answer to the problem of suffering requires that theists draw upon an expanded theism that includes the religion's particular theological teachings.[9] In particular, some explanations for suffering require that we take account of post-mortem compensation that God may offer to the sufferer. Religious sceptics are likely to dismiss such a manoeuvre as a case of putting the cart before the horse. They will no doubt protest that "thin theism" has not been shown to be warranted in the face of suffering. Why, then, should one give credence to the specific teachings of the Bible or some other holy book that purports to tell about God's providential guidance of the world? Marilyn Adams argues in response that what such explanations lose in theoretical economy they gain in increased explanatory power. In so far as a coherent, theologically expanded explanation offers resources to grapple with the problem of suffering that restricted theism lacks, they are worth considering. Scientists sometimes postulate the existence of theoretical entities long in advance of their having any experimental confirmation of their existence (the postulation of Uranus and neutrinos are famous examples) because of the explanatory power they offer. Explanatory power is also afforded by entities for which scientists have not yet – and may never – receive empirical confirmation, strings and dark matter among them. Analogously, theological explanations that appeal to God's relationship to persons in the next life, while not confirmable in this life, may offer advantages in increased explanatory power.

A Christian response to horrendous suffering

Marilyn Adams finds restricted theism unable to address the problem of horrendous evils such as the suffering of the cocaine baby. Within the Trinitarian theology of Christianity she finds resources restricted theism lacks. Christianity, unlike Judaism and Islam, teaches that three distinct yet equal divine persons, Father, Son and Holy Spirit together form one divine nature or essence. The Christian scriptures also state that "God is love". As the Catholic catechism puts it: "God himself is an eternal exchange of love, Father, Son, and Holy Spirit, and he has destined us to share in that exchange" (*Catechism of the Catholic Church*, 221). The Christian God, Adams explains, created beings that are simultaneously physical and spiritual, with physico-chemical processes that enable cellular reproduction and self-replication in a suitably accommodating natural environment, but also with minds and wills capable of higher-order consciousness and reciprocal love relationships. God, as love, wishes to be united with humans in a loving friendship. God desired greater intimacy with his creatures than was possible across the great ontological divide separating creator and creatures. That he might bring about greater loving communion between himself and humans, God took on a human nature and lived among us, enduring our travails, that he might identify with humans in the most intimate way possible.

By assuming a human nature God the Son became susceptible to hunger, thirst, fatigue, rejection, betrayal, humiliation, torture and an unjust death by crucifixion. He experienced a representative range of our suffering including its horrors. Now, however, the very horrors that threatened to deprive a life of meaning become the means of identifying with God. "Divine identification with human participation in horrors confers a positive aspect on such experiences by integrating them into the participant's relationship with God" (M. Adams 1999: 167). Marilyn Adams's claim is that from the vantage point of heaven, victims of horrors will recognize them as points of identification with God of such surpassing value that they would not wish them away. The victims of horrors will come to see their suffering as more than compensated for and overall part of a good and worthwhile life. "If postmortem, the individual is ushered into a relation of beatific intimacy with God and comes to recognize how past participation in horrors is thus defeated, and if his/her concrete well-being is guaranteed forever afterward so that the concrete ills are balanced off, then God will have been good to that individual despite participation in horrors" (*ibid.*: 168).

Marilyn Adams's theological explanation for suffering faces the following three objections (and others besides, no doubt). Granted that it is important for humans to love and identify with God, why does the point of our identification with God have to be at the point of suffering? Why did God not create a world in which we meet him only by sharing a rich variety of joys? Second, what about humans who suffer horrors and are driven to reject God or, for that matter, have never heard of the Christian God? Were such persons to wind up in hell, their life of horrendous suffering would be continued into eternity. Finally, what of Rowe's fawn? What provision is made for the suffering animals endure?

In response to the first objection, Adams's view is not meant to deny that many humans identify with God in this life by participating in his joy, by coming to see such beauty, goodness and love as comes to us in this life as gifts from God. Her particular concern is with those unfortunate persons whose lives on Earth are qualified largely by unmitigated suffering, in whom the world's joys are mostly absent. Even lives of horrendous suffering can be lives of meaning in virtue of God's solidarity with us as co-sufferer. But could God not have arranged the world so that horrendous suffering never arose in the first place, making our only avenue for identifying with God shared joy? Apparently not.

> Not even God could place human beings in a world like this without their being radically vulnerable to horrors. It seems to me that the metaphysically necessary constitution of created natures is something God has to work with and around in deciding whether and which sorts of things to produce in what circumstances. (*Ibid.*: 171)

In line with classical medieval metaphysics, Adams endorses the position that the metaphysical constitution of created natures was metaphysically necessary and not open to the inventiveness of the divine will. Not even, God, she tells us, could make fire a natural coolant. In like manner, humans with psycho-physical natures such as ours, placed in requisite environments for our survival, could not circumvent our vulnerability to horrific suffering.

What if, after suffering horrors in this life, one were consigned to an eternity of horrors in the next? A traditional Christian account of hell depicts it as a place of eternal, irrevocable conscious torment. How does Adams square her Christological theodicy with traditional teaching about hell? She does not. Adams finds the traditional Christian teaching about hell unjust, unfair and contrary to the nature of a loving God. She adopts the position of universalism, which is to say, one who denies that anyone goes to hell but that the scope and power of God's redemptive love will eventually draw all persons to himself (M. Adams 1993). What about animals? How does Adams account for their suffering? First, she denies that animals are capable of horrendous suffering, since they lack the cognitive wherewithal to interpret their lives as, on the whole, largely bereft of goodness. They do experience pain. From all appearances, a gazelle torn limb from limb by lions undergoes considerable pain. Nature is red in tooth and claw as the saying goes. Yet the cycle of predator and prey, of disease winnowing herds, of animals becoming extinct, should not be seen either as a horrendous evil or even as a gratuitous evil, but instead as a delicate balancing of the ecosystem. Suffering seems not only inherent in creating a sustainable ecosystem, but an inevitable part of the evolutionary development of higher-level sentient organisms. Recall our discussion from the first chapter regarding the extraordinarily narrow parameters for physical constants, initial conditions and physical laws necessary for human life to emerge and evolve into creatures like us. It is not unreasonable to think that only in a universe very much like ours – with its attendant suffering – could creatures such as ourselves arise. Peter van Inwagen thus claims:

> No one, I believe, would take seriously the idea that the highest subhuman animals, the immediate evolutionary precursors of

human beings, could have evolved naturally without hundreds of millions of years of ancestral suffering ... Pain would seem to be an indispensable component of the evolutionary process after organisms have reached a certain stage of complexity.

(2006: 119)[10]

Final responses to objections

We conclude this chapter by looking at the problem of divine hiddenness. The problem, again, is that a God perfect in wisdom, power and goodness would not allow sincere seekers after God to have their searches end in failure. If God were perfectly good he would disclose himself to all who earnestly seek him. Yet, says John Schellenberg, experience shows that many an earnest search for God ends in frustration. Therefore, the reasonable conclusion is that the God of theism does not exist.

As we have already seen, a general theistic strategy for addressing suffering is to pose some great good that God would forego were he to eliminate the particular instance of suffering under consideration. Human freedom is often proposed as a good God would sacrifice were he to disclose himself too forcefully. God must keep his "epistemic distance" if he is to preserve our capacity to respond freely to his overtures of friendship. Surely God could produce mass conversions the world over were a sonorous bass voice to boom from the heavens, intelligible in every language, announcing that in three minutes the God of the Abrahamic faiths will heal every ill person in the world. And if three minutes later all persons were indeed healed, surely no sincere seeker would refuse to acknowledge God's reality. But such a divine display would override human freedom and frustrate God's purposes in creating us, namely that we should be united to him in a relationship of reciprocal friendship. Goodness requires only that God give each person sufficient although less than conclusive information to acknowledge God.

Could God not reveal himself in some spectacular way just short of coercion that preserved our epistemic freedom in relation to God? Perhaps God could nudge each non-believing person in a way uniquely tailored to each person that would lead to suitably probable but not conclusive belief. Unfortunately, coercion can be as effective with probabilistic belief as with certain belief. Suppose a mugger shoves a hard cylindrical object in your back demanding your money, and you have background knowledge that only 50 per cent of muggings in your locale are conducted with real guns, and that only 5 per cent of persons mugged are actually shot. Most rational persons would still feel coerced to hand over their money, the low probability of harm notwithstanding (see Murray 2001).

The demand that God supply evidence sufficient to move all persons non-coercively to belief fails to give sufficient weight to the fact that how forcefully evidence strikes us depends on our having become suitably disposed to see and appreciate the evidence correctly. How we estimate evidence, as we saw in earlier chapters, involves the will, the seat of our cares, concerns, loves and attachments, and not just the intellect alone. If one strongly dislikes the idea of a God to whom one owes a debt of gratitude and to whom one is morally accountable, this dislike may colour one's assessment of the evidence. In this vein, Paul Moser (2008) distinguishes between "propositional" and "volitional" evidence for God's existence, the former concerned merely to show that God exists, the latter engaging our will, so as to draw us mind and heart into a relationship of filial love.

Moser offers a distinctively Christian response to the problem of hiddenness, the central claim of which is that God is not interested in providing humans with mere evidence of his existence, as if God were responsible to schedule routine cameo appearances throughout the world to assure its inhabitants that indeed he still exists. Drawing on the teachings of the Christian New Testament, Moser argues that God's goal in disclosing himself to us is to move us in heart and mind into an "I–Thou" relationship of filial love, whereby we are transformed into persons related to God in obedient friendship. In so far as God supplies evidence of his existence, it is not simply to spur mere mental assent to the fact of his existence, as if one's goal in gaining such knowledge were to answer correctly the "true-false" question "Does God exist?" Rather, says Moser, God wishes to encounter us on the level of direct experiential acquaintance that transforms our whole being and to move us to divine–human fellowship.

If, as Moser argues, God's purposes in revealing himself lie chiefly in bringing about an existentially gripping, life-changing personal relationship of obedience and trust in God, then God may have a number of reasons for remaining hidden. These reasons, says Moser, might include teaching people earnestly to yearn for "volitional fellowship" with God, removing human complacency about God's call on their lives, strengthening grateful trust and removing obstructive pride. God might even withhold his presence knowing that a premature overture to friendship might be rebuffed, much like a marriage proposal after a first or second date (*ibid.*: 107). One might rightly ask whether, before accepting an invitation to friendship with God, one first must come to believe that he exists and has the loving, relational character attributed to him. While Moser agrees that "filial knowledge of God's reality requires propositional knowledge that God exists" (*ibid.*: 126), God has no interest, says Moser, in supplying *merely* propositional evidence that doesn't lead to "filial knowledge". This more purposive evidence leading to the knowledge of experiential acquaintance – as opposed to mere notional assent – requires that those who receive it have the right orientation of mind and will, the lack of which may be reason enough for God to remain hidden.

Clearly Moser's solution to the problem of divine hiddenness goes beyond standard restricted theism, as it relies crucially on moral and theological notions particular to Christian theism. Nor does it escape Moser's notice that this sort of argument breaks with standard philosophical practice. But Moser recommends that the discipline of philosophy be revamped to make room for, nay to prioritize, questions treating of one's relationship to God and neighbour over the arcane and sometimes trivial concerns that preoccupy professional philosophers.

Summing up

Does the world's suffering show that belief in God is unreasonable? Or, as proponents of the various theistic defences argue, is belief in the theistic God reasonable despite the world's suffering? Theists think we lack adequate grounds to assert confidently that gratuitous evils exist, while atheists size up the evidence differently. Like so many protracted philosophical debates, this one has no obvious and decisive winner. We seem to have arrived at an impasse. In fact, partisans of both sides often admit that their opponent's position can be reasonably held. In his article "The Problem of Evil and Some

Varieties of Atheism", Rowe (1996), whose arguments figure centrally in this chapter, was content to call himself a "friendly atheist". Friendly atheism, in contrast to "unfriendly atheism", recognizes that theists are not irrational to size up the balance of probabilities as they do. Rowe himself thinks the balance of probabilities tilts in the opposite direction, hence his rejection of theism. Consider an analogous case. Based on extensive research using economic models she deems reliable, economist A believes that an economic recession will lift before the year's end. Economist B relies on slightly different models and, on the basis of extensive research, concludes that the recession will continue well into next year. While A differs from B, A need not think that B is irrational or unreasonable. In fact, A might admit that were she to size up the evidence as B does, she too would believe the recession more durable. But she *does not* estimate the evidence as B does and thus believes differently. Time will tell which of the economists was correct. The stand-off between atheists and theists is not so easily resolved.

8 The nature of God

Why philosophize about God?

If God exists, one is naturally led to ask what sort of being is God. Theists and non-theists alike have a stake in posing the question. Theists, of course, have in interest in knowing the central object of their devotion. Christians, for instance, claim that the highest state of heavenly beatitude consists in "seeing God face to face", of "knowing as we have been known". In his *Proslogion*, Anselm of Canterbury prays to God: "Lord, You give understanding to faith, grant me that I may understand, as much as You see fit, that You exist as we believe You to exist, and that You are what we believe You to be" (1998: 87). Anselm takes metaphysical investigations into God's nature to follow naturally upon one's desire to know better the being one worships. As a lover wishes to know all he can of the beloved, so Anselm wishes to know God, as God is the object of his heart's highest desire. At the very least, authentic devotion to God requires that one endeavour to think truthfully about God.

Some critics of theism urge careful study of the metaphysics of theism as a way of showing that the concept of an omnipotent, omniscient and omnibenevolent being is incoherent and, if incoherent, irrational.[1] We would not bother to investigate the intellectual credentials of the claim that in the remotest parts of Australia there reside animals that are simultaneously insect and mammal since, given what we know about the properties of each, we know this to be a physical impossibility. Anyone professing such a belief would be irrational. Analogously, critics of theism argue that the panoply of attributes traditionally ascribed to God constitute an incoherent set of properties. In philosophers' jargon, the properties traditionally ascribed to God are alleged by theism's critics to be "non-compossible", that is, incapable of being possessed by the same being at the same time. Regardless of one's motivation, metaphysical investigations into God's nature are philosophically rich in their own right, shedding light on the nature of necessity, being, time and a host of other concepts of general metaphysical interest.

The question of method

Before we examine some of God's attributes in detail, we must pose some questions about methodology. How do we gain knowledge of God or settle disputes about his nature? To what sources can we appeal to settle debates about God's nature? A long tradition dating back to ancient Greece suggests that our native cognitive capacities are capable of discerning God's existence as well as something of his nature, a sentiment, as we saw, that inspires the tradition of natural theology. Nature, in other words, provides a "general revelation" of God's existence and nature, partial although it may be. The world being what it is, and our cognitive powers being what they are, we can, according to this view, infer some important truths about God, such as that he exists, is one and is the creator of world.

If, however, God is as Pascal and other theists believe, infinitely good, wise and powerful, then it is also true that human reason will be unable to plumb the depths of the divine nature. For this reason, Jews, Christians and Muslims, point to God's "special revelation" of himself, given either in holy writings or to appropriate authorities, as the best source for informing our judgements about God's nature and his dealings with creation. So the Abrahamic faiths speak of God disclosing to prophets important information about his nature and purposes, which they then convey to the intended audience. Philosophers traditionally rest content to restrict their investigations into God's nature to what unaided reason can reveal. Theologians expand their evidential range to include special revelation. These are not strict divisions as, for instance, Aquinas thought that God specially reveals truths about himself that are in principle accessible to unaided reason, but which most people lack the ability, time and inclination to pursue.

Three approaches characterize most philosophical efforts to depict God's nature by relying on reason alone. "Creation theology" begins with the theistic belief that God is the creator and sustainer of the universe, and reasons "backwards" to determine what traits such a creator must possess to accomplish this creative feat. Obviously, a creator and sustainer of the world would have to possess tremendous power and intelligence. Intelligence betokens mind, and the age of the universe may signal that the cause of the universe also has a will: the two elements crucial to personhood. Consider that if the efficient causes of the universe have always existed in sufficient strength and order, one would expect the universe to have always existed. If the sufficient conditions for a fire in the fireplace are present, then there will be a fire. Yet, the universe has not always been here, but came into being roughly fourteen billion years ago. This has prompted some to infer that the creation of the universe was the work of an agent who "decided" when the universe should come into being.[2] Hume would no doubt remind us, however, that creation theology alone cannot help us to fix the fine points of our theology. Among other things, we cannot by creation theology alone determine if God is perfect in goodness, more or less likely to communicate with us, nor what steps humans should take to be rightly related to God. Is God perfect in goodness or good for the most part? Is he omniscient or might there be a few truths unknown to God? The "book of nature" does not supply ready answers to these questions.

"Comparative theology" tries to forge a composite portrait of God by examining the central insights gleaned about him from the world's major religions. On this view, all religions are best viewed as the products of humans endeavouring to orient themselves successfully to the divine. While religions invariably take on the trappings of the times and places where they arise and are practised, one might think it possible to forge a conception of God based on common insights gathered from them all. Perhaps a set containing the union of all claims made about God by the world's religions could supply a more or less accurate conception of God. Unfortunately, the world's religions say incompatible things about God. Theists say that God is one; Hindus say that God is many. Pantheists say the divine is impersonal; theists say the opposite. Muslims say God is transcendent, while animist or nature religions believe the divine to be immanent. The disagreements dividing the world's religions thus give us grounds for suspecting that comparative theology cannot establish any substantive "lowest common denominator" conception of God.

"Perfect being theology" capitalizes on the common theistic idea that whoever God is, he must be the unsurpassably greatest being in the universe. Perfect being theologians, then, depict God's nature simply by reflecting a priori on what must be true for God to be the maximally perfect being, as Anselm expresses it, "the being than which no greater can be conceived".[3] If God is the being than which no greater is possible, it follows that he has no equal or superior in wisdom, power, goodness or in any other property that contributes to his exalted status. But in what does such perfection consist? Philosophers disagree at many points about the nature of a maximally perfect being. Is it more perfect for God to be able to experience emotions or to be "impassible", as many medieval theologians believed? Will a perfect God sovereignly control every event that occurs or does God display greater power by coordinating his actions with those of genuinely free creatures? Can a perfect God change in any way or allow his actions to be "conditioned" or affected by those of his creatures? While perfect being theology may be our best approach to depicting the nature of God, our conflicting intuitions about the nature of a perfect being reveals a limitation for those wishing to offer a full account of God based on a priori reason alone. Perfect being theologians are allied in thinking that there is a considerable ontological gap between less than perfect humans and the being than which no greater can be conceived. This, along with the conflicting intuitions among perfect being theologians, should induce a healthy dose of intellectual humility about just how far human reflection goes toward providing a complete and accurate account of God's nature.

Another interesting question to ask is whether, in thinking about what God is like, anyone ever adopts the standpoint of pure philosophical reason. Human reasoners seldom, if ever, begin their thinking about God from an entirely neutral and dispassionate point of view, as if their cultural backgrounds, commitments and traditions were of no account. Perhaps it is more realistic to recognize that long before people begin to think philosophically about God, they are likely already situated in various religious, academic or social communities that inform their judgements. Most likely we test our convictions about God's nature (or the incoherence thereof) through a kind of "reflective equilibrium" that involves the ongoing modification of our views in the light of our encounters with the thinking of others, especially as those opinions differ from our own. In this respect, our thinking about God's nature is like our thinking about matters political and ethical: it will reflect the particular concerns of time and place. If this is true, then there is no reason to restrict ourselves to one or another *a priori* form of theorizing; rather, our conceptions about God's nature can potentially be informed by the insights of them all, and more besides, including the experiences we and others have of God. These questions of method aside, we turn now to examine the attributes theists frequently ascribe to God.

The classical conception of God

A once widely accepted "classical" account of God's nature emerged in the Judaeo-Christian scholastic tradition of the medieval period. This view, embraced by the leading lights of the period – Augustine, Anselm and Aquinas – shares with perfect being theology the goal of thinking about God in the most exalted terms, as a divine person possessing to the highest possible degree wisdom, power and goodness, and any other quality it is better to have than to lack. The classical view also takes special care not to depict God as subject to limitations or deficiencies of any sort. Consider that we are not now what we once were, bodily, intellectually, emotionally and in other respects. And as we suffer the vicissitudes of time we grow increasingly susceptible to declines in body and mind, eventuating in death. Surely we want to deny that God, as a maximally perfect being is subject to fragility, senescence, dependence and death. From this core intuition that a maximally great being cannot suffer limitations or deficiencies, a number of God's attributes come into clearer view.

First, God must *exist necessarily*, which means that God's existence differs from ours by not being dependent on anything or anyone else, or such as to be taken from him or lost in any way. God has always existed, will always exist and could not do otherwise than to exist. Also, whatever attributes God possesses, he possesses necessarily. For instance, God would be less than perfect if he had needed to study for a long time before acquiring omniscience or had needed to exercise vigorously before becoming omnipotent. God never had to "earn" or acquire his attributes. Whatever attributes God possesses, he has always had and will always have. From this it follows that God is *immutable*, that is, not subject to change. After all, if a being is "maxed-out" in wisdom, power, goodness and any other positive attribute, then no change would be a change for the better. From which it further follows that God's "emotional mien" does not change – he is *impassible*.[4] Although the Judaeo-Christian scriptures sometimes portray God as angry one moment and appeased the next, this is, strictly speaking, anthropomorphic according to the classical picture we are here describing.

God is *a se* – or, he has *aseity* – which is to say, everything that exists depends on him, but he in turn does not depend on anything else. God is wise. But if wisdom is a property that exists necessarily and independently of God, then God's being who he is, his having the nature he does, would depend on something outside himself, thus violating the aseity condition. According to the classical tradition we are here unpacking, God is not a being comprised of parts, physical, temporal or logical, for anything composed of parts would seem to be dependent on those parts and their proper configuration. The reasoning behind this claim is that if God's existence and nature depends on individual attributes and their being arranged in a certain way, then it is conceivable that those "parts" are subject to dissolution. A miscellany of springs, gears, hands and clock faces strewn about the room would not be a working clock; all parts must be present and in their proper relationships to be a working clock. But if God is a maximally perfect being, he cannot depend on his properties or attributes in a fashion analogous to the clock.[5] Thus God must be a perfect *unity*, or *metaphysically simple*.[6]

If God lacks physical parts he lacks a body, or, as the philosophers say, he is *incorporeal*. And if God lacks temporal parts – God's inner life does not consist of past, present and future – then he is *eternal*, or outside of time. The whole of time is immediately present to the unchanging divine consciousness. If you are starting to wonder what *can* be said of God according this tradition, it is this: God is his own metaphysically simple, unique act of perfect and unchanging being.

So the dominant picture of God according to scholastic philosophers and theologians looks like this: God is a necessarily existing person who is an essentially omnipotent, omniscient, omnibenevolent, *a se*, immutable, impassible, incorporeal, timeless and metaphysically simple act of perfect being. This "God of the philosophers" may look quite beyond our intellectual reach – we whose thinking is very much limited by space and time – and a departure from the God of popular devotion. In fact, so-called "negative theologians" insist that the gap between our cognitive powers and God's reality means that we can know only what God is not – not what he is. Aquinas is less pessimistic. While we cannot know God exhaustively, or as God knows himself, it does not follow that we can know nothing of God. Aquinas acknowledges that our accounts of persons and their properties, and the language we use to talk about them, are drawn from the everyday world of empirical experience and that in this world we never bump into metaphysically simple acts of perfect being. From this he does not conclude that we know nothing of God, but rather that we must describe God by way of analogy. For instance, when we say that humans exist and that God exists, the term "exists" is not being used in precisely the same sense in each case, since God is said to exist necessarily and we do not. But neither are the words entirely unrelated (or equivocal), as is the case when we say the word "bank" to refer to a side of a river and a repository of money. When we say that God and humans "exist", there is some overlap in meaning, but not strict equivalence (univocity) of meaning. When we say that humans are knowers and that God is a knower, again, we do not use the word "knower" in strictly the same way. For some of what humans know they know inferentially, but God does not have to reason from premises to conclusions; he has the totality of all truth immediately before the divine consciousness.[7]

The classical picture of God has come under intense scrutiny, in some cases leading to rejection. As we shall see below, this classical conception of God, particularly the aseity and immutability conditions, are difficult to defend in a world containing creatures with libertarian free will, whose choices condition the content of what God knows. Process theologians, following the lead of Alfred North Whitehead, embrace a "dynamic" conception of God, in which God's being develops in relation to the world around him.

As we shall see later, so-called "open theists" deny that God has perfect knowledge of the future choices of persons with libertarian free will. And philosophers such as Richard Gale think that a God of finite goodness, power and knowledge is preferable to the traditional account. It goes well beyond the scope of this chapter to explore all of these qualities ascribed to God. Since we have already explored aspects of God's goodness in our discussion of the moral argument and the problem of evil, we shall focus our discussion on the two other attributes deemed essential to minimal theism: power and knowledge.

Divine power

The doctrine of divine omnipotence says that God has the maximal degree of power it is possible to possess. Yet how powerful is God? The book of Job says that "the Lord ... can do all things" (Job 42:2) and, as the angel Gabriel says to Mary at the annunciation, "nothing will be impossible with God" (Luke 1:37). Do these passages mean that we should answer affirmatively the old schoolyard question: "Is God powerful enough to make a rock so big that he would be unable to lift it?" Can God make a round square? Before turning to these questions, recall the point made earlier that God's unsurpassable greatness requires that he embody every perfection essentially; that is, the perfections God has he cannot fail to have and still be God. If there were an infinitely powerful being who was also dim-witted and mean, then that being, however impressive his power, would not be God. Second, our judgements about the extent of God's power must be assessed in the light of his total nature, his goodness, wisdom, will, immateriality and so on. So, our question might be put more carefully by asking: "What does it mean to be perfect in power, while simultaneously possessing all the other attributes characteristic of divinity?"

God's omnipotence is typically analysed as his having the maximal possible power to bring about possible states of affairs. Thus stated, two conditions qualify God's perfect power. First, as Aquinas argued, being omnipotent does not require that God be able to bring about states of affairs that are logically or metaphysically impossible. For instance, God, who is the perfection of all being, cannot make it such that he both exists and does not exist simultaneously, for that would be logically impossible. Neither can he change the past, as that too, says Aquinas, would involve a contradiction (*Summa Theologiae* Ia, q.25, a.4). God cannot now make it the case that George Washington was not the first president of the United States, as that would imply that George Washington was and was not the first president of the United States. Philosophers commonly point out that when one utters a contradiction, one does not successfully identify some meaningful task that God cannot do. To say that God cannot bring it about that there exists a dimensionless cube is not to point out a limitation on God; it is merely to spout gibberish.

A second limitation on divine power – if it is a limitation at all – is that the scope of God's power be understood in the light of his other attributes. God is perfect in power, consistent with his being all-knowing and perfectly good. So it is no diminution of divine power to say that God cannot sin, as this would be contrary to his perfect goodness and thus a metaphysical impossibility. Humans can break promises, but God cannot. As strange as it may sound, humans can do things an omnipotent God cannot do, such as torture persons for sadistic pleasure. So God's power, and the rest of his attributes for that matter, must be understood by keeping the whole of God's nature in mind.[8]

Considerations of logic also militate against there being more than one omnipotent being at a time. For the sake of argument, suppose there are two omnipotent beings, A and B. A attempts to exercise its omnipotence by making a mountain in a particular location, while B attempts to exercise its omnipotence by making a plain in the exact same location. If both were successfully omnipotent, then neither would succeed in shaping the landscape to suit its own preferences. Each would be powerless to bring about a state of affairs that clearly falls within the scope of any omnipotent being's power. Therefore, each fails to be omnipotent. Thus, there cannot be two omnipotent beings (adapted from Hoffman & Rosenkrantz 2002: 168).

One might protest: "Shall the power of an infinite God be circumscribed by human logic?" Could not one claim, as Descartes seems to have done in his correspondence with Mersenne, that God is above logic and in fact invents all necessary truths? Were this the case, it would lead to the bizarre conclusion that God, if he so chose, could have made it such that $2+2=138$, with our concepts of the number two, addition and equality having just the meaning we normally give them. Setting aside the fact that we cannot impart any sense to such strings of words, other problems beset the view. Note first that a necessary state of affairs is one that obtains whether or not anyone acts to bring it about. If it is necessarily the case that ten is greater than two, then this is not something that God brings about (although the knowledge of this has always been among the things God knows). Additionally, if God could invent necessary truths then, as Alvin Plantinga points out, God would not have an essential nature, for none of the properties that characterize him would be *essential* or *metaphysically necessary* for him. God might just as well have adorned himself with different properties, for instance ignorance and moral turpitude (Plantinga 1980: 126). Furthermore, if God lacks a nature, then he must remain utterly inscrutable to us since, for all we know, God changes his nature on a regular basis. And if God is inscrutable, then he is not the sort of being one can look to for guidance, count on to keep his promises or be worthy of worship and devotion.

Our earlier discussion of the free will defence reveals another interesting limit on divine power. Not only cannot God do the logically impossible, there are also logically *possible* states of affairs that God cannot "strongly actualize" or directly bring about. One strongly actualizes some state of affairs by performing an action that directly brings about some state of affairs – turning on a light by flipping a switch, for example. Someone weakly actualizes an event by performing some act that indirectly brings the event about – turning on a light by asking someone else to flip the switch. So if I am genuinely free with respect to a wide range of morally significant actions, then whether I choose to act in a morally appropriate or inappropriate manner is up to me. If God directly causes me to refrain from acting immorally, then God strongly actualizes my action and I am not genuinely free. God cannot, consistent with my freedom, directly bring it about that I will choose not to act in some morally inappropriate way. Consider then, a world in which all its morally free inhabitants freely refrain from sinning for an entire year. While this is a logically possible world, not even an omnipotent God can directly bring it about. So we see that if God creates a world containing creatures with libertarian freedom, then there are further restrictions on divine power. This limitation on divine power is important as we consider the relationship between God's power and goodness.

Can God be free?

William Rowe, whose evidential argument from evil we considered in an earlier chapter, has posed an interesting objection to the traditional teaching that God is free with respect to creating the world (Rowe 2004). Following Leibniz, Rowe supposes there is a best of all possible worlds and that God is necessarily perfect in wisdom, power and goodness – the maximally perfect being. Then it follows, says Rowe, that God's goodness constrains him to create that world. If God must create the best of all possible worlds, then he is not free to refrain from creating a world – a clear limitation on divine power. If God lacks freedom, then he lacks what to Aquinas is a clear good, something that is better to have than to lack. Moreover, Rowe argues, if God could not do otherwise than to create, and to create the particular world he did, then he is not deserving of our praise and thanksgiving. Gratitude is owed to benefactors that give freely, not under compulsion. So why should we thank and praise someone for doing something he could not help but do? It would be like praising someone for having a pulse. To be clear, nothing external to God, no higher authority or law, compels him to create. Rather, it is his own internal nature, in particular his goodness, that Rowe says necessitates God's creating a world. A more disturbing consequence ensues from Rowe's claim that God must create the best of all possible worlds. If Rowe is right, this world, with all its attendant suffering, all its particular moral and natural evils, must be the best of all possible worlds. In short, either God is not free, a clear limitation on his power, or he is not perfectly wise or good.

Rowe is not the first philosopher to wrestle with the question of God's freedom in creating. Aquinas took up the question of God's freedom in creation, concluding that the creation of the world was what we would call today a libertarian free act of God. But as Norman Kretzmann has pointed out, there are necessitarian strains in Aquinas's thinking that challenge his commitment to God's freedom in creation (Kretzmann 1991a). First, "God necessarily wills his own being and his own goodness, and he cannot will the contrary" (*Summa contra Gentiles* I.80; 1975: 255). This essential willing is, however, contained *within* the divine being himself and does not necessarily issue forth in a created world. But Aquinas also endorses the neo-Platonist principle of Pseudo-Dionysius that God's goodness is essentially "self-diffusive" and thus productive of all being. If God must will his own goodness, and if goodness is necessarily self-diffusive, it is difficult to see how Aquinas can avoid God's having to create of necessity. Kretzmann thus parts company with Aquinas by concluding, as Rowe does, that goodness is necessarily self-diffusive, and that God must create a world.

Clearly, the freedom Rowe denies God possesses is libertarian freedom. Libertarians characteristically claim that free actions must include alternative possibilities, at the very least, that any free act is one in which the agent has the power to act or refrain from performing the act. One way to avoid Rowe's conclusion that God is not free is to ascribe to God a compatibilist freedom, which holds that free acts are compatible with their having been determined by the right sort of necessitating conditions. C. S. Lewis, although a libertarian with respect to human freedom, ascribes to God a freedom devoid of alternatives:

> The idea of what God "could have" done involves a too anthropomorphic conception of God's freedom. Whatever human freedom means, Divine freedom cannot mean indeterminacy between alternatives and a choice of one of them. Perfect goodness can never debate about the end to be attained, and perfect wisdom cannot debate about the means most suited to achieve it. The freedom of God consists in the fact that no cause other than Himself produces His acts and no external obstacle impedes them – that His own goodness is the root from which they all grow and His own omnipotence the air in which they all flower. (1962: 35)

While Lewis's ascription of compatibilist freedom may give one the satisfaction of saying that God is free, all of the troubling consequences of saying so remain: God *must* create, he must create this world with all its evils, and it remains problematic how we are to be grateful to God for what he could not help but do.

Against Lewis, one could argue that, while libertarian freedom is paradigmatically accompanied by alternatives, this is not a necessary condition of freedom. Suppose that by the end of her life, Mother Teresa had so habituated herself to acting compassionately that she was no longer able to refrain from attempting to help some suffering child she encountered on her daily rounds. Let us also suppose that Teresa's will was not always cemented in goodness, but that this condition was achieved through a lifetime of repeatedly and freely choosing to act compassionately even when it was possible for her to do otherwise. Finally, let us add that Teresa's compassionate actions originated with her will and not with any causes external to her, and that her will's being fixed in goodness was a state toward which she strove and, when achieved, identified with and fully endorsed. While Teresa's compassionate actions at the end of her life were without alternatives, it is hard to see why her acts of compassion at the end of her life were not free.[9] Could not something analogous to Teresa's end state simply be the state God has always been in? True, alternate possibilities figure prominently in Teresa's history and not God's, but if Teresa's latter-day compassionate actions display libertarian freedom without alternate possibilities, it seems plausible to think God's do too.

Why accept the claim that God must create the best of all possible worlds? For one, Rowe thinks the gap between the finite created being and the infinite uncreated being of God admits of an infinite number of degrees of separation, such that for any world God creates, he could create another that more closely approximates his own goodness. Rowe also invites us to suppose, for the sake of argument, that God creates a less than optimal world when he might have created a morally better world. Then, according to the intuition of perfect being theology, we could imagine a being greater than God who brings into being a morally superior world. But then it would follow that God is not the being than which *no* greater can be conceived – that title would go to the being capable of creating a world better than God's. So if there is no best possible world for God to create, then we must reject the existence of God as conceived in accordance with perfect being theology (Rowe 2004: 82–3).

Rowe's argument notwithstanding, there are several ways of thinking about what it means for a universe to be good that undermine the idea that there could be a best. Arthur Lovejoy, following the medieval idea that being is convertible (i.e. extensionally equivalent) to goodness, defends what he calls the "principle of plenitude". It is the thesis that:

> The range of conceivable diversity of kinds of living things is exhaustively exemplified, but also that ... the extent and abundance of creation must be as great as the possibility of existence and commensurate with the productive capacity of a "perfect" and inexhaustible Source, and that the world is better, the more things it contains.   (1960: 52)

If, as Lovejoy submits, the world is better the more things it contains, and if we assume that a world's stature is measured by how closely it reflects the goodness of its creator, then clearly there can be no best of all possible worlds. If the world is better the more things it contains, then God could always create another star, another grain of sand, another electron, and thereby enhance the goodness of the world. Even so, the gap between any created world, however good, and God's infinite goodness admits of an infinite number of degrees. "This means that omniscient, omnipotent God can no more choose the additively optimal set of parts than he can pick out the largest fraction between zero and one" (Kretzmann 1991b: 237). If the "best" universe is construed as one containing the most amount of overall value, then here too there can be no upper limit, since it is reasonable to think that whatever qualities contribute to the universe's value can always be added to and thus have no intrinsic maximum.[10] Similar remarks apply to Philip Quinn's (1982) proposal that a God perfect in power and goodness must create a world containing the maximal amount of *moral goodness*. For is it not possible that God add to the number of creatures one more, the balance of whose good choices increase the overall goodness? Even if one is convinced that it is coherent to speak of the best of all possible worlds, why rule out the idea that there are a host of worlds that tie for overall value and that God's freedom is preserved in being able to choose among them?

Yet a further difficulty with the position that God is obliged to create the best of all possible worlds is illuminated by the distinction between *logically possible* and *feasible* worlds. Logically possible worlds are those the complete description of which violates no laws of logic. Feasible worlds are logically possible worlds whose contours require that we take the choices of free creatures into consideration. Suppose God wants to create a world W containing a million inhabitants, all of whom voluntarily worship God. While this is certainly a logically possible world, it is not a world that God can *strongly actualize*, that is to say, directly bring about simply by divine fiat. Whether or not all one million people *freely* worship God – and thus whether or not God gets the world he most wants – depends on the free decisions of its inhabitants. One might suppose that if one batch of a million people fails to yield a satisfactory number of persons who freely choose to worship God, that he can substitute a different collection of free persons from whom he gets a more favourable ratio of worshippers to non-worshippers. Perhaps so. It is also possible, however, that no matter the collection of persons with which God chooses to populate his world, some will freely elect to reject rather than worship him. In which case, while the best world is logically possible, it is not feasible, since the facts about the free choices of its potential inhabitants precludes the realization of a better world. The implications of the distinction between logical and feasible worlds ought to be clear. It may turn out that the best of all possible worlds (say a world in which all its inhabitants are peaceable, just and loving) while logically possible is not a feasible world – not one that God can himself directly bring about.[11]

The paradox of the stone

But what about the stone? Let us clarify the problem. The paradox of the stone is often formulated as a dilemma: Either God can create a stone he cannot lift, or he cannot create a stone he cannot lift. If he can create a stone he cannot lift then he is not omnipotent in virtue of being unable to lift the stone. If he cannot create the stone then he is not omnipotent in virtue of being unable to create it. Either way, there is one task God cannot perform. Therefore, God is not omnipotent. Not even God can do what is logically contradictory, as we have already noted. But it is not clear that the task being posed for God by this dilemma requires that he do what is clearly contradictory. After all, if humans can build objects too big for them to lift, then why can God not do so? Is this dilemma merely a clever puzzle, or is it a potential *reductio* that threatens the very coherence of the concept of omnipotence? For if God lacks omnipotence, then by the intuitions of perfect being theology, there is no God.

One solution suggests that God can in fact create such a stone, but it poses a problem for him only if he decides to create it. Richard Swinburne argues that:

> The omnipotence of a person at a certain time includes the ability to make himself no longer omnipotent, an ability which he may or may not choose to exercise. A person may remain omnipotent for ever because he never exercises his power to create stones too heavy to lift, forces too strong to resist, or universes too wayward to control.   (1977: 158)

Were God to create the unliftable stone, it would, ironically, be his last act as an omnipotent being. But as long as he refrains from this particular action, he remains omnipotent (and, we might add, retains his divine status). On Swinburne's view, God is a being who could possibly suffer a diminution of his power. Perfect being theologians would no doubt insist that a being superior to Swinburne's God is imaginable, namely one who cannot be dispossessed of his power but who possesses maximal power essentially. And if God possesses omnipotence essentially, then, as George Mavrodes argues, the paradox of the stone is impossible. For God's creating a stone so heavy he subsequently will not be able to lift it logically reduces to "a stone that cannot be lifted by Him whose power is sufficient for lifting anything" (Mavrodes 1963: 222). Since it is no slight on omnipotence not to be able to bring about the incoherent, we really have no paradox of the stone.

We have compiled quite a list of things God cannot do: create a round square, break a promise, create the best of all possible worlds, undo the past and guarantee that the choices of free creatures will perfectly coincide with every logically possible creation scenario. Peter Geach thinks the word "omnipotent" is the wrong term to describe God's power, as it suggests to many that God can do anything whatsoever, and we see that this is not the case. Geach prefers the word "almighty", by which is meant that God is the most powerful being, without equal or superior in power. Is this sufficient for divinity? Is an almighty God perfect enough for the perfect being theologians? Here, perhaps, it is appropriate to recall the ontological gap separating God and humans. Intellectual humility requires that humans acknowledge that we lack the raw, ratiocinative horsepower to plumb the depths of the divine nature. To think otherwise, suggests Kierkegaard, to think that God's nature is utterly transparent to our powers of inspection, is to invite the objection that we have invented our own God.

Divine omniscience

To say God is omniscient is to claim that he knows all and only true propositions. But what should be included within the scope of "every truth"? Does God have exhaustive knowledge of the future? Does he, for example, know everything I will ever think or do? Does he have knowledge of alternative futures – futures that would have come about had humans made choices other than the ones they did? Can he know what I am experiencing when I am enjoying a good bottle of wine? Does the God who made sound waves, thus making music possible, know how Mozart's Jupiter Symphony goes? As we shall see, these questions lead some philosophers who consider them to reject aspects of the classical account of God's nature limned above.

Contrasting divine and human knowledge will take us a little way towards understanding the doctrine of divine omniscience. It will also reveal some of the philosophical questions the doctrine generates. Assuming that humans lack innate knowledge, that we are born blank slates, it follows that all our knowledge must be acquired. God, however, cannot be said to acquire knowledge, as this would imply that God was at some time deficient in knowledge. From this it follows that none of God's knowledge is inferential, for this would imply a movement of thought, from lacking some conclusion to acquiring one. Ascribing inferential knowledge to God would also imply that God changes and, if he changes, that he is not immutable as the classical conception of God would have it.

How does God know? An imperfect analogue for divine knowledge might be self-evident knowledge for humans. Humans do not reason to propositions such as $A = A$ or $10 > 2$. They are self-evidently obvious to suitably mature human reasoners. No sooner do we grasp what these claims mean, then we see that they are true and indeed must be true. For this sort of intuitive knowledge, said Locke, "the mind is at no pains of proving or examining, but perceives the truth as the eye doth light, only by being directed toward it" (*Essay Concerning Human Understanding* IV.ii.1; 1959: 176–7). God's mind, unlike ours, is in no need of being directed towards his knowledge; rather the totality of all knowledge is immediately, non-discursively, and occurrently before the divine mind, in one comprehensive intellectual vision. (Aquinas taught that, strictly speaking, God's knowledge does not even assume the form of discrete propositions, but that for God all truths form part of one comprehensive intellectual vision.) From this it follows that God, unlike humans, lacks memorial knowledge. He has no need to recall anything, since the entirety of God's knowledge is ever before his mind.

Yet a further difference between divine and human knowledge concerns the type of knowledge peculiar to divine and human knowers. The bulk of human knowledge is owing to perception. To know what a rose smells like or a banana tastes like is to have experiential knowledge that most philosophers think is not reducible to propositional knowledge. God, lacking a body, cannot have olfactory knowledge, kinaesthetic knowledge or other forms of experiential knowledge that require a body. Is this a deficiency in God's knowledge? Is God's omniscience threatened by his lack of a body, or should we rather say that the non-bodily manner of divine knowing is superior to that of humans? The classical tradition would deem it a deficiency, not a perfection, for God to acquire knowledge through sensations associated with bodily organs, since God does not acquire any knowledge, and to have sense organs would compromise God's aseity for the reasons already mentioned.

Our being temporal, embodied beings also makes possible what philosophers call "indexical knowledge", which locates our knowledge claims to a particular time, location, or to the unique first-person perspective each of us has of our own experiences. Knowledge *de praesenti*, as philosophers call it, is knowledge indexed essentially to some particular moment of time. A husband calls home to tell his wife "my plane is boarding right *now*". "My plane is boarding now" uttered at noon is not the same claim as "my plane is boarding now" uttered at midnight. What the indexical term "now" refers to changes with each utterance. If I tell you "My holiday starts tomorrow", uttered on 1 March, then I refer to 2 March. If I utter the same phrase on 2 March, I obviously refer to 3 March as the start of my holiday. Yet if God is eternal, that is to say, outside of time, how can he know such tensed truths – truths that stand in relations of past or future to the present? God, being perfect in knowledge, knows all truths. If he knows all truths then he always knows what time it is. But since the time is constantly changing, so would the content of God's knowledge. And if God is undergoing change, he cannot be immutable, as the classical conception of God insists.[12]

The other troublesome case for omniscience is posed by what philosophers call knowledge *de se*. Consider the claim "I think, therefore I am." Although the same expression can be uttered both by Descartes and me, what Descartes accepts when he utters it is not what I accept when I utter the same expression. The proposition I utter could be marked "private access only". But since God and I are distinct persons, how can he have knowledge from *my* first person perspective? Let us look at each problem in turn.

One might think that any tensed truth is easily convertible into a tenseless equivalent by using clock and calendar time. John's saying "Today is the first day of my holiday", can be expressed without the indexical term "today" as "John's holiday begins at 5pm on 15 June 2010". One might think that God's knowledge of a tenseless equivalent for every *de praesenti* expression would preserve his omniscience without compromising his timelessness. But are these expressions equivalent? Suppose that on 1 June 2010 you are hospitalized in a coma due to an unfortunate automobile accident. You awaken, and the first piece of information conveyed to you is that your brother John's holiday begins at 5pm on 15 June 2010. Do you know whether or not John has actually begun his holiday? No! Not until you know what the present date is. William Craig thinks a timeless God faces a predicament similar to our coma patient.

A being that knew all tenseless facts about the world, including which events *occur* at any date and time, would still be completely in the dark about tensed facts. He would have no idea at all of what is now going on in the universe, of which events are past and which are future. On the other hand, any being which *does* know tensed facts cannot be timeless, for his knowledge must be in constant flux, as the tensed facts known by him change.   (2001: 99)[13]

Jonathan Kvanvig defends God's ability to know the same propositional content we possess through our first-person and temporal perspectives, although not in precisely the same way humans know them. The difference between God and us rests not on whether God knows the same content we do, but *how* God knows it. Whereas we grasp this content of expressions using indexicals such as "now" *directly*, God grasps the same content *indirectly*. Kvanvig understands the indexical expressions such as "now", "today" and "yesterday" to express what he calls "the essence" of the moment in time to which it refers. An essence is a unique property or properties of a thing that make it the thing it is and differentiate it from all other things. Kvanvig argues that each moment of time has its own unique essence that makes it a unique moment of time, different from any other moment of time.

The notion of individual moments of time having an essence that uniquely identifies them is admittedly a strange notion. Perhaps the following analogy will help. Consider the colour spectrum, spreading out from red on one end, moving through orange, yellow, green, blue and purple on the other end. One could conceptually slice the colour spectrum into an infinite number of colour slices, each slice varying ever so slightly in hue or tone from the one next to it. Each infinitely thin slice of the colour spectrum would have it own unique colour – its own colour essence, if you will. Now, instead of slices of colour, think of slices of time having their unique essence, each moment differing in its properties from the moment nearest to it. Times, lacking hue and tone, make it difficult to see precisely in virtue of what each moment of time is marked out as unique. Moreover, Kvanvig's solution leaves us to wonder just whether it is hours, minutes, seconds, nanoseconds or some infinitesimally smaller unit of time that possesses a unique essence.

Consider again the indexical expressions "today is 1 March 2010" and "yesterday was 1 March 2010", uttered on 2 March. The uses of "today" and "yesterday" pick out the exact same time in March by referring to the same essence of time. Humans who move through time apprehend *directly* the essence of the moment referred to by the word "now" – by *being in the moment*, as it were – and as a result form a present tense belief. If a person grasps the essence of the moment at some time other than the present, what he knows will be expressed using some other tense. God, being timeless, grasps the essential content of our indexical expressions but does *not* form tensed beliefs in the way we do, that is as beings immersed in the flux of time. Kvanvig thus concludes:

> If God does not directly grasp any proposition including temporal aspects, it does not follow that He is not omniscient. For even if He only indirectly grasps all temporal moments, it is still the case that He can know all true propositions. Hence it might be thought that one can affirm the doctrines of time-lessness, immutability and omniscience by affirming that God indirectly grasps every temporal moment, and directly grasps none of them. (1986: 159)

Craig argues that Kvanvig's solution succumbs to the very objection he levelled against the reduction of tensed statements to un-tensed statements. For Kvanvig's "essences of time" don't indicate whether those times are past, present, or future. Moreover, if a time were essentially a past time, then it is impossible for it ever to be present, which Craig thinks is absurd. And if God is eternal, he could not timelessly grasp some essentially present moment without existing at that moment.

Edward Wierenga adopts a strategy similar to Kvanvig's to respond to the problem of *de se*, first-person knowledge (Wierenga 1989: 175–86). He modifies the account slightly by insisting that persons have *haecceities* or *individual essences* – essences that not only mark you as the kind of being you are but as the particular individual you are. While you share your human essence with millions of others, no one else has your *haecceity*. Wierenga proposes that we analyse my *de se* knowledge of, say, "I am looking at a mountain", as the acceptance of a proposition that implies the conjunction of my essence and the fact that I am looking at a mountain. Like Kvanvig, Wierenga denies that my first-person propositions necessarily include a privacy condition restricting knowledge of them to me. It is true both that my individual essence is a property I necessarily have and no other thing can possibly have, and that only

I can express my "I-propositions". But from the fact that only I can have my essence and only I can express the propositions entailing my essence, it does not follow, according to Wierenga, that only I can know my first-person propositions.

Both Kvanvig and Wierenga appeal to essences of moments of time and individual essences of persons to show how divine omniscience is compatible with first-person and temporally located knowledge. Many philosophers are suspicious of the metaphysically esoteric notions these thinkers invoke (see Chisholm 1981: 16–17). Even so, there is an underlying point each is at pains to make. From the fact that God does not gain knowledge in precisely the same way we do, via sensory organs arranged on the head, it does not follow that God does not have access to the same knowledge by other means. Consider an analogy. Suppose humans evolve to the point of being telepathic, making unnecessary the need to communicate our inner thoughts via sounds in the throat and flapping of the tongue. A genetic miscopy produces an unfortunate throwback, unable to communicate telepathically but only through speech. Miscommunication is frequent because he lacks a vocabulary perfectly suited to convey the complexity of thoughts, experiences and emotions so easily communicated telepathically. True, our throwback would have experiential acquaintance with the sensation of speech that his fellows lack, but surely this is no deficiency in the rest of the race. They have the same, arguably superior, knowledge through another modality. If Kvanvig and Wierenga are right, God stands in an analogous relation to us regarding tensed knowledge as the telepathic humans do to our genetic anomaly. Even if the problem of indexical knowledge can be squared with the classical conception of God, sceptics insist that the doctrine of divine omniscience faces its biggest challenge in being reconciled to human freedom.[14]

God's omniscience and human freedom

One of the main philosophical challenges posed by saying that God is omniscient rests not with the claim itself, but with its alleged implications for human freedom. If God knew from the foundation of the world that I will go to the zoo tomorrow, then it looks as though I am not free to act otherwise than as God foreknows. Plainly, God cannot be omniscient and also be mistaken in his belief that I will go to the zoo. Moreover, most of us think that the past is fixed and unalterable; past events are, to use philosophical terminology, "accidentally necessary". Not even God can now undo the fact that Winston Churchill was Prime Minister during the Second World War. So if God knew in the past that I would go to the zoo tomorrow, and he cannot be mistaken, then it seems impossible that I act otherwise than as God knows. To claim I could act otherwise, say, by going to the cinema instead, appears to entail either that I can cause God to have a false belief or that I have power to change the past and what God has always believed, claims that traditional theists cannot concede. And if I cannot act otherwise than as God knows I will act, then I am not free. So to affirm with classical theism that God is omniscient seems to require that we deny humans are free to choose among alternative courses of action.

For the sake of clarity and precision, let us examine a formalized argument of William Hasker's (1989: 69):

1. It is now true that Clarence will have a cheese omelette for breakfast tomorrow. [Premise]
2. It is impossible that God should at any time believe what is false, or fail to believe anything that is true. [Premise: divine omniscience]
3. Therefore, God has always believed that Clarence will have a cheese omelette for breakfast tomorrow. [From 1, 2]
4. If God has always believed a certain thing, it is not in anyone's power to bring it about that God has not always believed that thing. [Premise: the unalterability of the past]
5. Therefore, it is not in Clarence's power to bring it about that God has not always believed that he would have a cheese omelette for breakfast. [From 3, 4]
6. It is not possible for it to be true both that God has always believed that Clarence would have a cheese omelette for breakfast, and that he does not in fact have one. [From 2]
7. Therefore, it is not in Clarence's power to refrain from having a cheese omelette for breakfast tomorrow. [From 5, 6]

So Clarence's eating the omelette tomorrow is not an act of free choice.

Several details of this argument are worth highlighting. First, God is here depicted as believing in time – *before* Clarence eats an omelette. One view of God's eternality is that God has always existed, exists now and will always exist at all points of time. This view, called "sempiternality", differs from the classical idea of eternality in which God exists outside any temporal framework. As we shall see below, Thomists, among others, appeal to this classical notion eternality to reconcile God's omniscience and human freedom. Second, this argument depends on a principle of the fixity or the unalterability of the past. Before Lincoln became the sixteenth president of the United States, the fact of his being president was contingent – still somewhat malleable. Perhaps he could have chosen to remain a country lawyer. But now that he was in fact the sixteenth president, the truth has hardened, acquiring the force of necessity, so that not even God can undo this fact. Third, God's essential omniscience means that he believes infallibly; it is impossible that he believe something and it fail to be true.

A fourth crucial feature implicit in Hasker's argument is a "transfer of necessity principle".[15] If A is necessarily the case, and it is necessary that if A is the case, then B is the case, then it is necessary that B is the case ($\Box A$; $\Box$(If A then B); therefore $\Box B$). We can illustrate this with the weaker notion of physical necessity. Suppose climate conditions and the laws of nature make it necessary that (A): the temperature will drop below freezing tonight. It is also physically necessary that (B): if the temperature drops below freezing, the water in the birdbath will turn to ice. So (C): it is physically necessary that the water in the birdbath will turn to ice. The transfer of necessity principle has also been formulated as a "transfer of powerlessness principle". For if we are powerless to prevent the temperature from freezing tonight, and the water in the birdbath turning to ice is necessarily connected to the freezing temperature, then we are powerless to prevent the water in the birdbath from turning to ice (see Fischer 1989: 6ff.). The application to the case of divine foreknowledge is plain. If God knew yesterday that Clarence would eat an omelette tomorrow, then God's knowledge is now accidentally necessary. God's essential omniscience ensures that it is necessarily the case that, if God knew yesterday Clarence would eat an omelette tomorrow, then, according to the argument, it is necessary that Clarence eat an omelette tomorrow. Therefore, Clarence is not free to do other-wise than eat the omelette.

Some philosophers resort to drastic measures to solve our prob-lem, either by abandoning divine foreknowledge, jettisoning liber-tarian freedom or denying that there are truths about the future. Richard Swinburne holds that arguments such as Hasker's not only show that omniscience precludes human libertarian freedom, but worse yet, they also show that God lacks freedom. If God knows infallibly from the foundation of the world every decision *he* will make, then he too is not free to deviate from what he infallibly knows in the past about his own future plans and purposes. In order to accommodate the traditional belief that God is free, Swinburne limits God's knowledge to all propositions about the past, present and only those propositions about the future that are physically necessitated by the past.

> That God is omniscient only in the attenuated sense would of course – given that he is perfectly free and omnipotent – have resulted from his own choice. In choosing to preserve his own freedom (and to give freedom to others), he limits his own knowledge of what is to come. He continually limits himself in this way by not curtailing his or men's future freedom.
>
> (1977: 176)

God could have exhaustive knowledge of the future simply by decreeing all that will ever occur, although he refrains from this for freedom's sake. How, exactly, God succeeds in shielding himself from all that future knowledge is a mystery.

Similar to Swinburne's view is that of "open theism". Open the-ists affirm that God is omniscient, but circumscribe the scope of omniscience to exclude knowledge of the future free actions of free creatures. It is not that God voluntarily chooses not to peek into the future, as Swinburne suggests, but rather that the truth about my future free actions is indeterminate; no truth about my future free choices exists yet. Even so, open theists acknowledge that God knows much of the future, since much of it follows deterministi-cally from the laws of nature and the history of the universe. Also, God, being intimately familiar with our individual histories and psychologies, has highly probable beliefs about how we are likely to choose. Open theists also admit that some things will happen in the future simply because God decrees them to happen. So, on this view, God is like a playwright, who sketches the general contours of the plot, but leaves room for improvisation on the part of the actors. Theists in the Judaeo-Christian tradition argue that this view fails to account for God's prophetic knowledge of the future: for example, "before the cock crows, you will deny me three times," as Jesus prophesies of Peter.

One can also resolve the alleged incompatibility between divine foreknowledge and libertarian freedom by abandoning the latter, as do contemporary compatibilists. Briefly, compatibilists think it perfectly coherent to say that some human actions are both free and determined. Free actions, on this view, are those that arise unimpeded and uncoerced from our own interior wants and desires. What compatibilists deny, however, is that our own history and the laws of nature leave us free to have desires other than the ones we do. As I believe Bertrand Russell once quipped on this view, "you are free to do as you please, but you are not free to please as you please". More germane here is the theological variant of compatibilism, in which God's providential control of the world includes his determining the structure of our wants and desires. As Paul Helm puts it: "Not only is every atom and molecule, every thought and desire, kept in being by God, but every twist and turn of each of these is under the direct control of God" (1994: 22).[16]

Some philosophers, following remarks in Aristotle's *On Interpretation*, hold that God is in time but lacks knowledge of the future because, strictly speaking, there are no true statements about the future for God to know. And if there are no truths about the future, then one does not depreciate divine omniscience to say God does not know them. Why would someone say there are no truths about the future? One analysis of what it means to say a proposition is true holds that there are truth-bearers and truth-makers. A truth-bearer, such as the proposition "Stonehenge is in England" is *made* true by Stonehenge's actually being in England. By contrast, the proposition "Prince Harry will have four children" has no corresponding truth-maker, no *current* state of affairs to make the proposition true. So, strictly speaking, there are no truths about the future for God to know. Philosophical and theological problems beset this simple analysis of statements about the future. First, many other true statements we make, such as the universal generalization that "All crows are black" is not grounded in any current state of affairs, since the generalization is about all crows, past, present and presumably future. Second, this proposal runs counter to the traditional theistic claim that God not only knows the future, but prophesies to humans that certain events will take place.

Setting these drastic manoeuvres to one side, we turn to the three main solutions to the problem posed by God's infallible foreknowledge, all with roots in the medieval scholastic tradition.

The divine timelessness solution

Luminaries such as Augustine, Anselm and Aquinas claim that the problem of divine foreknowledge and human freedom is a pseudo-problem in so far as it suggests that God exists in time. Strictly speaking, God does not have *fore*knowledge. If God is outside of time, he is aware only of one eternal present, a single unvarying glance of all that ever happens. Again, imagine moments of time like the individual frames of a movie reel unwound from their spool and spread out in a line. Each frame could be labelled, t_1, t_2, t_3 and so on, where each "t" denominated a day, hour, minute or whatever slice of time one wishes. We humans could at a glance take in a few frames at most, but God, being omniscient, would be able to take in each and every frame with a single glance. No moment of time is any less available to his gaze than another. So God stands to the whole of time analogous to the way you and I do when observing some current event presently unfolding before us. Note, however, that merely to observe an event occurring is not thereby to cause that event to happen. The order of knowledge and the order of causation do not necessarily coincide. To update a common medieval illustration, from my vantage point atop a hill, I may observe two cars on the winding road below me, one going up, the other down. Due to their speed, the width of the road and the blind curve toward which they are approaching, I see that they are headed inescapably toward a collision. My presently watching this scene unfold does not, of course, cause it to occur. If this analogy is apt, then neither does God's all encompassing observation of the events of history efficiently cause those events.

The view that God is outside of time has problems of its own. Craig (2009), for instance, thinks that once God creates and then sustains a changing world moment by moment, he is implicated in time. A God outside of time poses additional problems for notions of providence, prayer and other sorts of divine–human interaction. If God is, as the medievals thought, a pure and perfect act of timeless being, then in what sense is divine and human dialogue possible? Christians speak of prayer as a divine–human dialogue in which God answers prayer *because* we prayed, that is, as a response to our prayer. But if God is outside of time, this account of divine–human dialogue is not possible. Others think the notion of a timeless God, with its perceptual metaphor of God passively perceiving each and every moment of time in a single, unchanging, comprehensive vision, fails to give God the freedom to act in creation, in particular, in the future. Suppose a student receives acceptances from three different universities and is trying to decide which to attend. She prays to God: "Lord, at which of the three universities will I have the best overall collegiate experience?" On the timelessness view, God sees only the choice our petitioner actually makes, not the alternative futures that would have transpired had she chosen to go elsewhere. So how can God answer this prayer?[17]

Even if one waives the vexing issues that accompany timelessness, it is not clear this move resolves the problem of divine omniscience and human freedom. Again, imagine God sees in one comprehensive vision each and every moment of my existence. In frame t_1 he sees my birth, in frame t_2 my wedding day, in frame t_3 my death. God's fixed, unchanging vision sees the moment of my death, and there is nothing I can do to alter God's unchangeable vision of what transpires in frame t_3. Linda Zagzebski (2007: 112) puts the problem in the form of the following argument:

1. God timelessly believes K and is infallible.
2. Nobody now can do anything about the fact that God timelessly believes K and is infallible.
3. Nobody can do anything about the fact that if God timelessly believes K and is infallible, then A will kill B on Saturday (what is next Saturday to us).
4. So nobody now can do anything about the fact that A will kill B on Saturday (what is next Saturday to us).

5. So *A* will not kill *B* freely.

If we can do no more to change God's timeless believing than we can his past believing, then it looks as though there is no advantage to the timelessness solution.

The Ockhamist solution: distinguishing between hard and soft facts

Is there a way to keep both divine foreknowledge and a robust account of human freedom? Marilyn Adams brought renewed attention to the work of late medieval philosopher William of Ockham, who argued that not all statements about the past are, strictly speaking, irrevocably true in a way that makes them accidentally necessary.

> Some propositions are about the present as regards both their wording and their subject matter (*secundum vocem et secundum rem*). Where such [propositions] are concerned, it is universally true that every true proposition about the present has [corresponding to it] a necessary one about the past – e.g., "Socrates is seated," "Socrates is walking," "Socrates is just," and the like.
>
> Other propositions are about the present as regards their wording only and are equivalently about the future, since their truth depends on the truth of propositions about the future. Where such [propositions] are concerned, the rule that every true proposition about the present has [corresponding to it] a necessary one about the past is not true.
>
> (Ockham 1983: 46–7)

The crucial distinction drawn by Ockham is that between what we now call "hard facts" about the past and "soft facts" about the past, only the former being accidentally necessary. Consider the proposition "The Second World War began in 1939"; it is strictly about the past and no one, not even God, can alter its being true. Now consider the claim "The Second World War began eighty years before I took my wife on a cruise". This claim is only partially about the past – "in its wording only", as Ockham put it – since it is also about how some fact in the past is related to a contingent future event over which I can yet exercise some power. I can make this claim, partially about the past, true by picking up the telephone and booking a cruise for my wife and myself. Statements of the form "God knew that S would do A" do not express irrevocably true hard facts about the past, but soft facts, whose truth is contingent on my free actions now or in the future. So it is false that God's having forever known about what I will do tomorrow is accidentally necessary in the sense that puts them beyond my counterfactual power.

Defenders of the distinction between hard facts and soft facts nevertheless admit that it is very difficult to specify exactly the difference between facts *strictly* about the past and those *not strictly* about the past, and between facts that are *accidentally necessary* and those that are not. John Martin Fischer summarizes an unsuccessful attempt to define soft facts by an "entailment criterion of soft facthood" forwarded by Marilyn Adams: "A fact F about t_1 is a soft fact about t_1 if and only if F's obtaining entails that something (contingent) occurs at some later time t_2" (Fischer 1992: 35). The problem, as Fischer points out, is that on the entailment criterion, every fact winds up being classified as a soft fact. To use Fischer's example, suppose that "John is sitting at t_1" – clearly a hard fact about t_1. John's sitting at t_1 entails that John does not sit for the first time at t_2, which entails the "not-happening" of "Jack sits for the first time at t_2". But because of the entailment criterion of soft facthood, one must now say that "John is sitting at t_1" is a soft fact, not a hard fact. And this point is generalizable: John is writing at t_1, John is laughing at t_1, Mary is laughing at t_1 and so on.

Alvin Plantinga analyses accidental necessity in terms of "counterfactual power over the past". Recall premise 4 of Hasker's argument: "If God has always believed a certain thing, it is not in anyone's power to bring it about that God has not always believed that thing. [Premise: the unalterability of the past]". So if God believed at t_1, some point in the past, that Clarence would eat an omelette at some later time t_2 (this coming Saturday), then, on Hasker's view, God's belief at t_1 is a hard fact. Not, however, if Clarence possesses "counterfactual power" over the past. That is to say, not if it was within Clarence's power at t_2 to do something such that *if he had done it*, then God would not have in fact held the belief he did at t_1. Suppose that Clarence is free on Saturday to eat an omelette or pancakes. He eats an omelette. Since God infallibly knows all future events, he would have believed at t_1, prior to Saturday, that Clarence would eat an omelette. So, as a matter of fact, Clarence's choice of an omelette coincides with what God foreknew. But does this mean, as Hasker argues, that Clarence was powerless to act otherwise? Not necessarily. If Clarence was free on Saturday to eat pancakes instead, then it was within his power on Saturday so to act that he *would have* brought it about that God believed at t_1 that Clarence ate pancakes instead. So if Clarence possesses counterfactual power over the past, God's knowledge at t_1 is a soft fact about the past, not a hard fact about the past, thus preserving Clarence's freedom.

The Molinist solution

One final, ingenious solution for reconciling divine omniscience and human freedom stems from the work of Luis de Molina, a sixteenth-century Jesuit philosopher, and is called Divine Middle Knowledge or, appropriately enough, "Molinism". Molinism's robust account of divine omniscience ascribes three "moments" or aspects to God's knowledge, two moments that are "before" God's decision to create a world (i.e. "pre-volitional" moments), and one "after". (There is no temporal progression, since God is outside of time, according to Molina.) First, and *logically* most prior, is the knowledge God has by his very nature as an essentially omniscient being. This "natural knowledge" encompasses knowledge of everything that it is logically possible to bring about, as well as knowledge of all necessary truths, such as the truths of logic and mathematics. The third and logically last moment is God's "free knowledge", arising from God's free decision to bring about one among the many possible worlds. Once God selects a particular creation scenario, then he has "post-volitional" knowledge of all the truths characterizing the world he has willed to create. Now, if God elects to populate his world with free creatures then, in order for God to get just the world he wants, he needs to know "in advance" how every free creature will choose in every circumstance in which it is free. So after God's natural knowledge, and logically prior to his free knowledge, is what Molina called God's "middle knowledge", for it is between the others in the logical progression of God's thinking about what to create. By his middle knowledge, God knows what philosophers call "the counterfactuals of freedom". These propositions are said to be contingently true, and have the form: If person S were in circumstances C, then S would freely do X in C. So before God creates a world, he knows for every possible free creature, in every situation in which it chooses freely, how it will exercise its power of free choice. So on this view, God has perfect foreknowledge of the world simply in virtue of his prevolitional knowledge plus his decision to create some particular world and some particular persons.

Advocates of divine middle knowledge think it confers interesting and important theological and philosophical advantages. In addition to knowing the actual future, God knows possible futures that would have come about had his creatures made free choices other than the ones they did, or had God populated the world with different free creatures. This knowledge gives God meticulous providential control over creation, for by knowing all the possible free creatures and all the choices they would make in any free situations they confront, God was able to populate the world with just those free agents whose free choices coincided with his purposes.

Molinism also offers a powerful explanation for some of the ways God providentially interacts with humans. Return to the earlier example in which you receive simultaneous scholarship offers from three different universities of equivalent stature. Suppose further that you pray to God, asking him to guide you to that university which will contribute to your enjoying the best overall collegiate experience. If God had only simple foreknowledge, that is, the ability to look into the actual future, all he can do is tell you about the choice you in fact will make. If God has middle knowledge, however, he can see how your life *would have* unfolded had you chosen differently and can thus better answer your prayer. The doctrine of divine middle knowledge also offers a solution to the apparent injustice of those theological perspectives that require one to hold certain doctrines as a necessary condition for enjoying eternal beatitude. How are babies who die in infancy or remote people who have never heard the required doctrines to qualify for the afterlife? The Molinist has a ready answer: God knows how such persons *would have chosen* had they heard the requisite teachings. Most importantly for our purposes, divine middle knowledge offers a way to reconcile divine omniscience and human freedom (see Craig 1987: 127–51).

Despite its apparent advantages, critics have not spared Molinism, attacking both its philosophical coherence and alleged theological advantages. Perhaps the most oft cited objection to Molinism is the so-called "grounding objection".[18] What makes the counterfactuals of creaturely freedom true? What makes it true and therefore possible for God to know, that "Had I not become a philosopher, I would freely have joined the mob"? How can there be a truth about what university my tenth child will select, since I do not have a tenth child? What makes statements about possible but non-existent creatures true?

Some of the typical ways of understanding the truth conditions for counterfactual statements do not appear to work for the counterfactuals of creaturely freedom. Suppose, contrary to fact: "If I had thrown the wine glass against a wall, it would have shattered". We know this must be true given the laws of nature and the inherent physical structure of the entities referred to. But counterfactuals of freedom cannot be grounded in physical necessitation or they would not be counterfactuals of *freedom*. Suppose you know me to be a somewhat dishonest character, and you wonder whether it is true that, "if I offered Wood £1,000, he would give me a grade of A for the class". It is reasonable to think that this is true because of deeply anchored, habitual tendencies in my character. But tendencies of character surely do not give one certain knowledge about what I *would* do, but only a probabilistic belief about what I *might* do, or *probably* will do. From time to time free agents do act out of character, after all. Critics of Molinism claim that counterfactual statements about what an agent might do or would probably do, do not give God the knowledge he needs for meticulous providential control of the world. Critics claim that truth-maker theory fares no better. Recall that truth-makers are that in virtue of which a proposition is true. So what makes the proposition "St Paul's Cathedral is in London" true is the state of affairs of St Paul's being in London. So, says the critic of middle knowledge, as there are no states of affairs, or truth-makers, that ground claims about my tenth child or other non-existent beings, we have no way to understand how such claims could be true and we can make no sense of what it would mean for God to know them.

Advocates of Molinism counter by claiming that they are more confident that there are true counterfactuals of creaturely freedom than they are of any theory that requires that counterfactuals have grounds, or truth-makers. Moreover, the critic's objection about a lack of grounds is founded on the false idea that grounds must take the form of concrete objects. But as we saw earlier, we express many sorts of propositions whose truth does not depend on the physical world being a certain way, but rather on some abstract state of affairs obtaining. Negative existentials, such as the claim "there are no dinosaurs", is true, but not because it is grounded in the way the world is now. Similar remarks can be made about moral truths such as "It is wrong to torture children", universal generalizations such as "All crows are black", or future-tense propositions such as "Astronauts will land on Mars in 2050". None of these propositions is true in virtue of the physical world being a certain way. As Fred Freddosso has proposed, just as past-tense statements are true because of the way the world was, and future-tense statements are true because of the way the world will be, perhaps counterfactual conditionals are true because of the way the world *would be*.

A second objection to Molinism is that the doctrine places unacceptable limitations on divine creativity. For according to Molinism, the counterfactual truths of human freedom are not made true by God, but by the free decisions of the agents whom they are about, otherwise they would not be truths of *freedom*. So when God goes to create the world, he does not make the contingent truths about creaturely freedom; they are already true independently of God's creative activity, and all God can do is select which among the array of truths he wishes to instantiate. It is as if God goes to the divine workshop to make a world and finds many of the raw materials available for his use are already in place. He is at liberty to use them or not, or to use only those that suit his purposes, but he is stuck with the materials on hand. This leads, as we have already seen, to some logically possible worlds not being feasible worlds. God may want to actualize a world in which all free creatures choose friendship with himself, but it is also possible that the counterfactuals of creaturely freedom do not align with God's preferences. Some find this an unacceptable limitation on both divine power and freedom.[19] Molinists deny that this limitation is significantly different than God's creative endeavours being constrained by the laws of logic and his own moral nature.

Perhaps these limitations would be acceptable if the doctrine of divine middle knowledge delivered all its alleged benefits. Robert Adams argues that the semantics of counterfactual conditionals calls into question the use God is said to make of middle knowledge. I am in fact married and a teacher of philosophy. But suppose I had not gotten married. Any number of things might have happened. If I had not gotten married, I might still have gone into philosophy, or maybe I would have run away and joined the French Foreign Legion, become a monk or a deep-sea explorer. And God is supposed to know which of these counterfactuals, if any, is true. How shall we understand the truth of "If I had remained a bachelor, I would have gone into philosophy"? The traditional analysis of counterfactual statements employs the core metaphor of proximity to the actual world. So if the history of the actual world remained just as it is with the lone exception of my remaining a bachelor, then what world is next in proximity (similarity) to the actual world? The answer "I would go into philosophy" is supposed to be correct in virtue of being in closer proximity than any alternative named above. But if proximity to the actual world is the basis on which we make sense of which among the many possible counterfactuals is the true one, then we must first know which is the actual world before we can determine which counterfactual is closest. But God is supposed to know which counterfactuals are true *before* he creates the actual world. So on this explanation, God cannot use the truths of counterfactuals in the way he is said to use them.

To see a related objection, recall our earlier example about choosing a university. If it is a free choice, then presumably God knew from the foundation of the world which university you would choose. In fact, he instantiated the world with you in it knowing in advance that you would make the particular free choices you do. So what good does it do you if God knows that you would have been happier had you chosen differently? He has created you precisely because he already knew how you would exercise your freedom. So it does not appear that Molinism even delivers one of its vaunted benefits.

In this chapter we have only scratched the surface of many intricate and profound issues that arise when we ask about God's omnipotence and omniscience. Matters would grow more complex still were we to have surveyed other traits ascribed to God, such as simplicity, impassability and immutability, to name but a few. We have seen that enquiring about God touches on most of the main areas of philosophical enquiry: logic, the nature of freedom, causation, time, knowledge and many more. Whether or not one believes in God, the philosophical issues generated by the traditional concept of God remain deeply challenging and rewarding to those who pursue them.

Conclusion

The debate concerning God's existence, like many debates in philosophy – the success of sceptical arguments, the nature of time, the moral permissibility of war and scores of examples like them – is a matter on which the best philosophical minds disagree. Partisans of both sides can be found who present and defend their arguments with rigour and sophistication, find these arguments compelling and at the same time seem to have a clear understanding of their opponents' views. From this we can, I think, derive several lessons. One obvious lesson is that this debate, like most debates in philosophy (indeed, like many debates in academia) is one for which we should not soon expect some final philosophical resolution. Nor can we insist that all parties who find themselves in such protracted debates simply suspend judgement, for this would require that most academics jettison many of their intellectual commitments. Besides, the very principle that mandates suspension of belief in the face of disagreement is itself a matter of disagreement, thus hoist on its own petard, as they say.

Second, a small dose of intellectual humility and generosity should help us to appreciate that persons of good mind and sincere will can be found on either side of the debate. This, in turn, should preclude quick dismissals of those with whom we disagree as silly, stupid or in open defiance of the most basic standards of rationality. Respect rather than ridicule for one's interlocutors is the only way forward. As noted earlier, William Rowe once described himself as a "friendly atheist". While persuaded by the arguments for atheism, Rowe was nevertheless able to appreciate how someone might rationally estimate the force of the evidence differently than he did. Likewise, "friendly theists" see and appreciate the force of their opponent's views, even if they judge the cases differently. The ability imaginatively to project oneself into the mindset of another should be seen as perfectly compatible with being firmly convinced that one's own views best capture the truth. Indeed, given the perennial debates to which the history of philosophy treats us, we should be surprised to find matters otherwise.

Some philosophical debates are such that it matters very little, if at all, for the course of our daily lives on which side of the debate we fall. It is hard to see how our preference for the A theory over the B theory with respect to time, or for the axioms of S4 over S5 in modal logic, obtrude into our daily lives except, perhaps, for those whose research centres around such debates. Many philosophical questions bear little, if at all, on how we live our lives. In other cases, our day-to-day lives must be lived in defiance of our philosophical convictions. Hume acknowledged that, while his philosophical reasoning made him sceptical (and melancholy!) about the uniformity of nature's laws, nature prevailed over philosophy and he continued to use the stairs to descend to lower levels of a building, just as sceptics about time continue to set alarm clocks and pedestrians partial to Zeno scurry to avoid oncoming buses.

Religious debates, like ethical debates, are not irrelevant to our lives, nor does nature force us to live in opposition to our preferred views – they are somewhere in between these. But they are, to use William James's term, "forced" in at least this limited sense: our lives will bear testimony to one side or the other, even if we plead ignorance of or disinterest in the subject. Tomorrow, we will live as vegetarians or not; we will support the political structures of our country or not; we will pray or not. Even if you have never considered the arguments for or against vegetarianism, your choices will situate you to receive the goods or suffer the harms that accompany the one side or the other. So too tomorrow we will either live as theists, who value a relationship of filial love to God as supremely important, or not. I believe Pascal is correct, to wit, that existentially we do not have the luxury of disinterest in whether or not there is a God, since daily existence forces us to live "as if" inclined to one or the other side. The fabric of our lives, the causes to which we devote ourselves, the way we think about matters moral, political and personal will, perforce, reflect the presence or absence of theistic convictions.

I have suggested at various places that the question of God's existence is a matter of the heart as well as the head. Here, the passions are in play. The question of God's existence is more like the question "Should I marry this person?" than "Can this proof be solved in less than fifteen steps?" The first question most assuredly benefits from clear thinking and accurate judgements about the character of one's potential spouse, but it is more than that.

Philosophers from Plato to Pascal to Plantinga argue that, when the intellect's highest truth coincides with our highest good, the dispositions of the will or heart, the structure of our loves and concerns, influences our thinking. If God exists, we are simultaneously pursuing the true and the good, the source of love and ultimate fulfilment, and the ground of all reality. Indeed, these thinkers agree that the truth comes into view only as we cultivate suitable dispositions of the will, since the good is partly constitutive of the true. Inasmuch as many atheists see religious belief as a social and intellectual harm, then advocating for atheism might also be viewed as the simultaneous pursuit of the true and the good. A. C. Grayling is typical here: "I look around the world today and see that the majority of conflicts in the world have their roots in religious passions. What are they arguing over? Faerie. It so dismays me that I could weep when I think about it. Religion is a cancerous tumour in the history of mankind" (2004: 30).

If the structure of our loves, cares and concerns bear upon our investigations into God's nature and existence, then they can work both for and against religious belief. A. J. Ayer was a lifelong and well-known atheist who, toward the end of his life, had a near-death experience in which he felt drawn to a source of light and goodness. Ayer reflected on this experience saying: "My recent experiences, have slightly weakened my conviction that my genuine death … will be the end of me, though I continue to hope that it will be" (Ayer 1994: 232). Notice that Ayer felt the evidential force of that experience as counting against his atheism, although not so much as to cause him to change his mind about God. Notice too that Ayer's estimate of the evidence is suffused with his hope that theism is not true. It is reasonable to think that the structure of Ayer's passions were in play as he estimated the relevance of his experience on his beliefs. As we saw in Chapter 5, Tolstoy's character, Raskolnikov, despondent at the course his life has taken, and suddenly finding himself the recipient of another's love, abandons his nihilism and opens to the divine. Suffice it to say, whichever position one adopts towards God is probably not done for entirely cerebral, dispassionate reasons. May we hope for ourselves and for those who disagree with us, that life's experiences allow our best intellectual efforts and our best loves to lead us to truth.

Notes

Introduction

1. Monotheism, the belief of the Abrahamic faiths, is the target of our investigation. Judaism, Christianity and Islam are united in thinking that God is the unsurpassably great, personal, creator of the world, who possesses all great-making qualities to the maximal degree possible, although their accounts of God differ on other points.

2. The philosopher John Searle, who was present at the dinner, recounts this story in *Mind, Language, and Society: Philosophy in the Real World* (New York: Basic Books, 1998), 36–7.

3. I say "roughly" because some theists, Pascal and Kierkegaard among them, deny that human reason can muster objective evidence that shows the truth of theism, yet they nevertheless recommend belief for practical or existential reasons.

4. In *Evidentialism: Essays in Epistemology* (Oxford: Oxford University Press, 2004), Earl Conee and Richard Feldman, offer one of the most thorough explications and defences of evidentialism that I know of. The word "justification" is a major term of appraisal among epistemologists. Significant controversy divides epistemology as to the necessary and sufficient conditions of a belief's being justified, or whether such conditions can even be provided. Many philosophers deny that having evidence and appreciating its probative force are necessary for a belief's being justified. Elements of these disputes will surface as our discussion unfolds.

1. Design arguments

1. C. Stephen Evans offers an excellent analysis of natural signs and the ways they move us to belief in *Natural Signs and Knowledge of God: A New Look at Theistic Arguments* (Oxford: Oxford University Press, 2010).

2. Arguments similar to Behe's can also be found in the work of microbiologist Michael Denton; see his *Evolution: A Theory in Crisis* (Bethesda, MD: Adler & Adler, 1985).

3. Francis Collins, the head of the human genome project, himself a theist, nevertheless sides with views such as Miller's against the claims of the intelligent design movement. See his *The Language of God: A Scientist Presents Evidence for Belief* (New York: Free Press, 2006), esp. ch. 8.

4. Robin Collins presents six solid cases of fine-tuning in his "Evidence for Fine Tuning, in *God and Design: The Teleological Argument and Modern Science*, Neil A. Manson (ed.), 178–99 (London: Routledge, 2003).

5. Naturalism, the view that nothing exists that is not a part of the natural world – and thus that there is no supernatural reality – does not entail that the natural world is irreducibly material. Perhaps the best physics about the ultimate constituents of matter shows, or will show, that something immaterial underlies the entire physical world, in which case there could be a non-materialistic naturalism.

6. This is not the same issue as (though it is related to) the so-called "hard problem" in the study of consciousness: if the world is made up entirely of matter, how do unconscious bits of matter result in conscious thought? The argument from reason attempts to account for a particular range of our conscious thoughts – those, for instance, that allow us to draw inferences from logical laws and to reason in truth-conducive ways.

7. Victor Reppert collects and assesses various forms of the argument from reason in C. S. Lewis's Dangerous Idea: In Defense of the Argument from Reason (Downers Grove, IL: InterVarsity, 2003). See William Hasker's "Unity of Consciousness Argument" in his *The Emergent Self*, 122–46 (Ithaca, NY: Cornell University Press, 1999).

8. Aquinas seems to have anticipated this line of argument in his fifth way: "Now whatever lacks intelligence cannot move toward an end, unless it be directed by some being endowed with knowledge and intelligence; as the arrow is shot to its mark by the archer. Therefore some intelligent being exists by whom all natural things are directed to their end; and this being we call God" (*Summa Theologiae* q.2, a.3; 1981: 14).

9. Plantinga is quoting Charles Darwin, letter to William Graham, Down, July, 1881, in *The Life and Letters of Charles Darwin Including an Autobiographical Chapter*, Francis Darwin (ed.) (London: John Murray, 1887), vol. 1, 315–16.

10. The notion that God must be invoked to account for our knowledge of necessary truths is at least as old as Augustine, who offers such an argument in *On Free Choice of the Will*, bks 2, 8.

2. Cosmological arguments

1. Craig, perhaps more than any other contemporary philosopher, has revived interest in the *kalam* argument. See his *The Kalam Cosmological Argument* (Eugene, OR: Wipf & Stock, 2000) and *Theism, Atheism, and Big Bang Cosmology* (Oxford: Clarendon Press, 2003).

2. An anonymous reviewer of this book noted that naturalists may be guilty of their own "naturalism of the gaps": that (naturalistic) science will ultimately explain that of which we are presently ignorant, and which looks rather theistic.

3. See David Hume, *Dialogues Concerning Natural Religion*, part IX, in *Dialogues Concerning Natural Religion and Natural History of Religion*, J. C. A. Gaskin (ed.) (Oxford: Oxford University Press, 1993), and Kant, *Critique* II, ch. 3, §5, "The Impossibility of a Cosmological Proof of the Existence of God".

4. This was a BBC radio debate between Bertrand Russell and F. C. Copleston, broadcast in 1948. Transcripts and audio files are available on the internet.

5. Rowe is quoted by Bruce Reichenbach in "Explanation and the Cosmological Argument", in *Contemporary Debates in the Philosophy of Religion*, Michael Peterson & Raymond J. Van Arragon (eds) (Oxford: Blackwell, 2004), 108.

6. Alexander Pruss and Richard Gale ("A New Cosmological Argument", *Religious Studies* 35[4] [1999], 461–76) have vigorously defended an argument from

contingency that uses a weak version of PSR, which requires only that for any contingently true proposition p, there is a possible world w containing the propositions p and q, such that q explains p. One could imagine Russell consenting more readily to the claim that it is *possible* that there is an explanation for the universe rather than the claim that there actually is one. Readers are invited to pursue objections to the weak PSR by Graham Oppy, "On a New Cosmological Argument", *Religious Studies* 36(3) (2000), 345–53, and Kevin Davey & Rob Clifton, "Insufficient Reason in the New Cosmological Argument", *Religious Studies* 37(4) (2001), 485–90. Pruss and Gale respond in "A Response to Oppy, and to Davey and Clifton", *Religious Studies* 38(1) (2002), 89–99.

3. The ontological argument

1. $\Diamond p \supset \Box \Diamond p$ and $\Diamond \Box p \supset \Box p$ are equivalent by contraposition. See Kenneth Konyndyk, *Introductory Modal Logic* (Notre Dame, IN: University of Notre Dame Press, 1986), 120. Most philosophers regard the distinctive axiom of S5 to be the claim that if it is possible that a proposition p is true in all possible worlds, then that proposition must be true in all worlds. See also Paul Herrick, *The Many Worlds of Logic* (Fort Worth, TX: Harcourt Brace, 1994), 316–17.
2. E. J. Lowe gives this rendition of Plantinga's modal ontological argument in his article "The Ontological Argument", in *The Routledge Companion to Philosophy of Religion*, Paul Copan & Chad Meister (eds) (London: Routledge, 2007), 338–9.
3. Interestingly, Gale's recent work with Alexander Pruss appears to have brought a change in Gale's thinking. While he continues to think that no being answers to the description of omnipotent, omniscient, omnibenevolent and necessarily existing (because he continues to think there are possible worlds where gratuitous evils occur that are inconsistent with a maximally perfect being), he does think there can be a finitely good, wise and powerful being who exists necessarily. As he puts it: "The danger of making God too perfect is that it makes him an impossible being, and thus not perfect after all". See "Why Traditional Cosmological Arguments Don't Work, and a Sketch of a New One that Does", in *Contemporary Debates in Philosophy of Religion*, Peterson & Van Arragon (eds), 114–30.

4. The moral argument for God's existence

1. See, for instance, The Five Precepts from *The Book of Discipline of the Sarvastivadins*, in *Buddhist Scriptures*, selected and translated by Edward Conze (Harmondsworth: Penguin, 1959) pt II, §1.
2. Proponents of non-relative virtues can readily admit that systems of virtues are subject to cultural shaping and background metaphysical beliefs about human nature and the conditions for human flourishing. Nevertheless, many virtue theorists contend that there remains a significant degree of overlap and cross-cultural similarity between traditions about general patterns of excellence as regards handling pleasure and pain, facing fear, the importance of friendship and other matters that are the subjects of virtue and vice. Especially helpful here is Martha Nussbaum's "Non-Relative Virtues", in *Moral Relativism*, Paul Moser and Thomas Carson (eds) (Oxford: Oxford University Press, 2001).
3. This form of a general moral argument is adapted from Robert Garcia & Nathan King, *Is Goodness Without God Good Enough?* (Lanham, MD: Rowman & Littlefield, 2009), 1.

4. We are setting to one side other supernatural but non-theistic explanations for features of the moral life. Hinduism and Buddhism, for example, explain moral accountability through the doctrines of reincarnation and karma.

5. I am indebted here to George Mavrodes, "Religion and the Queerness of Morality", in *Rationality, Religious Belief, and Moral Commitment*, Robert Audi & William J. Wainwright (eds), 213–26 (Ithaca, NY: Cornell University Press, 1986).

6. Charles J. Lumsden and E. O. Wilson describe epigenetic rules as "genetically determined peripheral sensory filters, interneuron coding processes, and more centrally located procedures of biased learning that affect the probability of acquiring one culturgen [transmittable behaviour] as opposed to another" ["Translation of Epigenetic Rules of Individual Behaviour into Ethnographic Patterns", *Proceedings of the National Academy of Sciences* 77[7] [July 1980], 4382].

7. Readers will recall the discussion regarding the argument from reason. If nature can play fast and loose with the truth here, why not elsewhere?

8. I am indebted to Alan Jacobs for this point.

9. Augustine long ago said "an unjust law is no law at all" (*On Free Choice of the Will*, bk. 1, 5).

10. Theists sometimes speak of humans having the power to imitate or emulate God by becoming agents whose actions and moral character conform to God's moral character. Thus, Robert Adams proposes that "things are excellent insofar as they resemble or imitate God .... God is the standard of goodness, to which other good things must in some measure conform, but never perfectly conform" (*Finite and Infinite Goods* [Oxford: Oxford University Press, 1999], 28–9).

11. An objective law can exist even though persons grasp its contents with greater and lesser degrees of understanding. The same could be said of the principles of mathematics. We may need tutoring to discover both sorts of objective truths.

12. Again, this is consistent with one's needing to be instructed to see these truths. Our capacity to apprehend *a priori* truths can be cultivated.

13. To say a claim is universally acknowledged is not to say that every single human on the planet attests to it. Infants, the mentally infirm and sociopaths, for example, may not affirm the claim in question. Others may instantiate an objective moral principle in their actions and attitudes without making the principle a matter of reflective consideration. Moral knowledge also comes in degrees, and typically requires study and reflection before one understands its content deeply.

14. Recall from Chapter 1 that philosophers sympathetic to "fine-tuning" arguments would deny that our life-permitting laws came about accidentally.

15. See Russ Shafer-Landau's *Whatever Happened to Good and Evil?* (Oxford: Oxford University Press, 2004), 77. As regards necessary truths, Robert Adams, among others, believes that God's existence "provides the best explanation for our knowledge of necessary truths", and that theists enjoy a theoretical advantage in explaining necessary truths. See his "Divine Necessity", in *The Virtue of Faith and Other Essays in Philosophical Theology* (Oxford: Oxford University Press, 1987), 209–20, esp. 218. See also Katherin Rogers, "Evidence for God from Certainty", *Faith and Philosophy* 25(1) (2008), 31–46.

16. Foucault's vision is explained in detail in *The Care of the Self: The History of Sexuality*, vol. 3, Robert Hurley (trans.) (New York: Vintage, 1986) esp. pt 2.

5. Religious experience and cumulative case arguments

1. *The Gallup Poll: Public Opinion 1986* (Wilmington, DE: Scholarly Resources, 1986).

2. Sometimes religious persons claim to experience God in a sunset or through a piece of music, which obviously do involve the senses. By extension, we might also include here devotional experiences, such as feeling "blessed" by prayers offered on one's behalf. Alvin Plantinga demurs from saying that all experiences of God are perceptual in character precisely because the perception of God is mediated by the perception of something else. See *Warranted Christian Belief* (Oxford: Oxford University Press, 2000), 182.

3. Alston and Swinburne's approaches are similar, but not identical. Alston's position concerns an entire doxastic practice of forming justified belief about God on the basis of religious experiences. Swinburne's principle of credulity treats individual experience–belief pairs. Jerome Gellman employs a principle closer to Swinburne's that he calls the "Best Explanation of Experience", or "BEE": "If a person, S, has an experience, E, which seems (phenomenally) to be of a particular object, O (or of an object of kind, K), then everything else being equal the best explanation of S's have E is that S has experience O (or an object of kind, K), rather than something else or nothing at all" (*Experience of God and the Rationality of Theistic Belief* [Ithaca, NY: Cornell University Press, 1997], 46ff.).

4. "Man cannot get beyond his true nature. He may indeed by means of the imagination conceive individuals of another so-called higher kind, but he can never get loose from his species, his nature; the conditions of being, the positive final predicates which he gives to these other individuals [i.e. God], are always determinations or qualities drawn from his own nature – qualities in which he in truth only images and projects himself" (Ludwig Feuerbach, *The Essence of Christianity*, George Eliot [trans.] [New York: Harper, 1957], 11).

5. Ironically, elements of Freud's theory and methodology, such as his teachings about Thanatos and Eros, and many of his claims about the subconscious have come in for severe criticism for lack of scientific grounding, as they are not subject to empirical cross-checks.

6. See Dennett's sketch of the natural origins of religions in Part II: The Evolution of Religion, in his *Breaking The Spell: Religion as a Natural Phenomenon* (New York: Penguin, 2006).

7. This is not to deny that our cognitive faculties can yield incompatible results. I might vividly remember placing my wallet on my dresser, while my eyes tell me there is no wallet there.

8. This argument follows Alston, *Perceiving God* (Ithaca, NY: Cornell University Press, 1991), 269–70.

9. I have always thought this an unfortunate analogy, inasmuch as one leaky bucket, placed inside another so that the metal of the second covers the hole of the first, will result in buckets that, in combination, hold water.

10. Richard Lewontin gives clear expression to one stream of anti-religious academic culture: "Our willingness to accept scientific claims that are against common sense is the key to an understanding of the real struggle between science and the supernatural. We take the side of science in spite of its failure to fulfill many of its extravagant promises of health and life, in spite of the tolerance of the scientific community of unsubstantiated just-so stories, because we have a prior commitment to materialism. It is not that the methods and institutions of science somehow compel us to accept a material explanation of the phenomenal world, but on the contrary, that we are forced by our apriori adherence

to material causes to create an apparatus of investigation and a set of concepts that produce material causes, no matter how counterintuitive, no matter how mystifying to the uninitiated. Moreover, that materialism is absolute, for we cannot allow a Divine Foot in the Door. The eminent Kant scholar Lewis Beck used to say that anyone who believes in God can believe in anything. To appeal to an omnipotent deity is to allow that at any moment the regularities of nature may be ruptured, that Miracles may happen" (Richard Lewontin, "Billions and Billions of Demons", *New York Review of Books* [9 January 1997], 28–32).

11. The importance of emotions for proper cognitive functioning is dramatically demonstrated in Oliver Sacks's well-known chronicle of Temple Grandin, a high-functioning autistic whose impairment prevents her from experiencing the same range of emotions experienced by normal adults. Because she does not experience many emotions that arise in everyday human interactions she fails to acquire a catalogue of emotional memories so vital to empathetic under-standing and consequently she fails to glean from these experiences lessons that strike most of us as obvious. Among other limitations, she is utterly unable to "read" people, to detect the nuances of vocal inflection, the ironies in people's conversation, the variations and reasons for their emotional displays, and the subtle social cues that tone of voice and gesture convey. She was unable to track the plot of Shakespeare's *Romeo and Juliet* due to the intricate play of motive and intention, and the meanings conveyed by intonation and gesture. As she herself puts it, "the emotional circuit's not hooked up". See Oliver Sacks's *An Anthropologist on Mars* (New York: Knopf, 1995).

12. See Robert Roberts & W. Jay Wood, "Proper Function, Emotion, and Virtues of the Intellect", in *Faith and Philosophy* 21(1) (2004), 3–24. The connection between emotions and intellect in the work of Jonathan Edwards, John Henry Newman and William James, is penetratingly explored in William Wainwright's *Reason and the Heart* (Ithaca, NY: Cornell University Press, 1995). The spe-cific role of emotions in religious understanding receives excellent treatment in Mark R. Wynn's *Emotional Experience and Religious Understanding* (Cam-bridge: Cambridge University Press, 2005).

13. Much of the time, getting the truth is entirely a matter of cognitive mechanics and does not depend at all on one's intellectual or moral character. As Jason Baehr points out, if I am sitting in a well-lit room at night and a power failure suddenly plunges me into total darkness, my belief that the lights went out does not depend on my being virtuously attentive, open-minded and so on.

14. Dostoyevsky's passage suggests that whether or not Raskolnikov's experience of love defeated his nihilism was in some measure up to him. This raises the prospect that the will plays an important indirect role in the way we accept and reject beliefs.

15. Her book offers a collection of some deeply personal and poignant stories of loss of belief, whereas Kelly Clark's *Philosophers Who Believe* (Downers Grove, IL: InterVarsity, 1993) offers accounts of philosophers who come have come to faith. In both books, one sees quite plainly that belief or non-belief, while an intensely intellectual matter, in not just a matter of cut and thrust dialectics.

6. Religious belief without evidence

1. Jeff Jordan's article on Pascal in *The Oxford Handbook to the Philosophy of Religion* pursues subtleties to the "many-gods" objection that I leave to one side.

2. To terminate enquiry into the truth of *p* is compatible with acknowledging that additional evidence could arise for or against *p*.

3. Hilary Kornblith, *Epistemology: Internalism and Externalism* (Oxford: Blackwell, 2001), will orient persons interested in pursuing some of the intricacies of the internalist–externalist debate.

4. Alvin Goldman rehearses some of internalism's gravest problems in "Internalism Exposed", *Journal of Philosophy* 96(6) (June 1999), 271–93.

5. These three terms, while not exactly synonymous, share a strong family resemblance to one another. See Alvin Goldman, "What is Justified Belief", *in Justification and Knowledge*, George Pappas (ed.), 1–24 (Dordrecht: Reidel, 1979); Alvin Plantinga, *Warrant and Proper Function* (Oxford: Oxford University Press, 1993); and Ernest Sosa, *A Virtue Epistemology* (Oxford: Oxford University Press, 2007), esp. ch. 2.

6. As our goal is to understand and assess Plantinga's Reformed epistemology, we need not address the objections commonly levelled against externalism. Readers interested in doing so may consult Laurence Bonjour, *Epistemology: Classic Problems and Contemporary Responses*, 2nd edn (Lanham, MD: Rowman & Littlefield, 2009), ch. 10.

7. Alvin Plantinga's reply is "Foundations of Theism: A Reply". *Faith and Philosophy* 3(3) (1986): 298–313

7. The problem of suffering

1. I refer to moral evil as applying to human actions, but it might also be extended to free non-human beings, such as angels. Some suffering arises due to the interplay of nature and human evil. A drought may bring famine to some spot on the globe, yet prosperous countries do not lack the resources to stave off starvation. That anyone should perish for lack of enough to eat may be due as much to selfishness as the vagaries of the weather.

2. "Alice laughed. 'There's no use trying,' she said 'one *can't* believe impossible things.' 'I daresay you haven't had much practice,' said the Queen. 'When I was your age, I always did it for half-an-hour a day. Why, sometimes I've believed as many as six impossible things before breakfast'" (L. Carroll, *Alice in Wonderland and Through the Looking Glass* [New York: Grosset & Dunlap, 1946], 221–2).

3. Rabbi Harold Kushner adopted this strategy in his popular best-seller *When Bad Things Happen to Good People* (New York: Anchor, 2004). This is also the strategy of Richard Gale, who thinks his cosmological argument "goes quite some way to justifying theistic belief", and who notes in reference to dealing with evil, "my task is easier because my God might be finite". See his "Why Traditional Cosmological Arguments Don't Work, and a Sketch of a New One That Does", in *Contemporary Debates in Philosophy of Religion*, Peterson & Van Arragon (eds), 130.

4. See John Hick's *Evil and the God of Love*, rev. edn (Basingstoke: Palgrave Macmillan, 2007). This point is ably defended by Michael Murray in "Coercion and the Hiddenness of God", *American Philosophical Quarterly* 30(1) (1993), 27–38.

5. Such cases constitute what Marilyn Adams calls "horrendous evils", defined as "evils the participation in which (that is the doing or suffering of which) constitutes prima facie reason to doubt whether the participant's life could (given their inclusion in it) be a great good to him/her on the whole". See her *Horrendous Evils and the Goodness of God* (Ithaca, NY: Cornell University Press, 1999), 26.

6. Hasker thinks this principle receives ample support from Judaeo-Christian scriptures and the traditions of ethical reflection they foster.

7. Perhaps Hasker sees Rowe's requirement on God as functioning analogously to karma and karmic debt. If I believe that all suffering persons undergo is neces-

sary for satisfying karmic debt and paving the way toward a better reincarnation, any efforts I extend to alleviate their suffering may thwart the satisfaction of that debt and the suffering will thus have to arise in some other way.

8. Adams builds into this story that the couple is unable to adopt and that they are wealthy enough to ensure that the child's needs will always be met without imposing a financial burden on anyone else.

9. Representative of this approach are Eleanor Stump, "Providence and Evil", in *Christian Philosophy*, Thomas Flint (ed.), 51–91 (Notre Dame, IN: University of Notre Dame Press, 1990), and Marilyn Adams, *Horrendous Evils and the Goodness of God* (Ithaca, NY: Cornell University Press, 1999).

10. See his Chapter 7, "The Suffering of Beasts". Michael Murray defends a related point that it is good overall for the cosmos to move from chaos to nomic regularity over an extended period of time. This, in turn, requires a gradual accumulation of complex states, of movement from lower animal to higher animal forms that eventuates in animal suffering. See his *Nature Red in Tooth and Claw: Theism and the Problem of Animal Suffering* (Oxford: Oxford University Press, 2008).

8. The nature of God

1. So concludes Anthony Kenny in the last chapter of *The God of the Philosophers* (Oxford: Oxford University Press, 1986).

2. This idea finds support in William Lane Craig, "The *Kalam* Cosmological Argument", in *Philosophy of Religion: A Reader and Guide*, William Lane Craig (ed.), 92–113 (New Brunswick, NJ: Rutgers University Press, 2002).

3. Thomas V. Morris, *Anselmian Explorations* (Notre Dame, IN: University of Notre Dame Press, 1987), and Katherin Rogers, *Perfect Being Theology* (Edinburgh: Edinburgh University Press, 2000) are both illustrative of perfect being theology and interesting for the different conclusions they reach about God.

4. To be precise, the classical tradition does not think that God has emotions, or "*passiones*", as this implies that God can be acted upon and changed by external events. Aquinas and other medieval theologians were willing to say that God has "*affectiones*", or affections such as love and joy, but that these are not subject to diminution or change by anything outside of himself.

5. We think in terms of subject and attribute. Persons are one thing and their distinct properties or qualities are conceptually distinct. And this is true, according to the classical tradition, of all persons except God.

6. Aquinas turns to the subject of God's simplicity immediately after question two concerning God's existence (See *Summa Theologiae* I, q.3.) Christopher Hughes offers a thorough examination of Aquinas's treatment of simplicity in *On a Complex Theory of a Simple God* (Ithaca, NY: Cornell University Press, 1989). The doctrine of simplicity turns out to be remarkably complicated. Hughes examines the special difficulties Christian theists face with the doctrine of the Incarnation – God the Son, the second person of the Trinity, taking on a human nature. Not only did God the Son take on a human nature, but in that human nature grew hungry, weary, angry and experienced other appetites and emotions common to humans. Furthermore, traditional Christian teaching says that Christ, the Son of God, retained his human nature, albeit in a glorified form, upon ascending to heaven. It is a matter of great perplexity how these claims about Christ are compatible with God's remaining eternal and immutable. See Hughes, *On a Complex Theory of a Simple God*, ch. 7, where he treats "The Incarnation and Change".

7. Ralph McInerny, *Aquinas and Analogy* (Washington, DC: Catholic University Press, 1999), offers an excellent introduction to Aquinas's account.

8. Of course, God's not having a body will also mean that there are many things humans can do that God cannot do.

9. Eleonore Stump argues for a position close to this in "Intellect, Will, and Alternate Possibilities", in *Christian Theism and the Problems of Philosophy*, Michael Beaty (ed.), 254–85 (Notre Dame, IN: University of Notre Dame Press, 1990).

10. See Bruce Reichenbach, "Must God Create the Best Possible World?", *International Philosophical Quarterly* 19 (1979). Reichenbach's arguments receive comment from Laura Garcia in "Divine Freedom and Creation", *Philosophical Quarterly* 42(167) (1992), 191–213.

11. Ed Wierenga pursues this line of argument in his "Perfect Goodness and Divine Freedom", *Philosophical Books* 48(3) (July 2007), 207–16. Alvin Plantinga made this limitation on divine power clear in *God, Freedom, and Evil* (Grand Rapids, MI: Eerdmans, 1977).

12. A powerful objection to God's being immutable and timeless was advanced to powerful effect in Norman Kretzmann, "Omniscience and Immutability", *Journal of Philosophy* 63(14) (Jul 14, 1966), 409–21.

13. Anthony Kenny made the same point earlier: "Knowing that 'Christ will be born' is true (roughly) throughout the years BC and that 'Christ has been born' is true throughout the years AD will not – *pace* Aquinas – enable one to know which of these two propositions is true *now*, unless one also knows the date" (*The God of the Philosophers* [Oxford: Oxford University Press, 1986], 48).

14. A Christian theological solution to indexical knowledge appeals to the doctrine of the Incarnation, whereby God the Son, the second person of the Trinity, takes on a human nature and lives among us. On the traditional doctrine of the Trinity, nothing is known by one person of the Trinity that is not known by another. We may suppose, then, what God the Son experienced in his earthly sojourn was fully communicated to the other members of the Trinity. Katherin Rogers offers this solution in *Perfect Being Theology* (Edinburgh: University of Edinburgh Press, 2000), 88ff.

15. This is Linda Zagzebski's term. See *The Dilemma of Freedom and Foreknowledge* (Oxford: Oxford University Press, 1991), 7.

16. Helm goes on to deny that God's direct control is mere efficient causation of the sort studied by physicists, although exactly what sort of causation God exercises remains a mystery on his account.

17. Thomas Flint surveys some problems with the timelessness view in *Divine Providence: The Molinist Account* (Ithaca, NY: Cornell University Press, 1998), 82ff.

18. Craig offers a detailed analysis of the grounding objection at www.leaderu.com/offices/billcraig/docs/grounding.html (accessed October 2010).

19. So-called "maverick molinists" accept that counterfactuals of freedom have their truth-value logically prior to God's acts of will, but want to maintain that God could have so acted that these counterfactuals would have had a different truth value from that which they actually have. See Thomas Flint, *Divine Providence*, 65ff., and Jonathan Kvanvig, "On Behalf of Maverick Molinism", *Faith and Philosophy* 19(3) (2002), 348–57.

Bibliography

Adams, M. 1993. "The Problem of Hell: A Problem of Evil for Christians". In *Reasoned Faith*, E. Stump (ed.), 301–27. Ithaca, NY: Cornell University Press.

Adams, M. 1999. *Horrendous Evils and the Goodness of God*. Ithaca, NY: Cornell University Press.

Adams, R. 1987. *The Virtue of Faith and Other Essays in Philosophical Theology*. Oxford: Oxford University Press.

Adams, R. 1999. *Finite and Infinite Goods*. Oxford: Oxford University Press.

Alston, W. 1991. *Perceiving God*. Ithaca, NY: Cornell University Press.

Anselm. 1995. *Proslogion*, T. Williams (trans.). Indianapolis, IN: Hackett.

Anselm. 1998. *Proslogion*. In *Anselm of Canterbury: The Major Works*, B. Davies & G. R. Evans (eds). Oxford: Oxford University Press.

Antony, L. (ed.) 2007. *Philosophers Without Gods*. Oxford: Oxford University Press.

Aquinas, T. 1975. *Summa contra Gentiles*. Notre Dame, IN: University of Notre Dame Press.

Aquinas, T. 1981. *Summa Theologiae*, Fathers of the English Dominican Province (trans). Westminster, MD: Christian Classics.

Aristotle. 1990. *Nicomachean Ethics*, 2nd edn, T. Irwin (ed.). Indianapolis, IN: Hackett.

Audi, R. & W. Wainwright (eds) 1986. *Rationality, Religious Belief, and Moral Commitment*. Ithaca, NY: Cornell University Press.

Ayer, A. J. 1994. "My Death". In *Language, Metaphysics and Death*, 2nd edn, J. Donnelly (ed.), 226–36. New York, NY: Forham University Press.

Barrett, J. 2000. "Exploring the Natural Foundations of Religion". *Trends in Cognitive Science* 4: 29–34.

Barrow, J. & F. Tipler 1986. *The Anthropic Cosmological Principle*. Oxford: Oxford University Press.

Beaty, M. (ed.) 1990. *Christian Theism and the Problems of Philosophy*. Notre Dame, IN: University of Notre Dame Press.

Behe, M. 1996. *Darwin's Black Box: The Biochemical Challenge to Evolution*. New York: Free Will Press.

Bonjour, L. 2009. *Epistemology: Classic Problems and Contemporary Responses*, 2nd edn. Lanham, MD: Rowman & Littlefield.

Boyd, R. 1988. "How to be a Moral Realist". In *Essays on Moral Realism*, G. Sayre-McCord (ed.), 181–228. Ithaca, NY: Cornell University Press.

Boyer, P. 2002. *Religion Explained: The Evolutionary Origins of Religious Thought*. New York: Basic Books.

Broad, C. D. 1967. "The Argument from Religious Experience". In *Problems and Perspectives in the Philosophy of Religion*, G. Mavrodes & S. Hackett (eds), 180–91. Boston, MA: Allyn & Bacon.

Calvin, J. 1981. *Institutes of the Christian Religion*, H. Beveridge (trans.). Grand Rapids, MI: Eerdmans.

Carroll, L. 1946. *Alice in Wonderland and Through the Looking Glass*. New York: Grosset & Dunlap.

Chambers, W. 1983. *Witness*. Quoted in M. Gardener, *The Whys of a Philosophical Scrivener*, 196–7. New York: Quill.

Chisholm, R. 1981. *The First Person*. Minneapolis, MN: University of Minneapolis Press.

Churchland, P. 1987. "Epistemology in the Age of Neuroscience". *Journal of Philosophy* 84: 548–9.

Clark, K. 1993. *Philosophers Who Believe*. Downers Grove, IL: InterVarsity.

Clark, K. J. & J. Barrett 2010. "Reformed Epistemology and the Cognitive Science of Religion". *Faith and Philosophy* 27(2): 174–89.

Clifford, W. K. 2006. "The Ethics of Belief". Anthologized in *Philosophy of Religion*, 3rd edn, M. Peterson, W. Hasker, B. Reichenbach & D. Basinger (eds), 109. Oxford: Oxford University Press.

Collins, F. 2006. *The Language of God: A Scientist Presents Evidence for Belief*. New York: Free Press.

Collins, R. 1999. "A Scientific Argument for the Existence of God". In *Reason for the Hope Within*, M. Murray (ed.). Grand Rapids, MI: Eerdmans.

Collins, R. 2003. "Evidence for Fine Tuning". In *God and Design: The Teleological Argument and Modern Science*, N. A. Manson (ed.). London: Routledge.

Collins, R. 2007. "The Teleological Argument". In *The Routledge Companion to Philosophy of Religion*, P. Copan & C. Meister (eds). New York: Routledge.

Conee, E. & R. Feldman 2004. *Evidentialism: Essays in Epistemology*. Oxford: Oxford University Press.

Conze, E. (trans.) 1959. *The Five Precepts* from *The Book of Discipline of the Sarvastivadins*, in *Buddhist Scripture*. Harmondsworth: Penguin.

Copan, P. 2008. "The Moral Argument". In *The Philosophy of Religion Reader*, C. Meister (ed.). London: Routledge.

Copan, P. & C. Meister (eds) 2007. *The Routledge Companion to Philosophy of Religion*. New York: Routledge.

Craig, W. L. 1987. *The Only Wise God*. Grand Rapids, MI: Baker Book House.

Craig, W. L. 2000. *The Kalam Cosmological Argument*. Eugene, OR: Wipf & Stock.

Craig, W. L. 2001. *Time and Eternity: Exploring God's Relationship to Time*. Wheaton, IL: Crossway.

Craig, W. L. (ed.) 2002a. *Philosophy of Religion: A Reader and Guide*. New Brunswick, NJ: Rutgers University Press.

Craig, W. L. 2002b. "The *Kalam* Cosmological Argument". In *Philosophy of Religion: A Reader and Guide*, W. L. Craig (ed.), 92–113. New Brunswick, NJ: Rutgers University Press.

Craig, W. L. 2003. *Theism, Atheism, and Big Bang Cosmology*. Oxford: Clarendon Press.

Craig, W. L. 2009. "Divine Eternity". In *The Oxford Handbook of Philosophical Theology*, T. P. Flint & M. C. Rea (eds), 145–66. Oxford: Oxford University Press.

Craig, W. L. & W. Sinott-Armstrong 2004. *God? A Debate Between a Christian and an Atheist*. Oxford: Oxford University Press.

Darwin, F. (ed.) 1887. *The Life and Letters of Charles Darwin Including an Autobiographical Chapter*. London: John Murray.

Davey, K. & R. Clifton. "Insufficient Reason in the New Cosmological Argument". *Religious Studies* 37(4): 485–90.

Davis, C. F. 1989. *The Evidential Force of Religious Experience*. Oxford: Oxford University Press.

Davis, B. & G. R. Evans (eds) 1998. *Anselm of Canterbury: The Major Works*. Oxford: Oxford University Press.

Dawkins, R. 1976. *The Selfish Gene*. Oxford: Oxford University Press.

Dawkins, R. 1986. "The Blind Watchmaker". In *The Blind Watchmaker: Why the Evidence of Evolution Reveals a Universe Without Design*. New York: Norton.

Dawkins, R. 1995. *River Out of Eden: A Darwinian View of Life*. New York: Basic Books.

Dawkins, R. 1997. In Conversation with Richard Dawkins. *The Evolutionist*: www.lse.ac.uk/collections/darwin/evolutionist/dawkins.htm (accessed September 2010).

Dawkins, R. 2006. *The God Delusion*. Boston, MA: Houghton Mifflin.

Dennett, D. 2006. *Breaking The Spell: Religion as a Natural Phenomenon*. New York: Penguin.

Denton, M. 1985. *Evolution: A Theory in Crisis*. Bethesda, MD: Adler & Adler.

Donnelly, J. 1994. *Language, Metaphysics, and Death*, 2nd edn. New York: Fordham University Press.

Dostoyevsky, F. 1993. *Crime and Punishment*, Pevear & Volokhonsky (trans.). New York: Vintage.

Evans, C. S. 2010. *Natural Signs and Knowledge of God: A New Look at Theistic Arguments*. Oxford: Oxford University Press.

Feinberg, J. & R. Shafer-Landau (eds) 1999. *Reason and Responsibility*, 10th edn. Belmont, CA: Wadsworth.

Feldman, R. & E. Conee 2004. *Evidentialism*. Oxford: Oxford University Press.

Ferris, T. 1997. *The Whole Shebang*. New York: Simon & Schuster.

Feuerbach, L. 1957. *The Essence of Christianity*, G. Eliot (trans.). New York: Harper.

Fischer, J. M. (ed.) 1992. *God, Foreknowledge and Freedom*. Stanford, CA: Stanford University Press.

Flew, A. 2005. *God and Philosophy*. Amherst, NY: Prometheus.

Flint, T. (ed.) 1990. *Christian Philosophy*. Notre Dame, IN: University of Notre Dame Press.

Flint, T. 1998. *Divine Providence: The Molinist Account*. Ithaca, NY: Cornell University Press.

Flint, T. & M. Rea (eds) 2009. *The Oxford Handbook of Philosophical Theology*. Oxford: Oxford University Press.

Foucault, M. 1986. *The Care of the Self: The History of Sexuality*, vol. 3, R. Hurley (trans.). New York: Vintage.

Freud, S. 1964. *The Future of an Illusion*, W. D. Robson-Scott (trans.). New York: Anchor.

Gale, G. 1990. "Cosmological Fecundity: Theories of Multiple Universes". In *Physical Cosmology and Philosophy*, J. Leslie (ed.). New York: Macmillan.

Gale, R. 1991. *On the Nature and Existence of God*. Cambridge: Cambridge University Press.

Gale, R. 2004. "Why Traditional Cosmological Arguments Don't Work, and a Sketch of a New One that Does". See Peterson & Van Arragon (2004), 114–30.

Gale, R. 2005. "On the Cognitivity of Mystical Experiences". *Faith and Philosophy* 22(4): 426–41.

Garcia, L. 1992. "Divine Freedom and Creation". *The Philosophical Quarterly* 42(167): 191–213.

Garcia, R. & N. King 2009. *Is Goodness Without God Good Enough?* Lanham, MD: Rowman & Littlefield.

Gardener, M. 1983. *The Whys of a Philosophical Scrivener*. New York: Quill.

Geach, P. T. 1989. "Omnipotence". In *Philosophy of Religion: Selected Readings*, W. L. Rowe & W. J. Wainwright (eds), 63–75. New York: Harcourt Brace Jovanovich.

Gellman, J. 1997. *Experience of God and the Rationality of Theistic Belief*. Ithaca, NY: Cornell University Press.

Gendler, S. & J. Hawthorne (eds) 2010. *Oxford Studies in Epistemology*. Oxford: Oxford University Press.

Goldman, A. 1979. "What is Justified Belief?". In *Justification and Knowledge*, G. Pappas (ed.), 1–24. Dordrecht: Reidel.

Goldman, A. 1999. "Internalism Exposed". *Journal of Philosophy* 96(6): 271–93.

Gould, S. J. 1989. *Wonderful Life: The Burgess Shale and the Nature of History*. New York: Norton.

Grayling, A. C. 2004. "A Man for all Reasons". *Philosophers' Magazine* 26: 28–30.

Guanilo 1995. "On Behalf of the Fool". In *Monologion and Proslogion with the Replies of Guanilo and Anselm*, Thomas Williams (trans.). Indianapolis, IN: Hackett.

Gutting, G. 1982. *Religious Belief and Religious Skepticism*. Notre Dame, IN: University of Notre Dame Press.

Hasker, W. 1989. *God, Time, and Knowledge*. Ithaca, NY: Cornell University Press.

Hasker, W. 1999. *The Emergent Self*. Ithaca, NY: Cornell University Press.

Hasker, W. 2008. *The Triumph of God Over Evil*. Downers Grove, IL: InterVarsity Press.

Hawking, S. 1988. *A Brief History of Time*. New York: Bantam.

Helm, P. 1994. *The Providence of God*. Downers Grove, IL: InterVarsity Press.

Herrick, P. 1994. *The Many Worlds of Logic*. Fort Worth, TX: Harcourt Brace.

Hick, J. 1989. *An Interpretation of Religion*. Basingstoke: Macmillan.

Hick, J. 2007. *Evil and the God of Love*, rev. edn. Basingstoke: Palgrave Macmillan.

Hoffman, J. & G. Rosenkrantz 2002. *The Divine Attributes*. Oxford: Blackwell.

Howard-Snyder, D. (ed.) 1996. *The Evidential Argument from Evil*. Indianapolis, IN: Indiana University Press.

Howard-Snyder, D. & P. Moser (eds) 2001. *Divine Happiness: New Essays*. Cambridge: Cambridge University Press.

Huchingson, J. E. (ed.) 1993. *Religion and the Natural Sciences*. New York: Harcourt, Brace, Jovanovich.

Hughes, C. 1989. *On a Complex Theory of a Simple God*. Ithaca, NY: Cornell University Press.

Hume, D. 1993. *Dialogues Concerning Natural Religion and the Natural History of Religion*, J. C. A. Gaskin (ed.). Oxford: Oxford University Press.

James, W. 1929. *The Varieties of Religious Experience*. New York: Random House.

Kant, I. 1961. *The Critique of Pure Reason*, N. Kemp Smith (trans.). New York: St Martin's Press.

Katz, S. (ed.) 1978. *Mysticism and Philosophical Analysis*. Oxford: Oxford University Press.

Kenny, A. 1986. *The God of the Philosophers*. Oxford: Oxford University Press.

Konyndyk, K. 1986. *Introductory Modal Logic*. Notre Dame, IN: University of Notre Dame Press.

Kornblith, H. 2001. *Epistemology: Internalism and Externalism*. Oxford: Blackwell.

Kretzmann, N. 1966. "Omniscience and Immutability". *Journal of Philosophy* 63(14): 409–21.

Kretzmann, N. 1991a. "A General Problem of Creation". In *Being and Goodness*, S. MacDonald (ed.), 208–28. Ithaca, NY: Cornell University Press.

Kretzmann, N. 1991b. "A Particular Problem of Creation". In *Being and Goodness*, S. MacDonald (ed.), 229–49. Ithaca, NY: Cornell University Press.

Kripke, S. 1977. "Identity and Necessity". In *Naming, Necessity, and Natural Kinds*, S. P. Schwartz (ed.), 66–101. Ithaca, NY: Cornell University Press.

Kushner, H. 2004. *When Bad Things Happen to Good People*. New York: Anchor.

Kvanvig, J. 1986. *The Possibility of an All-Knowing God*. New York: St. Martin's Press.

Kvanvig, J. 2002. "On Behalf of Maverick Molinism". *Faith and Philosophy* **19**(3): 348–57.

Lackey, J. 2010. "What Should We Do When We Disagree?" In *Oxford Studies in Epistemology*, T. S. Gendler & J. Hawthorne (eds), 274–93. Oxford: Oxford University Press.

Le Poidevin, R. 1996. *Arguing for Atheism*. London: Routledge.

Leslie, J. 1988. "How to Draw Conclusions From a Fine-Tuned Cosmos". In *Physics, Philosophy and Theology: A Common Quest for Understanding*, R. J. Russell, W. R. Stoeger & G. V. Coyne (eds). Vatican City: Vatican Observatory Press.

Leslie, J. (ed.) 1990. *Physical Cosmology and Philosophy*. New York: Macmillan.

Lewis, C. S. 1962. *The Problem of Pain*. New York: Macmillan.

Lewontin, R. 1997. "Billions and Billions of Demons". *New York Review of Books*, 9 January 1997, 28–32.

Locke, J. 1959. *An Essay Concerning Human Understanding*. New York: Dover.

Lovejoy, A. O. 1960. *The Great Chain of Being*. New York: Harper.

Lowe, E. J. 2007. "The Ontological Argument". In *The Routledge Companion to Philosophy of Religion*, P. Copan & C. Meister (eds), 338–9. London: Routledge.

Lumsden, C. J. & E. O. Wilson 1980. "Translation of Epigenetic Rules of Individual Behaviour into Ethnographic Patterns". *Proceedings of the National Academy of Sciences* 77(7): 4382.

Lycan, W. & G. Schlesinger 1996. "You Bet Your Life: Pascal's Wager Defended". In *Reason and Responsibility: Readings in Some Basic Problems of Philosophy*, 9th edn, J. Feinberg (ed.), 118–23. Belmont, CA: Wadsworth.

MacDonald, S. (ed.) 1991. *Being and Goodness*. Ithaca, NY: Cornell University Press.

Mackie, J. L. 1977. *Ethics: Inventing Right and Wrong*. Harmondsworth: Penguin.

Mackie, J. L. 1982. *The Miracle of Theism*. Oxford: Clarendon Press.

Mackie, J. L. 2001. "Evil and Omnipotence". In *God and the Problem of Evil*, W. L. Rowe (ed.), 77–90. Oxford: Blackwell.

Mann, W. (ed.) 2005. *The Blackwell Guide to the Philosophy of Religion*. Oxford: Blackwell.

Manson, N. (ed.) 2003. *God and Design: The Teleological Argument and Modern Science*. London: Routledge.

Martin, M. 1990. *Atheism: A Philosophical Justification*. Philadelphia, PA: Temple University Press.

Mavrodes, G. 1963. "Some Puzzles Concerning Omnipotence". *The Philosophical Review* 72(2): 221–3.

Mavrodes, G. 1978. "Real vs. Deceptive Mystical Experiences". In *Mysticism and Philosophical Analysis*, S. Katz (ed.), 235–58. Oxford: Oxford University Press.

Mavrodes, G. 1986. "Religion and the Queerness of Morality". In *Rationality, Religious Belief, and Moral Commitment*, R. Audi & W. J. Wainwright (eds), 213–26. Ithaca, NY: Cornell University Press.

Mavrodes, G. & S. Hackett (eds) 1967. *Problems and Perspectives in the Philosophy of Religion*. Boston, MA: Allyn & Bacon.

McCabe, H. 1991. *God Matters*. Springfield, IL: Templegate.

McGinn, C. 1999. *The Mysterious Flame: Conscious Minds in a Material World.* New York: Basic Books.

McInerny, R. 1999. *Aquinas and Analogy.* Washington, DC: Catholic University Press.

Meister, C. (ed.). 2008. *The Philosophy of Religion Reader.* London: Routledge.

Mellor, D. H. 2003. "Too Many Universes". In *God and Design: The Teleological Argument and Modern Science*, N. Manson (ed.). London: Routledge.

Miller, K. 2000. *Finding Darwin's God: A Scientist's Search for Common Ground Between God and Evolution.* New York: Harper Perennial.

Mitchell, B. 1973. *The Justification of Religious Belief.* Oxford: Oxford University Press.

Morris, T. V. 1987. *Anselmian Explorations.* Notre Dame, IN: University of Notre Dame Press.

Morris, T. V. 1992. *Making Sense of It All: Pascal and the Meaning of Life.* Grand Rapids, MI: Eerdmans.

Moser, P. 2008. *The Elusive God: Reorienting Religious Epistemology.* Cambridge: Cambridge University Press.

Moser, P. & T. Carson (eds) 2001. *Moral Relativism.* Oxford: Oxford University Press.

Mother Teresa 2007. *Mother Teresa: Come Be My Light: The Private Writings of the Saint of Calcutta*, B. Kolodiejchuk (ed.). New York: Doubleday.

Murray, M. 1993. "Coercion and the Hiddenness of God". *American Philosophical Quarterly* 30(1): 27–38.

Murray, M. (ed.) 1999. *Reason for the Hope Within.* Grand Rapids, MI: Eerdmans.

Murray, M. 2001. "Deus Absconditas". In *Divine Happiness: New Essays*, D. Howard-Snyder & P. Moser (eds), 62–82. Cambridge: Cambridge University Press.

Murray, M. 2008. *Nature Red in Tooth and Claw: Theism and the Problem of Animal Suffering* Oxford: Oxford University Press.

Nagel, T. 1997. *The Last Word.* Oxford: Oxford University Press.

Nussbaum, M. 2001. "Non-Relative Virtues". In *Moral Relativism*, P. Moser & T. Carson (eds), 199–225. Oxford: Oxford University Press.

Ockham, W. 1983. *Predestination, God's Foreknowledge, and Future Contingents*, 2nd edn, M. McCord Adams & N. Kretzmann (trans.). Indianapolis, IN: Hackett.

Oppy, G. 1995. *Ontological Arguments and Belief in God.* Cambridge: Cambridge University Press.

Oppy, G. 2000. "On a New Cosmological Argument". *Religious Studies* 36(3): 345–5.

Oppy, G. 2006. *Arguing About Gods.* Cambridge: Cambridge University Press.

Pappas, G. (ed.) 1979. *Justification and Knowledge.* Dordrecht: D. Reidel.

Pascal, B. 1995. *Pensées*, A. J. Krailsheimer (trans.). Harmondsworth: Penguin.

Peterson, C. & Seligman, M. 2004. *Character Strengths and Virtues: A Handbook and Classification.* New York: Oxford University Press.

Peterson, M. & R. Van Arragon (eds) 2004. *Contemporary Debates in the Philosophy of Religion.* Oxford: Blackwell.

Peterson, M., W. Hasker, B. Reichenbach & D. Basinger (eds) 2006. *Philosophy of Religion: Selected Readings*, 3rd edn. Oxford: Oxford University Press.

Plantinga, A. 1974. *The Nature of Necessity.* Oxford: Clarendon Press.

Plantinga, A. 1977. *God, Freedom, and Evil.* Grand Rapids, MI: Eerdmans.

Plantinga, A. 1980. *Does God Have a Nature?* Milwaukee, WI: Marquette University Press.

Plantinga, A. 1983. "Reason and Belief in God". In *Faith and Rationality: Reason and Belief in God*, A. Plantinga & N. Wolterstorff (eds), 16–93. Grand Rapids, MI: Eerdmans.

Plantinga, A. 1986. "Foundations of Theism: A Reply". *Faith and Philosophy* 3(3) (July): 298–313.

Plantinga, A. 1993. *Warrant and Proper Function*. Oxford: Oxford University Press.

Plantinga, A. 1995a. "Précis of Warrant: The Current Debate and Warrant and Proper Function". *Philosophy and Phenomenological Research* 55(2): 393–6.

Plantinga, A. 1995b. "Reliabilism, Analyses, and Defeaters". *Philosophy and Phenomenological Research* 55(2): 427–64.

Plantinga, A. 2000. *Warranted Christian Belief*. Oxford: Oxford University Press.

Plantinga, A. & N. Wolterstorff (eds) 1983. *Faith and Rationality: Reason and Belief in God*. Grand Rapids, MI: Eerdmans.

Pritchard, D. 2005. *Epistemic Luck*. Oxford: Clarendon Press.

Pruss, A. R. & R. M. Gale 2005. "Cosmological and Design Arguments". In *The Oxford Handbook of Philosophy of Religion*, W. Wainwright (ed.), 121–2. Oxford: Oxford University Press.

Pruss, A. R. & R. M. Gale 1999. "A New Cosmological Argument". *Religious Studies* 35(4): 461–76.

Pruss, A. R. & R. M. Gale 2002. "A Response to Oppy, and to Davey and Clifton". *Religious Studies* 38(1): 89–99.

Quinn, P. L. 1982. "God, Moral Perfection, and Possible Worlds". In *God: The Contemporary Discussion*, F. Sontag & M. D. Bryant (eds), 197–215. Barrytown, NY: Rose of Sharon Press.

Quinn, P. L. 1985. "In Search of the Foundations of Theism". *Faith and Philosophy* 2(4): 469–486.

Rawls, J. 2009. "On My Religion". In *A Brief Inquiry into the Meaning of Sin and Faith*. Cambridge, MA: Harvard University Press.

Rees, M. 2003. "Other Universes: A Scientific Perspective". In *God and Design: The Teleological Argument and Modern Science*, N. Manson (ed.), 210–20. London: Routledge.

Reichenbach, B. 1979. "Must God Create the Best Possible World?" *International Philosophical Quarterly* 19: 203–12.

Reichenbach, B. 2004. "Explanation and the Cosmological Argument". See Peterson & Van Arragon (2004), 97–114.

Reppert, V. 2003. *C. S. Lewis's Dangerous Idea: In Defense of the Argument from Reason*. Downers Grove, IL: InterVarsity.

Roberts, R. C. & W. J. Wood 2004. "Proper Function, Emotion, and Virtues of the Intellect". *Faith and Philosophy* 21(1): 3–24.

Rogers, C. 1961. *On Becoming a Person*. Cambridge, MA: Riverside.

Rogers, K. A. 2000. *Perfect Being Theology*. Edinburgh: Edinburgh University Press.

Rogers, K. A. 2008. "Evidence for God from Certainty". *Faith and Philosophy* 25(1): 31–46.

Rommen, H. A. 1998. *The Natural Law: A Study in Legal and Social History and Philosophy*, T. R. Hanley (trans.). Indianapolis, IN: Liberty Fund.

Rowe, W. L. 1975. *The Cosmological Argument*. Princeton, NJ: Princeton University Press.

Rowe, W. L. 1984. "Evil and the Theistic Hypothesis: A Response to Wykstra". *International Journal for Philosophy of Religion* 16: 95–100.

Rowe, W. L. 1988. "Response to Hasker's 'The Necessity of Gratuitous Evil'". Paper presented at the Central Division of the American Philosophical Association in Chicago (April).

Rowe, W. L. 1996. "The Problem of Evil and Some Varieties of Atheism". In *The Evidential Argument from Evil*, D. Howard-Snyder (ed.), 1–29. Indianapolis, IN: Indiana University Press.

Rowe, W. L. (ed.) 2001. *God and the Problem of Evil*. Oxford: Blackwell.

Rowe, W. L. 2004. *Can God Be Free?* Oxford: Oxford University Press.

Rowe, W. 2005. "Cosmological Arguments". In *The Blackwell Guide to the Philosophy of Religion*, W, Mann (ed.) 103–7. Oxford: Blackwell.

Ruse, M. & E. O. Wilson 1993. "The Evolution of Ethics". In *Religion and the Natural Sciences*, J. E. Huchingson (ed.), 308–13. New York: Harcourt, Brace, Jovanovich.

Russell, B. 1917. *Mysticism and Logic*. London: Allen & Unwin.

Russell, B. & F. C. Copleston [1948] 1964. Debate on the Existence of God. BBC radio. Reprinted in *The Existence of God*, J. Hick (ed.). Basingstoke: Macmillan.

Russell, R. J., W. R. Stoeger & G. V. Coyne (eds) 1998. *Physics, Philosophy and Theology: A Common Quest for Understanding*. Vatican City: Vatican Observatory Press.

Sacks, O. 1995. *An Anthropologist on Mars*. New York: Knopf.

Sayre-McCord, G. (ed.) 1988. *Essays on Moral Realism*. Ithaca, NY: Cornell University Press.

Schacter, D. 2001. *The Seven Sins of Memory*. Boston, MA: Houghton Mifflin.

Schellenberg, J. 1993. *Divine Hiddenness and Human Reason*. Ithaca, NY: Cornell University Press.

Schellenberg, J. 2004. "Divine Hiddenness Justifies Atheism". See Peterson & Van Arragon (2004), 30–41.

Schwartz, S. (ed.) 1977. *Naming, Necessity, and Natural Kinds*. Ithaca, NY: Cornell University Press.

Searle, J. 1998. *Mind, Language, and Society: Philosophy in the Real World*. New York: Basic Books.

Shafer-Landau, R. 2004. *Whatever Happened to Good and Evil?* Oxford: Oxford University Press.

Silk, J. 1994. *A Short History of the Universe*. New York: Scientific American.

Sontag, F. & M. D. Bryant (eds) 1982. *God: The Contemporary Discussion*. Barrytown, NY: Rose of Sharon Press.

Sosa, E. 2007. *A Virtue Epistemology*. Oxford: Oxford University Press.

Strawson, P. 1982. "Freedom and Resentment". In *Free Will*, Gary Watson (ed.), 59–80. Oxford: Oxford University Press.

Stump, E. 1985. "The Problem of Evil". *Faith and Philosophy* 2(4): 392–423.

Stump, E. 1990a. "Providence and Evil". In *Christian Philosophy*, T. Flint (ed.), 51–91. Notre Dame, IN: University of Notre Dame Press.

Stump, E. 1990b. "Intellect, Will, and Alternate Possibilities". In *Christian Theism and the Problems of Philosophy*, M. Beaty (ed.), 254–85. Notre Dame, IN: University of Notre Dame Press.

Stump, E. (ed.) 1993. *Reasoned Faith*. Ithaca, NY: Cornell University Press.

Swinburne, R. 1977. *The Coherence of Theism*. Oxford: Oxford University Press.

Swinburne, R. 1979. *The Existence of God*. Oxford: Oxford University Press.

Swinburne, R. 1996. *Is There a God?* Oxford: Oxford University Press.

Swinburne, R. 2004. *The Existence of God*, 2nd edn. Oxford: Oxford University Press.

Taylor, R. 1963. *Metaphysics*. Englewood Cliffs, NJ: Prentice-Hall.

Tomberlin, J. E. (ed.) 1991. *Philosophical Perspectives 5: Philosophy of Religion*. Atascadero, CA: Ridgeview.

Tooley, M. 1991. "The Argument from Evil". In *Philosophical Perspectives 5: Philosophy of Religion*, J. E. Tomberlin (ed.), 89–134. Atascadero, CA: Ridgeview.

Tryon, E. P. 1990. "Is the Universe a Vacuum Fluctuation?" In *Physical Cosmology and Philosophy*, J. Leslie, (ed.). New York: Macmillan.

van Inwagen, P. 2006. *The Problem of Evil*. Oxford: Oxford University Press.

Wainwright, W. 1995. *Reason and the Heart*. Ithaca, NY: Cornell University Press.

Wainwright, W. (ed.) 2005. *The Oxford Handbook of Philosophy of Religion*. Oxford: Oxford University Press.

Watson, G. (ed.) 1982. *Free Will*. Oxford: Oxford University Press.

Wierenga, E. 1989. *The Nature of God*. Ithaca, NY: Cornell University Press.

Wierenga, E. 2007. "Perfect Goodness and Divine Freedom". *Philosophical Books* 48(3): 207–16.

Wiesel, E. 1985. *Night/Dawn/Day*. Northvale, NJ: Jason Aronson.

Wilson, E. O. 1975. *Sociobiology: The New Synthesis*. Cambridge, MA: Harvard University Press.

Wykstra, S. J. 1996. "Rowe's Noseeum Argument from Evil". In *The Evidential Argument from Evil*, D. Howard-Snyder (ed.), 126–50. Bloomington, IN: Indiana University Press.

Wynn, M. R. 2005. *Emotional Experience and Religious Understanding*. Cambridge: Cambridge University Press.

Zagzebski, L. 1991. *The Dilemma of Freedom and Foreknowledge*. Oxford: Oxford University Press.

Zagzebski, L. 2007. *Philosophy of Religion*. Oxford: Blackwell.

Index